Their Greatest Hour

The Rearguard Action of the 12th Lancers, Dunkirk 1940

Philip Watson

Foreword by Her Majesty the Queen

Helion & Company

To Gill

To my wife Gill, who has had to put up with much over the last 42 years. Gill married me when I was a Trooper, long before I had any prospects and she has shared my life not only as a military wife, but as a mother who was left to bring up our four boys as work often took me away from home. She has had to endure endless years apart with much worry as we served and moved in an uncertain and violent world. In place of family holidays, she has had countless visits to war cemeteries, tramped over miles of battlefields as holidays morphed into battlefield tours. Also, she has seen my reference library grow to unreasonable proportions.

I really do 8.23.1

Helion & Company Limited
Unit 8 Amherst Business Centre
Budbrooke Road
Warwick
CV34 5WE
England
Tel. 01926 499 619
Email: info@helion.co.uk
Website: www.helion.co.uk
Twitter: @helionbooks
Visit our blog at blog.helion.co.uk

Published by Helion & Company 2023
Designed and typeset by Mach 3 Solutions (www.mach3solutions.co.uk)
Cover designed by Paul Hewitt, Battlefield Design (www.battlefield-design.co.uk)

Text © Philip Watson 2023
Images © as individually credited
Maps A to D drawn by George Anderson © Helion & Company Ltd 2023

ISBN 97-8-1804514-96-2

British Library Cataloguing-in-Publication Data.
A catalogue record for this book is available from the British Library.

For details of other military history titles published by Helion & Company Limited contact the above address or visit our website: http://www.helion.co.uk.

We always welcome receipt of book proposals from prospective authors.

Contents

List of Images

Portraits

(post nominal letters as of May 1940)

Photographs

Sketch Maps in Text

The following maps were derived from Stewart, *History of the XII Royal Lancers and Spearman*:

Colour Section Contemporary Maps

All maps are France and Belgium 1:50,000, Series M703 (GSGS 4040), U.S. Army Map Service, 1937

Abbreviations

ACC TC	Armoured Car Company Tank Corps
ADC	Aide-de-Camp
AFV	Armoured Fighting Vehicle
BEF	British Expeditionary Force
CACR	Cavalry Armoured Car Regiment
C-in-C	Commander-in-Chief
CRA	Commander Royal Artillery
CWGC	Commonwealth War Graves Commission
DLM	*Division* Légère *Mécanique*
DR	Despatch Rider
ESO	Embarkation Staff Officer
GHQ	General Headquarters
GOC	General Officer Commanding
HE	High Explosive
HMSO	His/Her Majesty's Stationery Office
IWM	Imperial War Museum
JNCO	Junior Non-Commissioned Officer
LAD	Light Aid Detachment
LO	Liaison Officer
NCO	Non-Commissioned Officer
OODA	Observe, Orientate, Decide, Act
QM	Quartermaster
RAF	Royal Air Force
RAMC	Royal Army Medical Corps
RASC	Royal Army Service Corps
RQMS	Regimental Quartermaster Sergeant
RE	Royal Engineers
RFC	Royal Flying Corps
RHA	Royal Horse Artillery
RHQ	Regimental Headquarters
RLMT	Royal Lancers Museum Trust
RMO	Regimental Medical Officer
RSM	Regimental Sergeant Major

RTC	Royal Tank Corps
RTO	Regimental or Rail Transport Officer
SHQ	Squadron Headquarters
SNCO	Senior Non-Commissioned Officer
SQMS	Squadron Quartermaster Sergeant
SSM	Squadron Sergeant Major
TNA	The National Archive

Acknowledgements

This volume would not have been written if the author had not been asked to assist The Royal Lancers with their Battlefield Study (Exercise DUNKIRK LANCER 2022). I am immensely grateful to Lieutenant Colonel (Ret'd) Nick Everard, Lieutenant Colonel Will Richmond and Major Tom Pritchard for their invitation to assist the serving Regiment in understanding the relevance of their history. The study was originally scheduled for 2020, to coincide with the 80th Anniversary, when the Regiment was to have been joined by the Duchess of Cornwall. Sadly, this became another casualty of COVID-19 but the study eventually took place in September 2022.

The study was delivered by two external guides (both ex-Lancers): Alan 'Chippy' Woods (late 17/21L) and the author (late 9/12L). Alan was responsible for delivering the operational overview and setting the broader context. His knowledge, enthusiasm, and passion for the subject place him among the very best Battlefield Tour Guides that I have met and had the pleasure of working with and he sets the bar high for those who aspire to follow in his footsteps.

I am also indebted to Lieutenant Colonel (Ret'd) Dick Taylor (late RTR) for his work on armoured cars in his seminal *Armoured Warfare in the British Army 1914-1939* (2022). It shifted my own perspective from mechanisation to modernisation. His more balanced approach to the transition away from horses, and the real reasons behind it, helpfully removes the pro-horse bias from the discussion.

The book would not be the same if it were not brought to life by the faces of those whose stories we have told. This would not have been possible without the encyclopaedic knowledge of Mrs Angela Tarnowski, the curator of The Royal Lancers Museum at Derby. Also, the Royal Lancers Museum Trust (RLMT) for their permission to quote from their diaries and use their photographs. As always, I remain indebted to Colonel (Ret'd) Noddy Stafford CMG for his hours of proof-reading and guidance in bringing this book to fruition.

I am also grateful to the following for permission to use their images: Marlborough College (photo of Andrew Roddick); Rupert Mann (Edward Mann medal group); the Museum of the Royal Monmouthshire Royal Engineers (David Smith photograph) and Dominic Warre for permission to use photos from his father's photo album. I would also like to thank Chris and Annette Booth for allowing me to use the photos of the 12th Lancers at Froyle House.

The last Regimental history which sought to bring the story to life was written by Colonel (Ret'd) Richard Charrington in *Spearmen*, which set the tone for the Regimental history books to follow. History, where possible, should be a 'warts and all' tale which does not seek to filter out mistakes and errors, lest false lessons be learned. He recognised that a human story full of colour and life is more likely to be read while at the same time removing the 'dry bones' stigma from the subject. In the writing of *Spearmen*, he drew upon many unpublished sources and I am grateful to him for his generosity in sharing those he did not use. I also credit him for the title of the book.

I am humbled that Her Majesty the Queen (who is now The Colonel-in-Chief of The Royal Lancers) has agreed to write the Foreword to the book. I hope she feels that I have represented her father (Major Bruce Shand) in a way that she would recognise. His diaries were a joy to read and were written with a lightness of touch that did much to bring the events of those extraordinary three weeks to life.

As Colonel-in-Chief of The Royal Lancers and the daughter of a 12th Royal Lancer, I am enormously proud of the Regiment's long and illustrious history. While Phil Watson's *Their Greatest Hour* recounts only twenty-one-days of fierce operations in the Lancers' 334-year life, their rear-guard activity during the retreat to Dunkirk was their zenith. Being on the back foot, as the British Expeditionary Force was then, often brings out one's true colours and it is testament to the Regiment that this story is one of discipline, loyalty, and fearlessness in the face of the enemy.

Having had great difficulty persuading my father to write a war memoir, *Previous Engagements*, I know, only too well, how challenging it is to document military manoeuvres. His autobiography is both self-deprecating and entirely modest – he did not even mention his first, of two, Military Crosses! With this in mind, I am thankful that *Their Greatest Hour* forms both a personal history of my father and also that of his Regiment. This historical account, formed from a combination of all available sources, immortalises the 12th Royal Lancers' five battle honours and nineteen gallantry awards - including my father's previously unmentioned Military Cross.

Warfare is chaotic and confusing, and for all but two members of the Regiment, about whom you will read, this was their first engagement with an enemy. Sadly, aside the military mastery, mistakes were made and friends were lost. While there are elements of the campaign that are particularly painful to read, I am grateful to Phil for his candid and un-censored narrative.

Amidst the stories of bravery and selflessness, there is nothing more humbling than to read of the Regiment's family spirit. My father spoke so fondly about this close bond with his fellow Officers and soldiers, and I know this ethos remains central nowadays. If my father had the opportunity to visit The Royal Lancers today, I know he would immediately recognise those amongst his number.

Death or Glory.

Camilla R

Introduction

Oh, there are Voices of the Past
Links of a broken chain,
Wings that can bear me back to times
Which cannot come again –
Yet God forbid that I should lose
The echoes that remain!
Proctor[1]

Without the Twelfth Lancers, only a small part of the Army would have
reached Dunkirk.
Shand[2]

There can be few military stories which have been written about in such great detail. The story of Dunkirk has found its way into the British consciousness, to such a degree it has come to epitomise the very essence of Britishness at times of national hardship.

The phrase 'Dunkirk Spirit' has been used to define the British character. Cartoons of the day re-defined the abbreviation of the British Expeditionary Force (BEF) to mean Bravery, Endurance, and Fortitude! This has been the prevailing national narrative of May 1940. A story of small boats that came to the rescue of a stranded Army on the beaches of Dunkirk: brave soldiers who would have died or been captured had it not been for the flotilla that came to their rescue. This is supported by strong images of stoic British soldiers waiting patiently on the beaches for deliverance.

Historians have subsequently identified other factors which contributed to the success of Operation DYNAMO. These include the mild weather and calm sea, as well as the use of the East Mole for the large ships. The smoke which hung in the air as a result of the German shelling and bombardments helped mask the BEF's activities, and Hitler's earlier somewhat unexpected *Halt Befehl* gave the hard-pressed expeditionary force time to consolidate abridgehead at Dunkirk. However, if Gort's statement as quoted by Shand is true, that 'without the Twelfth Lancers only a small

---

1   A.A. Procter, 'Voices of the Past,' in *Legends, and Lyrics: a Book of Verses* (1892), pp.107-108.
2   B. Shand, *Previous Engagements* (1990), p.62.

part of the Army would have reached Dunkirk,' then it would appear there is another element of the story which is still to be told. It was to account for the five Battle Honours the Regiment would win in just 21 days.[3]

The 12th Lancers Regimental History was written in 1950 and has been complimented by the autobiographies of Henry de la Falaise, Bruce Shand, and Tim Bishop. Occasional fragments of the story appear in the articles and the obituaries of the soldiers of 1940 in the *Regimental Journals*. It is striking that these unpublished letters and diaries, as well as the audio recordings held by the Imperial War Museum (IWM), have never been brought together in a single story.

The catalyst for this book was the requirement to assist in the delivery of a battlefield study for The Royal Lancers. It became apparent during the research phase of the planning that material was abundant but not together in one place. The extent of the role that the 12th Lancers played in June 1940 had escaped me, to my surprise.

In an attempt to understand why this story had not been told before, considering the volume of works published on the wider subject, I conducted a study of the history (historiography) to try and understand how the story had been previously written and more significantly the Regiment's relationship with its story (see Appendix IV). My conclusion is that, notwithstanding the Regiment's achievements, they were set against a background of strategic failure. In most cases, those who carried the Regimental narrative after the war chose to focus on the desert and Italy where their actions did not have a negative context and where, as individuals, they served with equal distinction.

It became apparent that the story had a modern military relevance as The Royal Lancers were once again in the wheeled armoured car role, doing a similar job to 1940, with a vehicle which had similar limitations. The role of Major Bruce Shand and his part in our history had been well-known amongst the regimental historians, as had the father-daughter relationship with the then Duchess of Cornwall. There had always been a close relationship between the Duchess and the Regiment, although on a discreet and private level. The Battlefield Study was conducted after the state funeral for Her Majesty The Queen, which resulted in the sad but understandable consequence that the Duchess of Cornwall, by now the Queen Consort, was unable to join the Regiment on the Study. It was clear that this was a story with modern relevance, and that it was a story that not only did people care about, but people might read beyond the boundaries of the Regiment.

The single purpose of this volume is, therefore, to draw together 'the echoes that remain' and to publish the definitive account of the 21 days in 1940 in order that the story can be told for the first time in its entirety and be of appeal to a wider audience.

The narrative is a human one punctuated with deeds of great daring. Those who were there admit that errors and mistakes were made, and at times they were scared.

---

3   Quote from Broadcast made over the British Forces Network in Germany in January 1959, in *12L Regimental Journal* (1959), p.50.

The historians who relate the broader story also overlook the genuine friendship and love the officers and men had for each other. The Regiment of 1940 was a very special organisation, and this was their greatest hour.

In the course of writing this book, some editing has been required when diaries contained the phonetic spelling of place names or the alternate use of spellings resulting from French and Belgian maps. Where confusion was a possibility, correct or alternate spellings have been included to assist with indexing. In addition, all the map references quoted (number in brackets) are obtained from relevant war diaries and relate to copies of issued colour maps, which also accompany the text.

This story did not begin in May 1940. It began a decade earlier when the Regiment exchanged its horses for the armoured car.

PAW
28th July 2023

1

Modernisation – Still the Same Spirit

The role of armoured cars especially in highly mobile warfare was emphatically that of the old cavalry screen.
Shand[1]

The armoured car regiment was a reconnaissance unit. It was the eyes and ears of the Army… sometimes delaying them, but never getting involved … Very roughly it did the old cavalry's job on a wider scale and at a higher speed.
Bishop[2]

Armoured fighting vehicles will in the future reign supreme over the open spaces of the world which were once such a favourable battleground for the cavalry.
Charrington[3]

Above all, do not let us be led astray, as has often happened before, by the verbose prophesies of those opponents of the cavalry arm who are but wise in their own conceit.
Barrow[4]

Is this the beginning of the end or the end of the beginning?
Pitman[5]

1   Shand, *Previous Encounters*, p.74.
2   T. Bishop (ed. B. Shand), *One Young Soldier: The Memoires of a Cavalryman* (1993), p.50.
3   *Cavalry Journal* (July 1927), p.430.
4   G. Barrow, 'The Future of Cavalry' in *The Cavalry Journal* (April 1929), p.184.
5   T.T. Pitman, 'Back to the Chariots' in *The Cavalry Journal* (April 1928), p.306.

Cavalry Mechanisation

The actions of the 12th Lancers in 1940 cannot be viewed or understood in isolation from the previous decade which spanned the years between the two wars. Very few of the Regiment would serve in both wars, but those who served during this period were the generation of Lancers who would link the horse and the armoured car. The two were simply different platforms on which to conduct the same role, and these would be the men that went to war in 1939. George Kidston-Montgomerie, who joined the Regiment in 1926, stated that every SNCO in the Regiment except one had First World War medal ribbons.[6]

Still the Same Spirit by Gilbert Holiday Stewart, (*History of the XII Royal Lancers*)

The post-First World War period from a cavalry perspective is usually viewed through the single prism of mechanisation which is a cavalry euphemism for the demise of the horse. This was caught up in a broader, and obsolete, argument that the majority of the cavalry were resistant to change. This does not mean that some individuals were not reactionary and the news was received with a mixture, of shock,

6   Kidston-Montgomerie, George Jardine: (Oral history)/Imperial War Museums <iwm.org. uk> (accessed 11/11/22).

Farrier SSgt H.G. Spencerley's 12L Lancer Enlistment papers and 8H Discharge papers 1931.
(Author's collection)

sadness, and personal difficulty when it came to losing the horse. That said, very few officers chose to leave and the vast majority saw it through together. The older soldiers who were either too old to retrain or who simply had the equestrian skill sets of saddlers, saddle-tree makers, shoesmiths, rough-riders and farriers were still required by the rest of the cavalry and moved to other regiments.[7]

For others, their reservations went much deeper. Some thought it was just a 'dangerous fetish' and there was strong opposition from two specific regiments: The Bays and The Greys, although not the 12th Lancers.[8] The machine versus horse argument was for the most part an 'argument between partisans,' however, General Sir George Barrow (who had been Allenby's Intelligence Officer in 1914) saw the key

7   Kidston-Montgomerie, George Jardine: (Oral history)/Imperial War Museums <iwm.org. uk> (accessed 11/11/22); Horsburgh-Porter, Andrew Marshall: (Oral history)/Imperial War Museums <iwm.org.uk> (accessed 11/7/22). Compare in the *12L Regimental Journal* (1928) and (1932), the two Regimental Rolls, noting the absence of cavalry tradesmen and the addition of new mechanised related appointments.
8   A.R. Mulliner, 'Cavalry Still an Essential Army' in *The Cavalry Journal* (October 1927), p.647; See, Taylor, *Armoured Warfare*, pp.142-143.

issue as being intellectual and linked to the cavalry spirit. He concluded in a lecture to Bristol University in 1929 on the 'Future of the Cavalry' that:

> Whatever the organisation of this mobile arm of the future, the spirit which animates it will remain the spirit of mobility, mobility of the mind and of the body. We shall never see again great masses of cavalry charging knee to knee; but so long as war remains, so long will cavalry or their exact mechanical equivalent.[9]

Barrow's definition of the cavalry spirit was one of offensiveness, underpinned by the mobility of the mind and body. In presenting this lecture, he thought people would suspect him of being biased towards the horse, however, he thought if that were the case, then the very 'predisposition' gave him the 'justification' to do so and presented the argument beyond the platform to be used.[10] The main debate regarding mechanisation in the cavalry was conducted in *The Cavalry Journal*.

The article carried in its July 1927 edition outlined the recent changes in cavalry organisation, stating that the recent statement by the Secretary of State for War that the 'small savings made on the cavalry' would be used to 'modernise and improve its fighting value.' Although it was agreed in principle, the main concern was the level of depletion in the 'home establishment' of men and horses that would be required to obtain the 'greater mobility and firepower' it sought.[11] It was disbandment and amalgamation that was the most serious threat to the cavalry post-1918, not mechanisation. Barrow, in his overall championing of the cavalry, thought that if the reason for the reduction was to be based on its performance in the previous war, then:

> For God's sake don't let us blame the cavalry or use this as an argument that its day is passed and gone forever. If it is to justify its continued existence the cavalry must move in unison with the ever-changing conditions of modern warfare… Above all, do not let us be led astray, as has often happened before, by the verbose prophesies of those opponents of the cavalry arm who are but wise in their own conceit.[12]

If this period is viewed purely from a mechanisation perspective, it has an inherently negative bias and overlooks the other innovations and the overall modernisation of the cavalry. The journey to modernisation for the Lancers began with Army Order 392, issued in December 1927, which finally abolished the lance as a weapon of war for regiments in the British Army.[13] This was not the first time the lance had been withdrawn from service and it had already once been reduced to a ceremonial weapon

9   Barrow, 'The Future of the Cavalry', p.379.
10   Barrow, 'The Future of the Cavalry', pp.365-379.
11   *The Cavalry Journal* (July 1927), p.409.
12   Barrow, 'The Future of Cavalry', p.184.
13   *12L Regimental Journal* (April 1927), p.27.

before its final withdrawal. Field Marshal Roberts withdrew the lance from service during the Boer War in late October 1900 and, in March 1903, Army Order 39 was issued:

> Regiments of cavalry will, in future, be armed with the carbine (or rifle) and sword. Regiments of lancers, dragoon guards, and dragoons will retain the lance as at present, but it will only be carried on escort duty, at reviews, and other cere-monial parades, not on guard, in the field, at manoeuvres, or on active service.[14]

The lance debate had been long and bitter. It had been discussed in both the Press and Parliament and was driven by Roberts. However, when Roberts was retired along with his appointment as C-in-C, those in the pro-lance lobby rose to prominence again and in 1909, Army Order 158, reinstated the lance as a weapon of war:

> With reference to Army Order 39 of 1903… regiments of Lancers will in future carry the lance, not only on escort duty and at all reviews and other ceremonial parades but also on guard, during training, at manoeuvres and, when so ordered, on field service.[15]

When viewed in isolation, Roberts can be seen as anti-cavalry and anti-*arme blanche,* but in truth, Roberts was an Army reformer who had seen the Army through the Boer War and reinforced many lessons that had been forgotten. This coincided with a change in the balance of power in Europe and the rise of Germany and therefore divided the Army's focus between its colonial responsibilities and the threat from the continent. Like all change, there was opposition from well-placed dominant voices, but even the final Army Order contained an element of pragmatism, 'when so ordered,' and left the door open and passions were appeased. The main threat to the Army and its reforms was fiscal restraints when all reforms would be balanced against cost and many financial cuts would be framed from a position of achieving operational efficiency.

One of the largest savings to be made was the closure of the Cavalry Depot at Canterbury in June 1927. This meant that all recruits would be sent direct to regi-ments to conduct their training, something which impacted upon all the cavalry regi-ments.[16] Also, in an attempt to decrease the weight carried on a horse and therefore extend the range of the cavalry, the Morris 6-wheeler cross-country lorry was issued to the 1st Line Transport of cavalry regiments. Major Harold Charrington (who was

---

14 Anglesey, *A History of the British Cavalry, 1816-1919, Vol. 4: 1899-1913* (1986), p.236; Army Order 39 dated March 1903.

15 See, Anglesey, *A History of the British Cavalry, Vol. 4;* S. Badsey, *Doctrine and Reform in the British Cavalry 1880–1918* (2008); S. Jones, *From Boer War to World War, Tactical Reform of the British Army, 1902-1914* (2013).

16 *The Cavalry Journal* (July 1927), pp.410-411.

serving with the 12th Lancers) thought this would be 'a great improvement.'[17] This initiative sought to achieve an improvement in operational efficiency while at the same time reducing the number of horses which were expensive. There were those, of course, who suggested that it might be viewed as mechanisation by the back door. The Army also sought to improve the regiment's firepower by increasing the number of machine guns from four to eight and sought a replacement for the Hotchkiss gun as it was seen to be 'unreliable.' The 12 that were recommended would only be issued on the outbreak of war.[18]

On 10th March 1928, while the regiment was on Command Manoeuvres, it was announced by the Army Council that the 12th Lancers and 11th Hussars would mechanise and become Cavalry Armoured Car Regiments (CACR).[19] Therefore, in the overall story of cavalry mechanisation, the first two regiments would convert to armoured cars and would be the only two regular Army units to do so. This in itself was partly wrapped up in fiscal savings and the modernisation of the cavalry. However, since there were no further mechanisations between 1928 and 1935, the balance would appear to favour modernisation rather than simple cost-cutting.[20]

A second statement followed a month later confirming that their names would not be changed and that they would retain their titles, seniority, and traditions:

> *They say there ain't no difference, and we are still Hussars,*
> *and Lancers (in the Army List) equipped with Armoured Cars,*
> *But now the order has come to us, clearly, it appears*
> *That 'enceforth we shall just be called the Armoured Car-biniers.*[21]

The decision had been made that the Royal Tank Corps (RTC) would hand over its armoured cars and their role would be assumed by the cavalry.[22] Some thought that the regiments were given the choice to either mechanise or amalgamate.[23] However, the reality was much simpler, and that was that the two regiments that were selected were chosen purely on their 'juniority,' as had been the case in the cavalry amalgamations six years earlier. With both the 12th Lancers and 11th Hussars being the two junior regiments of the cavalry remaining (unamalgamated), it was no surprise that

---

17   *The Cavalry Journal* (July 1927), pp.427.
18   *The Cavalry Journal* (July 1927), pp.409-410.
19   *12L Regimental Journal* (April 1927), p.6.
20   See, Taylor, *Armoured Warfare*, pp.142-143.
21   Taylor, *Armoured Warfare*, p.145 and *12L Regimental, Journal (October 1928)*, p.17. A deliberate play on words.
22   Savill, Kenneth Edward: (Oral history)/Imperial War Museums <iwm.org.uk> (accessed 03/08/22).
23   9/12L Lecture notes: Corps Recce Study Day, 'Salvation of the BEF 10-31 May 1940' (1985), p.12; Horsburgh-Porter, Andrew Marshall: (Oral history)/Imperial War Museums <iwm.org.uk> (accessed 03/08/22).

they were subsequently chosen to re-role.[24] However, Major General Pitman (Colonel of the 11th Hussars) stated in *The Cavalry Journal* that while deploring the loss of the horse, this fate was better than any other form of amalgamation and he saw an advantage in being in at the beginning of the process.[25]

The news was carried in the newspapers four days later under the headline 'Machine Guns For Sabres':

> Sir Laming Worthington-Evans, presenting the Army Estimates in the House of Commons, announced that the cavalry divisions of the Army were undergoing a revolutionary change, the first big step towards the ultimate disappearance of the horse from the battlefield.[26]

This statement did not take into account that there were many areas where only the horse and mule could operate, or that troops from the dominions and Empire would still need them. Secondly, on mobilisation to war, it would be these organisations who would join the Allies with their animals. Also, he did not consider that for at least a decade the cavalry would be a hybrid organisation of both horses and machines and that they would need to and should operate together.[27] Lastly, there was still discussion regarding whether it was necessary to mechanise the whole of the cavalry or whether the organisational change that was required was more a matter of getting the horse-machine proportions right.[28]

The organisational change and how an armoured car regiment would look, once it had received its full allocation of vehicles, was published in a later *Regimental Journal* for the benefit of the Old Comrades:

> The Regiment is at present organised into a Headquarters Wing and 3 squadrons each of HQ and 2 sections. The personnel of the Headquarters Wing is very similar to that of a mounted unit i.e., Headquarters and Orderly Room Staff, Band, Transport, Police, etc. Total Strength 134 as compared with 125 in a cavalry regiment. That of the squadrons is considerably less i.e., 6 × officers, 101 × other ranks as compared with 6 × officers and 140 × other ranks. The total strength of the Regiment is therefore 455 (includes 24 × officers) i.e., 94 × other ranks less than in old days.[29]

24   Pitman, 'Back to the Chariots', p.306; *12L Regimental, Journal* (October 1928), p.33.
25   Pitman, 'Back to the Chariots', p.307.
26   *Aberdeen Press and Journal* – Wednesday 14th March 1928.
27   E.G. Hume, 'Mechanical Aids to Cavalry' in *The Cavalry Journal* (July 1935), p.181.
28   E.G. Hume, 'Some Thoughts on Modern Reconnaissance' in *The Cavalry Journal January* (1928), p.211.
29   *12L Regimental Journal* (October 1930), pp.20-21.

The article then went into great detail regarding the composition of the vehicle fleet and how they were to be used and distributed in the Regiment:

> The regimental establishment of mechanical vehicles is as follows: Fighting Vehicles, 34 × armoured cars. Reconnaissance, and Message-Carrying Vehicles. 16 × Austin, 2 Seaters. 30 × motorcycles. (Triumph and Douglas). RHQ, 1 × 6-wheeled Tourer. Transport, 3 × Leyland 3 × Ton Lorries, 6 × wheeled. 7 × Morris and Crossley 30 cwt. Lorries, 6 × wheeled, Instructional Vehicles, 3 × Rolls-Royce Chassis. Signal Vehicles. 4 × 6-wheelers, fitted with wireless, to operate which 1 × officer and 32 × other ranks, to be permanently attached from the Royal Corps of Signals.[30]

These vehicles are allocated as follows:

> RHQ. 1 × Rolls-Royce armoured car for Commanding Officer. 1 × 6-wheeled Tourer. (For Adjutant and Orderly Room Staff). 6 × Motorcycles. 4 × Austins. 1 × 30 cwt Lorry. Each squadron has 11 × Rolls-Royce Armoured Cars. 8 × motorcycles. 4 × Austins, 2 × 30 cwt. 6-wheeled lorries, 1 × 3-Ton 6-wheeled lorry. 1 Rolls-Royce training chassis. Squadrons are organised in two sections each of five armoured cars, the remaining armoured car being the Squadron Leader's armoured car. Austins, motorcycles, and lorries on squadron establishment are not allotted to sections, but normally each section will always be given at least one Austin, for Section Commander's use, and three motorcycles, one for section HQ, and one for each sub-section. A section detached for any period over 24 hours would usually have a 30 cwt. lorry attached to it to carry spare petrol, water, tyres, food, ammunition, etc. Each section is commanded by a subaltern and is divided into two sub-sections, each of two cars, the fifth car being the Section Leader's car. With only four subalterns in each Squadron, only one sub-section in each section is commanded by an officer, the other being commanded by a sergeant. Cars are manned by crews of four.[31]

It is interesting to note that the Regiment had formed an HQ Wing (the forerunner of the HQ Squadron) for the first time. The overall establishment was smaller (and therefore costs were saved), the HQ element had grown, and the squadrons had become smaller. Also, even at this early stage, the armoured car was used for fighting and not for reconnaissance. This debate extended beyond the British cavalry as ultimately the decisions would also affect the British-Indian cavalry regiments. Lieutenant Colonel Hume wrote concerning his thoughts on mobile forces in the future, again viewing the role of the cavalry in a spirit of offensiveness and opportunity:

30   *12L Regimental Journal* (October 1930), pp.20-21.
31   *12L Regimental Journal* (October 1930), pp.20-21.

Is it not true that armoured fighting vehicles in a mobile offensive role are to a very great extent weapons of opportunity? To develop their maximum effect, they require a chance of surprise; when handled correctly in relation to the ground and the general situation, their mobility may often enable them to create this opportunity and, when it has been achieved, their mobility again adds greatly to the effectiveness of their action, which can be carried through before countermeasures are possible. It is essential therefore that early and accurate information, and control of a suitable area for mobile concealed manoeuvre, should be obtained: but, when opposed to an equally equipped adversary, these can only be secured by a more prompt and skilful use of mobility – made possible by superior communications, organisation, training, and leadership.[32]

However, when it came specifically to the armoured car, Hume's vision of its use was prophetic:

The essential point in the preliminary rapid exploitation of the mobility of armoured cars, and the forestalling of enemy reconnaissance, is the very great delaying power of a modern armament, on suitable ground, which results in an economy of Force, hence the great advantage of arriving first, both from the point of view of screening, and also for gaining secrecy, choice of ground, and the initiative for offensive action, when the situation develops. Once a screen is established on suitable ground supported where necessary by light tanks and artillery, the deployment of considerable Force will be necessary in order to break through.[33]

Hume and Barrow were not the only individuals who saw the cavalry offensive mindset as being ideal for the role, and therefore the decision to give the role to the cavalry was correct. Pitman observed:

This end can only be obtained by the addition of mechanical devices, and the authorities have realised rightly that mechanised forces require the cavalry spirit and quick-thinking brains. Where can these better be found than in our present cavalry who are officered and manned by the very best class in the Army? If the cavalry of the future are to have the power of breaking through the enemy's screen to gain information, armoured cars in considerable numbers are a necessity, and it has been decided that the unit best suited to perform the task required is a regiment.[34]

32   E.G. Hume, 'Some Thoughts on Mobile Forces of the Future' in *The Cavalry Journal* (January 1930), p.36.
33   Hume, 'Some Thoughts on Mobile Forces of the Future', p.34.
34   Pitman, 'Back to the Chariots', p.306. Also see Hume, 'Mechanical Aids to Cavalry', p.181.

The argument could also be made that the Royal Tank Corps (RTC) were not the most suitable to conduct the role. Colonel W.D. Croft RTC, in the 1926 edition of *The Cavalry Journal*, wrote of the challenges that the RTC officer faced:

> The first requisite of all Tank Corps personnel is a trained eye for the ground; it is essential for the leaders, and necessary even down to privates. In the case of the leaders, this training can best be cultivated out of school, either in the hunting field or on shikar. The former method is undoubtedly the best, but unless a man is sufficiently well-mounted to take his own line-and how few there are who can do this! He will not acquire that instinctive eye for the country to anything like the same extent which can be acquired by the second method. Unfortunately, opportunities for stalking are out of reach of the majority of Tank Corps officers, and, although pottering about with a gun is good practice, it does not offer the same opportunities for quick decisions as stalking.[35]

The remainder of the article is based around working in conjunction with mounted cavalry and at no point does he suggest or consider that the armoured car role should be assumed by the cavalry. However, Croft did suggest that, notwithstanding the statement in the *Field Service Regulations*, the role of strategic reconnaissance was to be conducted by the RAF. He thought there should be no 'embargo' and, when this could not be achieved by the RAF due to weather conditions, then this information could be gained by ground reconnaissance. This would enable the General Staff to get those 'priceless little items of information' to 'piece together the enemy's plan.' Croft also wrote:

> The most strenuous period of their employment will be in the earliest stages of the campaign. The further they can go before getting touch with the enemy the better chance will they have to being utilised to their fullest extent.[36]

Again, like Hume, it was another prophetic statement and was to be exactly how the 12th Lancers would be used in May 1940. However, the future was a decade away and the priority was to assume the role.

35   W.D. Croft, 'Notes on Armoured Cars' in *The Cavalry Journal* (January 1926), p.160. Note D. Taylor has an alternate contention 'that a true eye for the ground can only be obtained in the vehicle that one goes to war in, due to the height/commander's perspective, and its individual mobility characteristics.' The author's contention is to link the cavalry mounted spirt of aggression, opportunity and mental agility to mechanised reconnaissance.
36   Croft, 'Notes on Armoured Cars', pp.163-164.

Don't Worry it will be a long time before they can do without us by Gilbert Holiday
(*The Cavalry Journal*, July 1927)

Regimental Mechanisation

The two regiments had to approach mechanisation from two different start points. The 11th Hussars were in Aldershot. Following the announcement, in the absence of a real-time operational role, they were able to send the majority of their officers and men to the Royal Tank Corps Depot at Bovington and Lulworth for conversion training. They held their last mounted parade on 10th April 1928 and took receipt of their armoured cars from the 12 Armoured Car Company Tank Corps (ACC TC), beginning their training in early 1929.[37] For the 12th Lancers, however, their task was

37   Taylor, *Armoured Warfare*, p.147, p.206.

complicated by geography and their role as they were stationed in Helmieh, Egypt, and would not be able to send the Regiment *en masse* to the RTC Depot as the operational commitment still had to be fulfilled.

Upon receipt of the order to mechanise, the Lancers took a professional and pragmatic approach to the challenge. Field Marshal Birdwood, the Colonel of the Regiment, wrote that 'standing still and regretting is no good when advance is essential... the reputation of the 12th Lancers will still be further increased.' The Commanding Officer, Lieutenant Colonel Harold Charrington, said 'let us all get down to our new job just as we got down to it on our feet during the greater part of the First World War and that we are still a part of the Cavalry Corps, retaining our old titles, traditions, privileges, and retaining the old spirit which has kept the 12th Lancers second to none.'[38] Major Andrew Horsbrugh-Porter thought Charrington 'took to it like a duck to water.'[39] However, Kidston-Montgomerie stated that when Lieutenant Colonel Blakiston-Houston heard rumours of mechanisation, before handing over to Charrington, he put it more bluntly:

> We've been given this role and it's a very important role. And you're damn well going to do it. I won't have you bloody well bellyaching.[40]

The Regimental Colonel of the 11th Hussars, like Birdwood, added his weight to the challenge and wrote in *The Cavalry Journal* 'that the future and the *esprit de corps* and fine cavalry spirit for which these two regiments have been distinguished for the last 200 years will be preserved, and there is little doubt that they will maintain their high position in cavalry circles which they have held for so many years.'[41]

When it came to the practicalities of mechanisation, the 12th Lancers did it in phases, meaning that for some time the Regiment would be both mechanised and mounted. As part of the cavalry's earlier modernisations, B Squadron, under the command of Captain Herbert Lumsden, had already converted to be the Regiment's Machine Gun Section. This decision was based on the fact that they already had the Regiment's machine guns and therefore it seemed logical that they should be the first to mechanise. Their existence as the Machine Gun Section was described as 'short and merry' (1st January to 8th May) and Horsbrugh-Porter thought they were already 'the Regiment's elite.'[42]

B Squadron noted that the first time they fired the machine gun from a moving armoured car was a 'vastly different proposition' from firing it from the ground on the

38   Stewart, *History of the XII Royal Lancers* (1950), pp.319-320.
39   Horsburgh-Porter, Andrew Marshall: (Oral history)/Imperial War Museums <iwm.org.uk> (accessed 11/11/22).
40   Kidston-Montgomerie, George Jardine: (Oral history)/Imperial War Museums <iwm.org.uk> (accessed 11/11/22).
41   Pitman, 'Back to the Chariots', p.307.
42   *12L Regimental Journal* (October 1928), p.33 and Horsburgh-Porter, Andrew Marshall: (Oral history)/Imperial War Museums <iwm.org.uk> (accessed 11/12/22).

tripod. They thought their results were 'fairly satisfactory,' with 29 gunners achieving a first-class standard, 22 second and 5 third. They wrote that they were 'determined to do better' the following year.[43] This self-assessment was based on their results in the ground-mounted role when 86 out of the 89 personnel had achieved marksman the previous year.[44] A Squadron, which had been watching B Squadron, stated that they were proud of the way our 'armoured carbineers have come on in the last few months':

> The 12 cars on parade in the morning are, indeed, a sight worth seeing, and to watch the busy men of B dashing around in their suits of dungarees, spanner in one hand and cotton waste in the other very nearly takes the sting from the fact that A will be losing their horses in another nine months' time. C Squadron handed their horses over on 2nd April and they are, so it is said, not sorry.[45]

Having the dual role immediately highlighted to the soldiers the difference the armoured car would make to their daily lives, and the fact you could 'lock the garage door on a Friday and forget about it till Monday morning,' so the benefits to the younger men were not difficult to sell. When asked what the Regiment's opinion was of mechanisation, Horsbrugh-Porter said that 'in reality it was inevitable and in truth 'no one wanted to go to war on a horse… and the day of the horse was done.' When asked what the opinion of the young officers was, he stated that 'their opinion did not count at all' and that the opinions of 'junior officers up to the age of 26 are completely not worth listening to.'[46] Captain Fenton stated that soon the talk was about 'carburettors and all the many parts of the car,' and it was 'the youth and flexibility of mind of the majority of the men' that enabled them to 'absorb the new technical training.'[47] Also, the new trade pay scales for soldiers who undertook conversion training helped to smooth the transition:

> *Head right wheel in second gear.*
> *That is the word of command we shall hear,*
> *When the Cavalry change their swords for spanners*
> *And learn to drive for the extra "tanners."[48]*
> *When 'stables' blow, they all will grin,*
> *For their "water and feed's" in a four-gallon tin.[49]*

43   *12L Regimental Journal* (October 1928), p.30.
44   *12L Regimental Journal* (October 1928), p.33.
45   *12L Regimental Journal* (May 1928), p.37; 11xArmoured cars from 5 ACC TC and HQ Wing 1 Armoured Car in, *12L Regimental Journal* (May 1930), p.9.
46   Stewart, *History of the XII Royal Lancers*, p.320; Horsburgh-Porter, Andrew Marshall: (Oral history)/Imperial War Museums <iwm.org.uk> (accessed 11/07/22).
47   W. Fenton in Stewart, *History of the XII Royal Lancers*, p.320.
48   Reference to six-pence.
49   *12L Regimental Journal* (May 1928), p.35.

At the end of B Squadron's conversion training Charrington, who was now commanding the Regiment, submitted his report:

> This Squadron has now completed preliminary training with the 3 ACC TC, has taken over the full complement of armoured cars, and is now functioning as a complete Squadron in the field (less than three months from the date it commenced mechanisation). It is now capable of carrying out tactical exercises, both by day and night, over varying types of country, both by itself and in coop-eration with mounted troops. I am completely satisfied with the standard of driving, mechanical knowledge, and tactical skill so far displayed. Of the 97 OR's on the establishment of this Squadron, 47 have been trained as armoured car drivers, 12 as motorcyclists, 6 as six-wheel lorry drivers, 2 as Ford car drivers, 1 as 3-ton lorry driver, 4 as vulcanisers, 2 as fitters, 4 as technical storeman and clerks. All are capable of performing their duties efficiently.[50]

The report clearly articulates the level of conversion training that was required well beyond the crewing of the armoured cars. Drivers and technical tradesmen were needed to support a mechanised squadron in the same way saddlers and shoesmiths had done when the Regiment was mounted. The final part in the chapter on the Regiment's conversion would see Lumsden depart for Staff College.[51]

The whole mechanisation process took place between May 1928 and December 1929 with the training and armoured cars coming from both 3 and 5 ACC TC.[52] The Regiment was equipped with two variants of the Rolls-Royce Armoured Car, 1920 and 1924 models. They were virtually identical, except for the mounting for the turret-mounted Vickers machine gun.[53] In the May 1928 edition of the Regimental journal, there was an anonymous article entitled 'Gunnery from Armoured Fighting Vehicles,' in which it stated that unlike artillery or ground mounted machine guns, machine gun firing from a moving armoured car should be 'considered to be an art.' This was attributed to amongst other things, the moving vehicle and the ever-changing range of the target, something they would find difficult in practice.[54]

On 14th November 1929, the Regiment held Moy Day to say, 'Farewell to the Horses.' That said, it was not a true farewell as the significance of the horse to the officers had not been lost and Shand stated that as a 'sop' the Regiment retained 48 horses for the officers, who were also allowed to retain their grooms.[55]

It was during this period, before the whole Regiment had been converted, that nine cars of B Squadron commanded by Major Hornby were sent to Palestine on

50   H.V.S. Charrington in *12L Regimental Journal* (May 1928), pp.9-10.
51   *12L Regimental Journal* (May 1928), p.39.
52   Taylor, *Armoured Warfare*, p.206.
53   Stewart, *History of the XII Royal Lancers*, p.321.
54   *12L Regimental Journal* (May 1928), p.16.
55   Shand, *Previous Engagements*, p.17; Stewart, *History of the XII Royal Lancers*, p.321.

internal security duties for two months at the end of 1929. During this period, they were employed on patrols and raids, sometimes in conjunction with the infantry, but more often working alone. The hours were long, and it was hard work, but it was 'a useful introduction to their new role' and this made them the first cavalrymen to use the armoured car in an operational role.[56] This was not the only operational deployment the Regiment would conduct from Egypt and, in October 1931, a half-squadron under Captain Burne was again involved in internal security duties in Cyprus. During their five weeks of deployment, the Squadron did not come into contact with the rioters but had to content themselves with 'exerting a good moral effect.'[57]

Armoured Car Reconnaissance

Even though the Regiment had received its full allocation of 34 armoured cars, its training was hampered by the lack of transport and they were still waiting for their Leyland-equipped wireless trucks. By November 1930, the Regiment was in a position to start a period of 'intense' training which took the form of long reconnaissance patrols into the desert. Each squadron in turn would go out, taking the opportunity to cover different areas of Egypt, the Libyan Desert, the Alexandra coast and east as far as Sinai. One patrol was covered in great detail by the accompanying Medical Officer, Major Dun, who went with Major Rawnsley's A Squadron in October 1932. The patrol consisted of:

> Ten Rolls-Royce armoured cars, one wireless Leyland, three Austin Seven cars and six motorcycles. A total of six lorries of the unit and attached RASC carried the supplies and water reserve. Two RAOC workshop lorries, equipped with endless appliances and spares, accompanied the column. In addition to this, two armoured cars and some transport vehicles proceeded through the blue and yellow, straight across the heart of the desert to join us at Siwa. During the Summer of 1932, plans had been made for the necessary dumps and supplies of water, petrol, oil, and mechanical spares required en route. These were now put into force, liaison with the RAF effected and arrangements made for aeroplanes to keep in touch with the column and convey urgent supplies and spares, in case of break-down on impassable desert surfaces.[58]

The Regimental History reported that wireless communications were maintained with RHQ at Hemiech and the detachment in Alexandria, sometimes achieving ranges of over 500 miles. However, it did not say how difficult it was to do so, but Dun described what he saw:

---

56 Stewart, *History of the XII Royal Lancers*, p.321.
57 Stewart, *History of the XII Royal Lancers*, p.324.
58 T.I. Dun, *From Cairo to Siwa* (1933), pp.15-16.

Watch the wireless crew, one man on the roof erecting the tall mast by screwing it into place with four men on the ground, adjusting the guy ropes... We were kept in touch with Alexandria and Cairo, where similar units were functioning. It was rumoured that in a lighter joyous moment, one message sent out by us caused a bend in the wireless pole. I spent half an hour that night, inside the wireless lorry, watching the wireless staff working. Atmospherics were very pronounced, and a single message had to be tapped out repeatedly before it was correctly interpreted in Cairo.[59]

The Rolls-Royce armoured car was never designed to be used in the desert and water was one of their main concerns. The Lancers came up with a modification which would alleviate some of the problems:

The consumption of water by one of these armoureds in desert running is great. A condenser pipe is fitted to collect the steam vapour into condensing tanks, but even so, seven gallons in a day's running is not unknown. Each armoured is self-contained as regards water, rations, primus stove, first aid outfit and blankets. Within such a narrow space with flags, machine gun, and other necessary gadgets, it looks like a jigsaw puzzle fitting everything in. Water on the trip was conserved carefully, each armoured having one 12-and-a-half gallon fantassie [sic], a brick-shaped, metal camel tank with a screw top. One Thornycroft lorry was carrying 25 fantassies, approximately 312 gallons, in reserve.[60]

When the reconnaissance of the Siwa had been completed, Dun wrote that for him 'the lessons learned had been well worthwhile. This reconnaissance of 1,136 miles, for 21 days, over a terrain of sand, stones, and mud, was an excellent test of endurance for man and machine. It was not a joy ride, but one enjoyed every moment of it. Our speed averaged below 11 miles an hour and necessitated spells of all-out driving.'[61] Later when the Regiment returned to England these manoeuvres and patrols continued. Shand observed:

Told to take a troop of three armoured cars and two DRs to some remote part of the Kingdom [East Anglia] for a couple of days and keep in touch on the wireless. It was a good experience. Disasters occurred, not always reported back and loyally forgotten by those soldiers who had to suffer for my shortcomings, but probably I learnt more than I realised on these outings.[62]

59   Dun, *From Cairo to Siwa*, p.21.
60   Dun, *From Cairo to Siwa*, p.20.
61   Dun, *From Cairo to Siwa*, p.51.
62   Shand, *Previous Encounters*, p.17.

However, these outings did not go without serious incident and in 1932, Trooper Symonds was tragically killed in a training accident which involved an armoured car. This was possibly the first such cavalry fatality.[63] After two operational deployments, an intense period of training and the long desert patrols, the Regiment had quickly become masters of their new role and in 1933 the Regiment's Annual Report read:

> The Regiment was well commanded, well officered, and well administered. There is a strong Regimental spirit and the WOs and NCOs, and men are keen, intelligent, and smart… and efficiency goes on increasing.[64]

By 1934, the War establishment of armoured car regiments had been finalised. It was to be a regiment of 38 armoured cars, with three squadrons each with three troops of three cars. At the time it was considered to be flexible, offered good mobility and firepower and was not 'too unwieldy.' However, the net result was that the Regiment in a war would now only be able to field half the number of reconnaissance patrols that were generated by the old mounted-establishment. The mounted section of four men who were able to operate separately became the vehicle crew, and as such were all confined into one small space. At the end of the same year, the Regiment rotated with the 11th Hussars, and the Regiment returned to Britain leaving two NCOs and 69 men with the Hussars, as the priority for manning was Egypt. On their departure the High Commissioner stated:

> You have achieved an unexampled and unprecedented success over an exceptionally long period which is all the more creditable since in the course of it you have had to adapt yourselves to an internal change of far-reaching character.[65]

Horsbrugh-Porter saw the six years in Egypt as where the Regiment 'learnt its role, free from the interference from the War Office.'[66]

When the Regiment disembarked in Britain, they took over the 11th Hussars' Lanchester armoured cars. These were different from the Rolls-Royce in that they were six-wheeled armoured cars, slower and more robust. The armoured car was fitted with three machine guns, a Vickers .50 and .303 in the turret and a second .303 in the hull. Later, the hull-mounted machine gun in the Troop Leader's armoured car was removed to make space for the fitting of the No. 9 wireless set. This was a significant enhancement to the capability of the Regiment as now it had wireless communications to all its troops. It had always been the aspiration to fit the wireless to the armoured car as early as 1929, but the issue had simply been the size of the wireless.

---

63   Taylor, *Armoured Warfare*, p.148.
64   Stewart, *History of the XII Royal Lancers*, pp.325-326.
65   Stewart, *History of the XII Royal Lancers*, p.327.
66   Horsburgh-Porter, Andrew Marshall: (Oral history)/Imperial War Museums <iwm.org. uk> (accessed 11/08/22).

The only wireless suitable was currently carried on a lorry, and a size reduction would have resulted in a reduction in range. The cavalry understood that it would only be a matter of time before technology produced wirelesses that could be fitted into an armoured car, but for some, the wireless would always remain 'a novelty and even an object of suspicion.'[67] The impact on the Regiment was that whereas previously the wireless equipment in the lorries had been operated by members of the Royal Signals, now that the wireless had been fitted into the armoured cars, the cavalry would need to be trained to operate them, something which only affected the Cavalry Armoured Car Regiments. Shand stated that the Regiment had for what was in 'those days, a very sophisticated familiarity with the use of radio communications.'[68]

No sooner had the Regiment arrived back in Britain than it was sent on its third operational deployment. On 2nd January 1935, a grouping from the Regiment formed up under the title of D Squadron. The grouping was commanded by Captain Smith consisting of five officers, 60 soldiers, and eight Lanchester armoured cars. The half-squadron deployed to the Saar Plebiscite on mainland Europe which had been managed by the League of Nations since 1920. The Squadron was billeted in the 'Karl Kaiser Restaurant on the outskirts of Saarbrücken, and their role was to conduct patrols during the decision-making process of whether the region was going to stay with France or revert to Germany.'[69] The transition went without incident and the Squadron returned to Britain on 23rd February, with congratulations from the OC of the British Contingent who said that 'Smith and his officers could not have done better... they had some difficult patrols... they have been grand.'[70] The people of the Saar eventually voted unanimously to join Germany, which meant the return journey through France for the armoured cars was significantly different to the one they made two months earlier, Sergeant Bryant recalled that:

This proved to be a very different journey from the outward one. The crowds of people were still there but this time they were very antagonistic towards us, hissing, jeering, and throwing the odd stick or stone at us. Typical frog![71]

As one chapter of post-First World War history was closing, another conflict was looming. The war clouds were now rising again in Europe and in 1936, Italy invaded Abyssinia, and in November of the same year, the Regiment (less A Squadron) was sent back to Egypt to reinforce the garrison.[72] This was as a direct result of Mussolini

67   R. Chenevix Trench, 'Wireless with Cavalry', in *The Cavalry Journal* (January to October 1929), pp.559-560; Shand, *Previous Encounters*, p.17.
68   Shand *Previous Encounters*, p.17.
69   J.W. Bryant, *Some Thoughts at Sunset*, pp.21-24.
70   Stewart, *History of the XII Royal Lancers*, p.328.
71   Bryant, *Some Thoughts at Sunset*, p.24.
72   The personnel from A Squadron were used to bring the other squadrons up to establishment.

strengthening his garrisons in Libya. When the Regiment arrived, they shared their old camp in Helmieh with the 11th Hussars. The Regiment spent time patrolling the border between Egypt and Libya and guarding the RAF's forward landing grounds.[73] However, when not patrolling, lack of spares prevented any effective Brigade or Regimental training but it did introduce desert operations to those who had joined the Regiment since its return to Britain. During the period, B Squadron became a part of the Mobile Force, a force commanded by Brigadier Friend, someone who the Regiment would seek support from later in 1940. By Christmas 1936, the Regiment was complete again in Britain and it would be its first full year at home for a decade.[74]

By 1938, the Regiment was on its third type of armoured car. It seemed to change each time they moved and before each operation. Running parallel to the churn of vehicle types, the Regiment was learning and developing its tactics in both European and Imperial policing operations. The point at which this all came together was in 1938 when Captain Willis was on detachment in Palestine with the Trans-Jordanian Frontier Force and was decorated for his action in command of a squadron of armoured cars 'for gallant conduct and courageous, cool, and skilful leadership while in charge of three troops during an action near Beisan on 2nd December 1938.'[75]

In 1939, the Regiment would see its Lanchesters replaced by the Morris (CS9) armoured car. Its arrival was greeted with mixed reception, Shand described it as 'not very remarkable' and flimsy, while Gort stated that by the time they went to war it was 'obsolete.'[76] The subsequent negative comments were primarily based on its later performance in 1940. Historically, it is difficult to find any attributable quotes, however, when Freddie Hunn was asked if he had ever heard the Morris referred to as the suicide box, Hunn stated that it was not a phrase used in the 12th Lancers. Hunn said, in comparison to the Lanchester, the Morris was smaller, faster, had a lower profile, was more reliable, had better fuel consumption than its predecessor and each vehicle was fitted with wireless. The reality for the older soldiers was that they had to convert to the new vehicle each time and now that all armoured cars were fitted with wireless, all crew members were taught how to operate it. However, in addition the designated wireless operators were also taught Morse code.[77] Despite both pre and post-war personal opinions, all the armoured cars were similar, wheeled, lightly armoured, armed with machine guns, and latterly a perceived anti-tank capability. It would be with these limitations, blended with their mounted cavalry background, that would drive the new armoured car doctrine.

73   Bryant, *Some Thoughts at Sunset,* p.26.
74   Stewart, *History of the XII Royal Lancers,* pp.330-331.
75   TNA WO 373/92/164.
76   Shand, *Previous Encounters,* p.25; B. Shand, 'May 1940: A Memory', in *The Delhi Spearman* (1990), p.151; Gort, *Second Despatch* (25 July 1940), p.5931.
77   Hunn, Frederick: (Oral history)/Imperial War Museums <iwm.org.uk> (accessed 11/7/22).

New Morris Armoured Cars attached from 12th Royal Lancers, Budleigh, 1939 (c) Online collection NAM. 1975-03-63-1-33 <https://collection.nam.ac.uk/detail. php?acc=1975-03-63-1-33>

Armoured Car Doctrine

During their initial conversion training to armoured cars from the Depot and ACC TC, the two regiments soon discovered that it did not include tactical training. This was something they would have to learn for themselves.[78] On the subject of tactics manuals to assist in training, Colonel Kenneth 'Kate' Savill (a subaltern in 1938) stated that the new armoured car units did not have manuals like *Cavalry Training 1 and 2*, but they gradually evolved their 'training on the lines of the original cavalry training.' If there was a manual, he did not remember seeing it, although he thought the responsibility lay with the Commanding Officer and Squadron Leaders to communicate their content.[79]

In truth, there was no shortage of doctrine, but it tended to reflect the ownership of the armoured cars at the time of their production. The *Tank and Armoured*

---

78   Taylor, *Armoured Warfare,* p.146.
79   Savill, Kenneth Edward: (Oral history)/Imperial War Museums <iwm.org.uk> (accessed 03/08/22).

Car Training (Provisional) doctrine from 1921 to 1927 reflected its RTC origins and it saw the armoured car and tank doctrine being 'experimental and as a trial.'[80] It aimed to establish 'broad principles' on which 'common doctrine could be based' and expected considerable developments. Interestingly it saw the armoured car and the tank representing 'different stages in the development of the same idea' based on fire-power, mobility, and protection. It thought 'that in the future it might be possible to eliminate the disabilities of both types of AFVs and it might produce a single type combining the best qualities of both.'[81]

By 1931, there was a re-issue of *Armoured Car Training* and the combined reference to the tank had been removed. Evidently, this was the point when the RTC relinquished its responsibility and the publication was no longer provisional.[82] In 1937, the cavalry issued two publications *Cavalry Training (Horsed)* and *Cavalry Training (Mechanised), Armoured Cars.* Whereas the RTC saw the link between the tank and the armoured car, the cavalry saw the link to the horse. In the section on 'the leading of reconnaissance detachments,' and on the rules and guidance it stated that they, 'are the same as those laid down for cavalry, in *Cavalry Training (Horsed).*'[83] It emphasised the 'prompt transmission of information' and drew reference to the presence of the No. 9 set which can communicate between the Royal Signal section attached to RHQ and the section HQs.[84] In addition to referencing *Cavalry Training (Horsed), 1937,* under the section 'the conduct of an armoured car patrol,' it also referenced *Cavalry Section Leading 1934* again, drawing on its mounted origins where responsibility was placed on NCOs.

The *Regimental Journal* indicated that Charrington had been influential in forming the new doctrine and shaping it from a cavalry perspective:

> Glory for his part in formulating the tactical doctrine for armoured cars and also for setting the standards for the acceptance of the mechanised role to which all cavalry regiments have been since committed.[85]

Charrington wrote three articles for *The Cavalry Journal* in 1927, prior to his taking command of the Regiment, called 'where the cavalry stands today.' The purpose was a brief historical review of its use set against a background of uncertainty regarding its future place in the Army. In his concluding statement, he recognised the importance of aircraft and the necessity for infantry to operate in thickly wooded or mountainous

80   HMSO, *Armoured Car Training: Training and War 1921 (Provisional)* and HMSO, *Tank and Armoured Car Training, Vol. 2, War, (Provisional), 1927.*
81   *Tank and Armoured Car Training Vol. 2, War (Provisional),* Chap. 2, Sect. 9, para. 1-2, p.14.
82   HMSO, *Armoured Car Training War, Vol. 2, 1931.*
83   HMSO, *Cavalry Training (Horsed) 1937;* HMSO, *Cavalry Training (Mechanised) Pam. No. 1 – Armoured Cars, 1937,* p.19.
84   *Cavalry Training (Mechanised),* pp.20-22.
85   *The Delhi Spearman* (1964), p.44.

areas. He wrote that the cavalry would need to 'co-operate closely with the infantry and that is how it should be organised, trained, and equipped. Charrington saw it being achieved through mechanisation and that 'armoured fighting vehicles will in the future reign supreme over the open spaces of the world which were once such a favourable battleground for the cavalry.'[86]

However, this was not the first time that the Army had needed to modernise. This was something that the whole Army had done since the introduction of modern weapons (rifled and magazine-fed weapons with smokeless powder), but it had had little impact on the cavalry as a means of doing their work differently had not been available and the horse could not be replaced. The main impact on the Army during its period of modernisation had been the change in its formations which became more dispersed as the battlefield became larger, affecting its ability to command and control its soldiers. It was realised as early as 1877 that command would have to be delegated if opportunities on the battlefield were to be seized by initiative.[87] This change in command philosophy was not without its opponents, although it did find its way into the doctrine and training.

This was reflected in the overarching doctrine in training which remarked, 'that due to the nature of modern weapons the decentralisation of command was going to place increasing responsibility on junior commanders.' The benefits of decentralisation and the possibility of having to generate a large Army in war from a small peace-time cadre were recognised. The *Training Regulations* stated that on mobilisation to war the rapid expansion of the Army would mean in the future that 'all commanders were to train NCOs for work in a higher grade than that which they hold… Sergeants must be prepared to command troops in war, they will certainly do it.'[88] The formal transition from central to decentralisation was a journey each element of the Army had to make and arms such as the light infantry and cavalry, which had always operated at distance from their commanders, already had a culture of trust and initiative. For them, this transition was just a formalisation of what they had already had to do out of tactical necessity. It was something the 12th Lancers had embraced: Shand remarked that when he had been in trouble, the Adjutant, instead of informing the Commanding Officer:

> Judiciously handed me over to certain SNCOs who took my education in hand and tactfully but firmly directed my floundering steps. They were very competent nannies with a decidedly un-nannylike capacity for beer.[89]

86   H.V.S. Charrington, 'Where the Cavalry Stands Today' in *Cavalry Journal* (January 1927), pp.18-25 (April 1927) pp.173-183; (July 1927), pp.419-430.
87   HMSO, *Field Exercise 1870*, pp.58-63, pp.102-107, pp.113-115, pp.205-271, pp.236-245 and p.277.
88   HMSO, *Training Regulations 1934*, Chapter 2, Section 14, paras. 1 and 2, p.22.
89   Shand, *Previous Engagements*, pp.15-16.

The Regiment of 1939

The Regiment pre-mobilisation was based in Britain and manning for all home-based regiments was always an issue, as the regiments on Imperial duty were always maintained at full manning to the detriment of those serving at home. In 1934, when the Regiment returned to Britain, it was 71 men short. During the period 1934-1938, only four subalterns had been commissioned.[90] In early 1939, the government introduced 'limited National Service' and the 12th Lancers was one of the regiments selected for this intake. Although this solved the officer manning issue from a numerical perspective, it effectively produced a cohort of 13 militiamen all of whom were Second Lieutenants.[91]

This was the 12th Lancers of 1939, a regiment with 11 years of experience on three different types of armoured cars. It was a regiment short of men whose troops were to be led by young officers, of whom 11 were from the 13 original militiamen. The Regiment had been involved in the development of its doctrine with its origins based on mounted cavalry and had retained its cavalry spirit. This was a result of all the officers of captain and above and all the SNCOs who had originally enlisted and trained as a mounted cavalrymen.[92] Not only had the Regiment had to embrace the armoured car, but every man had also been taught to use the wireless which was still very much in its infancy. During the intervening years, all those who had served during the First World War timed out, so by the time the Regiment embarked in 1939 only the Commanding Officer and the Padre had seen service in the previous World War. However, it had deployed four times in its armoured cars on both Imperial and European policing operations and had developed its own residual operational experience. The Regiment was to be commanded by Lumsden, a man who had commanded the first squadron in the Regiment to be mechanised and had since attended Staff College.

Shand thought that the whole process of mechanisation and the transition to armoured cars had 'been commendably smooth thanks to the capability all round and the imagination from the top.' The resulting effect was that the Regiment was described as a 'highly efficient entity, highly skilled,' and full of personalities.[93]

90   Stewart, *History of the XII Royal Lancers*, p.327 Bishop, *One Young Soldier*, p.45.
91   *The Delhi Spearman* (1989), p.138; TNA WO 167/452 lists: Brinton, Holford, Hon. Noel-Buxton, Earl of Inchcape, de Zoete, Bishop, Henderson, Hall, Windeler, Robinson and Mann. During the Spring of 1939 the deteriorating international situation forced the British government under Neville Chamberlain to consider preparations for a possible war against Nazi Germany. Plans for limited conscription applying to single men aged between 20 and 22 were given parliamentary approval in the Military Training Act in May 1939. This required men to undertake six months' military training, and some 240,000 registered for service. See *Conscription: The Second World War* <https://www.parliament.uk/about/living-heritage/transformingsociety/private-lives/yourcountry/overview/conscriptionww2/> (accessed 01/09/22).
92   9/12L Lecture notes: Corps Recce Study Day, 'Salvation of the BEF 10-31 May 1940', pp.14,16.
93   Shand, *Previous Engagements*, pp.17,19; G. Blaxland, *Destination Dunkirk: The Story of Gort, Army* (1973), pp.9-10.

2

Personalities

With such a fine group of men as associates, life was more than agreeable, and the weeks went by swiftly, filled with our daily routine.
Falaise[1]

The following brief pen portraits are the personal opinions of Henry de le Falaise and Lieutenant Bruce Shand supplemented by lines from their obituaries.[2]

Lieutenant Colonel Herbert Lumsden MC (Commanding Officer)

Young, in his early 40s, always in perfect physical trim and he embodied the spirit of the Regiment. Extraordinarily intelligent, with an extremely penetrating mind, he was a superior type of officer. He had gone through Staff College and served with distinction in the First World War. His gallantry in action had won him the Military Cross with the RHA. There was not a trooper, NCO, or officer in his Regiment whom he did not know intimately and whose real worth he had not accurately rated. He saw through people and could quickly and accurately size them up. I never knew him to make a mistake about anyone. In military matters, his foresight was near to being uncanny. In manoeuvres, he seldom was at fault in figuring out what moves the enemy was going to make. He had a faculty that seemed amazing for taking measures to counteract what they attempted or did and sometimes it struck us, even before the other fellow himself had figured his course. A strict disciplinarian, he was nonetheless eminently just; he invariably always saw the human side.[3] He had a very sharp mind, a very smart appearance and possibly a greater tolerance of human error than

1   H. de la Falaise, *Through Hell to Dunkirk* (1943), p.7.
2   Shand, *Previous Engagements,* passim and Falaise, *Through Hell to Dunkirk*, passim.
3   Falaise, *Through Hell to Dunkirk*, pp.2-3.

his predecessor (who may well have concealed it). Ambitious, but blessed with humour and humanity.[4]

Major Andrew Horsburgh-Porter (A Squadron Leader)

One of the stars of the Regiment. A Wykehamist, lanky, high-strung polo player of 34, with a generous share of Irish and Spanish blood, brave, with something of a temperament. Fearless, enterprisingly bold, a born leader and full of cavalry dash. Horses were his hobby; he was an expert on all kinds of racing and could, without omitting one, rattle off the names of the winners of the Grand National and the weights the horses carried. A real gambler at heart, you felt that he would stake on a toss of the martial dice if challenged, his life and that of the officers and men of his Squadron, without batting an eye. He was the kind who rides his mount ruthlessly and hard, without pity for man, including himself, or beast, in order to win any game. Erratic, with a sometimes-uncontrollable temper under provocation, he was either very kind or very stern with his command. There was also another side to his character, a very charming side. I don't think the subalterns of his Squadron ever found that; perhaps because he did not intend them to. But I was privileged to have several glimpses of it, with the result that I became devoted to the man and would have gladly yielded the ultimate sacrifice for him if need be.[5] He 'always evinced great cavalry dash… the epitome of a free-range officer.'[6]

Major William Browne-Clayton (B Squadron Leader)

A saturnine officer from County Carlow, Andrew Horsburgh-Porter's brother-in-law. I think he suffered from some liver complaint which made him somnolent and frequently testy and with his rather yellow complexion, he looked like a Victorian satirical novelist's idea of an Indian Army officer.[7]

Captain Dozy Willis MC (C Squadron Leader)

An idiosyncratic soldier if ever there was one. Dressed almost invariably in an old box-cloth coaching coat that had belonged to his uncle and a red side hat, he treated the enemy and senior officers with an impartial and refreshing lack of respect.[8]

4   Shand, *Previous Engagements*, p.20.
5   Falaise, *Through Hell to Dunkirk*, pp.3-4.
6   Shand, *Previous Engagements*, p.21 and p.32.
7   Shand, *Previous Engagements*, p.38.
8   Shand, *Previous Engagements*, p.38.

Major John Erne [John Crichton, 5th Earl Erne] – North Irish Horse (Second in Command – A Squadron)

John Erne was not a regular officer and had recently come over from England. Attached to the Regiment only temporarily, he would soon have to return to Northern Ireland to take command of a newly formed armoured car regiment. His father had been killed in action in the last war. John, as he was known to us in the Mess, was a keenly attractive-looking Irishman in his middle thirties. Gifted with enormous charm, he was a most likeable character. Extremely quiet and calm, he kept his emotions in curb at all times, even under trying conditions. He was my conception of a thorough gentleman, of what an ideal gentleman should be. The fact that he bore one of the oldest titles of Ireland and England and was a peer of the realm apparently inclined him all the more strongly to be democratic and amiable to everyone. John's heart was in the right place. He always thought first of other people's feelings and the welfare of the men of the Squadron before his own. There was not a man in the whole outfit who would not have gone through hell and high water for his Lordship, the Earl.[9]

Major W.H. 'Bill' Mabbott (Quartermaster)

Shand described Mabbott as 'beloved and enormously capable.'[10] Bill had joined the Regiment in 1919. By 1936 he became RSM and in 1938 Quartermaster. It was said that it fell to him to supplement the mobilisation plan in 1939. That everything went smoothly and without fuss on the Q side was only to be expected from a department run by Bill Mabbott. So well had he organised his staff that when, in May 1940, the Regiment went into battle, although Bill was cut-off from it, there was never a hitch in administrative arrangements – proof of his foresight, planning and training. On return from leave, Bill was retained at Le Havre to command the troop at the Base Troops. He did not depart with the Regiment at Dunkirk but survived the sinking of the ill-fated RMS Lancastria when it was sunk on 17th June 1940, a week after the Regiment had been evacuated. A senior officer swimming in the water saw him still on the side of the ship which was sinking rapidly and shouted at him to jump receiving the reply – "I will be with you in a minute but have another 40 men to get off." A man of great courage who all through his life served his Sovereign and his Regiment without thought for himself. He was awarded the MBE and two Mentions in Despatches for his magnificent services during the War… and he was loved by us all.[11]

---

9   Falaise, *Through Hell to Dunkirk*, pp.4-5.
10   Shand, *Previous Engagements*, p.9.
11   *12L Regimental Journal* (April 1949), p.115; *The Delhi Spearman* (1980), p.85.

Lieutenant Bruce Shand (1 Troop Leader – A Squadron)

Tall, fair-headed, blue-eyed and a little over 20, he initially impressed persons who did not know him well as being a wealthy dilettante. Though naturally indolent and insouciant, he could also, you felt, exhibit abundant courage, born of possession of real stamina if he deemed it worth the effort. He chose to cause one to believe that things military bored him inordinately. Perhaps they did. But it stood out that his troop was one of the best and that, on manoeuvre, he was the ablest of them all. I had supreme faith in Bruce, for I was confident that in a pinch he would never lose his head. He could be depended upon to do the right thing, even if it might be his pose to enact a hero's role with a slightly bored smile.[12] He was thought to be a 'very nice person' and was known to 'bend the rules a little to make life a little more comfortable.'[13]

Second Lieutenant Peter Arkwright 11th Hussars (2 Troop Leader – A Squadron) – DoW 24/5/40[14]

Tall and comely above the average in a masculine way, he looked about 18 although he was a little above 20. Always smiling and happy he savoured life and delighted in making his troopers happy. He was in charge of the Squadron's sports and outdoor games. In his love of beauty and cleanliness, he encouraged his men to grow flowers in front of their billets. This was imitated by the other troops, and the little village in which we were billeted rapidly turned into a Spring flower show. He also displayed eager ingenuity as a soldier and could usually be counted upon to spring a totally unexpected surprise during manoeuvres on those who represented the enemy. I was in command of a foot patrol one night, my object being to try to capture his armoured car, which was guarding a railroad crossing, or at least to put it out of action. It was pitch-dark. After crawling on my stomach over water-soaked ploughed fields with my patrol, we finally surrounded his car. I was about to give the signal to leap to the attack when hundreds of flashes and a terrific noise like the cracking of a hundred rifles burst upon us. He had secretly bought packets of Chinese fire-crackers and laid them all over the ground surrounding his position, linked them all together and touched them off from his car when he heard us nearby. It may not have been according to the military Hoyle of night manoeuvres, but it made us laugh and proved that we had not fooled him for one minute. I have described this trifling episode only because I think it provides an excellent notion of his character and his manner of doing things. To him, war was a game, and he was determined to enjoy it, to get as much fun from it

---

12   Falaise, *Through Hell to Dunkirk*, p.5.
13   Bryant, *Some Thoughts at Sunset*, p.28.
14   Arkwright is recorded as a 11H by the CWGC. Therefore, his death is not included in the overall total for 12L.

as he could, like the good sport he was.[15] A natural soldier, he had a completely unaffected character and was loved by his men.[16]

Second Lieutenant Andrew Roddick (3 Troop Leader – A Squadron) – KIA 25/5/40

Andrew Roddick was a recent arrival from England, only 21 years old, not tall, with fair hair and light blue eyes. He was intelligent beyond the average, with a real sense of humour and sharp wit which amused us all. He would have us believe that his prime ambition was to sit in front of a fire, housed on his landed estate, reading the *Farmers' Gazette*, or, with the help of a glass of port of approved vintage doze over the staid columns of *The Times* in a deep chair in his old-fashioned and ultra-exclusive club in London. He was a graduate of an agricultural school. Farming was his hobby, and he would give us to understand that the price of hogs was of much more vital interest to him than soldiering in the mucky fields of northern France. But the truth was that he was really eager to be a crack officer and was rapidly learning his trade and doing it with a twinkle in his eye and in a manner which, combined with his other agreeable attributes, made him a high favourite in the Squadron. He was a brave, lovable lad. Roddick was Lumsden's wife's nephew. Sergeant Lewis, the troop sergeant, later wrote to Roddick's parents saying, 'that he was held in great esteem by all of us, they had confidence in the decisions he made, that he led them well and 'was responsible for several successful actions against the enemy.'[17] Shand thought him like his uncle, 'a man of humour, humanity, and a permanent twinkle in his eye.'[18] His school wrote that 'he had always been a great fighter. Here we remember him for his unyielding honesty and cheery kindliness, and as one of the best and best-liked of Captains. At Cambridge he won a Distinction in Agriculture and meant to farm; his whole heart was in it, and he loved every minute of it, studying French methods in his odd moments in France.'[19] Lumsden wrote 'he was a grand boy and a great success as an officer. Although he had only been in the Regiment for a short time, he was loved and respected by all. He was a born leader of men and would have been a great success as a soldier, as he always put his work and his men first. It was strange that one who so disliked taking life should have been killed whilst himself necessarily killing Germans.'[20]

15   Falaise, *Through Hell to Dunkirk*, pp.5-6.
16   Shand, *Previous Engagements*, p.36.
17   Letter The Royal Lancers Museum Derby.
18   Shand, *Previous Engagements*, p.36.
19   *The Marlburian, July 1940* (vol. LXXV no 986).
20   Lumsden in *The Marlburian, July 1940* (vol. LXXV no. 987).

Second Lieutenant Tim Bishop (A Squadron – SHQ subaltern)

Handsome, trim, and elegant. As a result of parental disagreement, he had left Stowe to enlist in the Life Guards, eventually obtaining what was called an 'A' Cadetship to Sandhurst, joining us with several other young officers in the latter part of 1938. Before the war, life in the ranks of the Household Cavalry was much as it must have been in Victorian times, with unbelievably rigid discipline and considerable hardship. The hours spent cleaning horses and accoutrements were infinite and Tim used to say that even young soldiers looked 20 years older than they actually were. I think he was lucky in that having a little money he could get a lot of this work done for him by others, but the standards set by the 'Plungers' were those by which he lived, giving a certain old-fashioned austerity to part of his nature. He could write attractively and was a gifted artist, like his beautiful sister, Molly Scott. All his armoured cars had friezes and frescoes inside them of sporting scenes and one only wishes they could have been preserved. He was also an effective, sympathetic and polished rider, with a wide knowledge of horses. In later life, he became a well-known and respected judge of hunters. I could have wished for no better companion in the hazards ahead of us: blessed with a keen sense of the ridiculous, he was an infallibly competent soldier without any overdoses of enthusiasm.[21]

Second Lieutenant Basil Hall (Transport Officer – A Squadron)

Basil Hall was not a regular career officer and was originally a trooper in the Inns of Court Regiment. On the outbreak of war, the Regiment became the 101st Officer Cadet Training Unit and he was commissioned in early 1940, along with Alan Windler and Ander Henderson.[22] A lawyer by profession, he had recently joined us. Very intelligent and well-read, he always displayed an eagerness to help others and was notably precise in his duties. He was a type quite apart from the other officers, a sturdy reliable John Bull.[23] Erudite… who handled the logistic complexities… with infinite patience and skill.[24]

Second Lieutenant John Clark-Kennedy (2 Troop Leader – B Squadron)

'Haywire' was commissioned on 25th August 1938 and joined the 12th Lancers at Tidworth. He initially failed the medical as a result of his poor eyesight but was

---

21   Shand, *Previous Engagements*, p.37.
22   Hall Diary, p.1.
23   Falaise, *Through Hell to Dunkirk*, p.7.
24   Shand, *Previous Engagements*, p.36.

allowed to join on the account that he could see alright with his glasses. John felt that he had only passed the entrance exam as it was during the Munich crisis and the 'rumblings of war.'[25] In those days he possessed five things that made an instant impression: a pipe, thickish glasses, an ancient cream Rolls Royce and, as certain officers painfully discovered, a powerful punch and formidable temper. Known as 'Haywire' in his youth, he went to France as a troop leader in October 1939. At the Battle of Arras, he was wounded when his car was knocked out while trying to reach another car already hit. John had two cars shot from under him in France and he was awarded the Military Cross for his gallantry. The *Regimental Journal* of 1960 stated that 'new troop leaders anxious to learn the secret, often used to sidle up to him with sly questions about troop tactics.' During the war John was to have four more cars shot from under him in the desert.[26]

Second Lieutenant Peter Miller-Mundy, (4 Troop – B Squadron)

'Potter' was larger than life and twice as colourful, a subaltern's dream and a Commanding Officer's nightmare. He was already something of a legend when he joined B Squadron of the 12th from the Supplementary Reserve. He was quite fearless and some of his exploits as 4 Troop Leader in France, when he won one of the best Military Crosses of that campaign, are in the *Regimental History*. We can only hope that his Saintly namesake met Peter with a big Havana, a glass of Kummel and a backgammon board.[27]

Second Lieutenant Edward Mann (Troop Leader – C Squadron)

Ned Mann was from Malvern, went to Sandhurst, joined the 12th Lancers in 1938, and served with the Regiment throughout the war, being in command of a squadron for the latter half of it. In 1940, as a subaltern, he was awarded the Distinguished Service Order for an exploit of great coolness and gallantry which materially delayed the German advance to Dunkirk and contributed towards the safe withdrawal of the BEF. He subsequently fought in North Africa and Italy, receiving the Military Cross, and being decorated by the Americans. He possessed a charming personality, and imbued with great natural gaiety he was the least pompous of people and certainly the best of friends. He was highly capable and quite unruffled by adverse circumstances. He was the last person to court popularity, but one doubts if anyone in the Regiment

25   *An Officer and a Gentleman: The Life of John Clark Kennedy 1918-2020* (2012), pp.6-8 <https://www.carsphairn.org/CarsphairnArchive/files/original/ c9db07c01e683d6261b500c81fd24c7f.pdf> (accessed 14/11/22).
26   *The Delhi Spearman* (2009), pp.107-108.
27   Obituary by Clark-Kennedy in *The Delhi Spearman* (1982), p.52.

was more liked or respected.[28] After his death, The Edward Mann Memorial Prize was set up in his memory and the sum of £20 was to be awarded on the recommendation of the Commanding Officer and presented by the Trustees of the Memorial Fund 'to an officer who has distinguished himself in the world of sport.'[29]

Second Lieutenant Piers Edgecumbe (Phantom Force) – KIA 27/5/40

Charming and dreamy. The Continental and North American idea of an English aristocrat is benevolent and forgetful.[30]

RSM (later Major) Major E.C. 'Fred' Fox

A man of inexhaustible energy and brilliant ability; few people knew that in 1942 he was offered a posting to the 11th Armoured Divisional Staff, which might have led him to far higher ranks. However, Fred, against the advice of his Commanding Officer, refused. He reckoned that the 12th Lancers meant more to him than promotion and in forming the war-time offshoot of the Regiment he was determined to make it a success; and then continue to serve the 12th Lancers. His devotion and loyalty to his Regiment may have stemmed from the fact that as a young soldier he had absorbed the atmosphere created by Blakiston-Houston, Lawrence, and Mabbott. 'Fred' owed his nickname to the leading jockey at the time of his joining. He became a proficient horseman and won the young Soldiers' Cup for his skill with the sword, lance, and revolver. But the rifle was his real weapon. For years he coached and shot with the rifle team. Always gay, efficient and immaculate, he went to war as Squadron Sergeant Major and shortly became RSM to Herbert Lumsden. He enjoyed a dashing solo action in his armoured car near Mount St. Eloi, then in 1941 promoted to Quartermaster. He helped Colonel Ian Smith form the 27L and was the backbone of that Regiment in Italy.[31]

Henry de la Falaise (Marquis de La Falaise de La Coudraye) (*Agent de Liaison – A Squadron*)

Of an ancient and, I think, impecunious family, he had fought with gallantry in the First World War, receiving not only the *Croix de Guerre* but also the coveted *Médaille*

28   Obituary in *12L Regimental Journal* (1960), p.6.
29   *The Delhi Spearman* (1966), p.109.
30   CADOGAN No. 117413 (1917-1940).
31   *The Delhi Spearman* (1982), p.78.

Militaire, and was badly wounded. Extremely smart and well-dressed at all times, he had a strong resemblance to a film star of those days called Adolf Menjou, though I believe the latter had no French blood. Henry's knowledge of the celluloid world and Hollywood, in particular, was encyclopaedic as he had gone to make his fortune there very soon after the war, employed at one time by Joseph Kennedy, subsequently American Ambassador in England, of whose early commercial activities he painted the most lurid and terrifying picture. He had not made his fortune, although he had managed to marry in succession the leading Hollywood actresses Gloria Swanson and Constance Bennett. By 1940 he had long been rid of the former and was now disenchanted with the latter and was hoping to wed a charming and very rich South American, Emmita Rodriguez. Constance Bennett was being difficult about the divorce but just before the Blitzkrieg started Henry received incontrovertible evidence of her adultery. His only fear, and nothing else seemed to alarm him during the next three weeks, was that he might lose these vital papers. Happily, they reached England with him. It was a real pleasure to have him with us: good-tempered and good-mannered, amusing and with time for everyone and with a generosity of spirit not always apparent in his compatriots, the 'Marquess,' as the troops called him, was an enormous asset, especially as Andrew [Horsburgh-Porter] had great respect for him and consequently acted in a more restrained manner than hitherto. Henry was highly conscientious in smoothing over matters with the inhabitants of Foncquevillers when difficulties arose over billets, drunken troops and so on.[32]

In his obituary in *The Delhi Spearman* it said that he was never ruffled, even when he saw his country falling in ruins, he kept the gaiety and the sang-froid of his aristocratic background. And the officers realised that in Henri they had seen the perfect flower of Medieval *'noblesse oblige.'* Coming back from Dunkirk to the Cavalry Club, he changed his clothes and nipped back to Paris just in time to take his wife over to America where he wrote a book about his experiences. He had a long and happy life and was always fond of the 12th Lancers.[33]

32   Shand, *Previous Engagements*, p.26.
33   *The Delhi Spearman* (1973), p.80.

Lieutenant Colonel Herbert Lumsden MC.
(RLMT)

Major Andrew Horsburgh-Porter. (RLMT)

Captain Dozy Willis MC. (RLMT)

Captain Ronald Kennard (Adjutant).
(RLMT)

Henry de la Falaise. (*Through Hell to Dunkirk*)

Lieutenant Bruce Shand, 1945.
(*Previous Encounters*)

2nd Lieutenant Tim Bishop. (Front cover *One Young Soldier*)

2nd Lieutenant John Clark-Kennedy.
(RLMT)

2nd Lieutenant Peter Miller-Mundy.
(RLMT)

2nd Lieutenant Piers Edgcumbe. (The grave of Second) Lieutenant Piers Richard Edgcumbe rededicated in France. (CWGC)

Left: 2nd Lieutenant Andrew Roddick. (1936 Cotton XI detail STG Roddick, Marlborough College)
Above: 2nd Lieutenant Basil Hall. (<https://www.telegraph.co.uk/news/obituaries/military-obituaries/army-obituaries/8539616/Sir-Basil-Hall.html>)

2nd Lieutenant David Smith. (*Castle and Regimental Museum, Monmouth* <https://www. peoplescollection.wales/discover/query>)

2nd Lieutenant Edward Mann. (RLMT)

RSM Fox. (RLMT)

RQMS James. (RLMT)

SSM Tree. (RLMT)

Sergeant Booker. (RLMT)

Sergeant Freddie Hunn. (BBC Two – Britain's
Greatest Generation, Then and now: the
Greatest Generation in pictures – Major
Freddie Hunn MBE)

Sergeant Ditton. (RLMT)

Sergeant Lewis. (RLMT)   Sergeant Pearton. (RLMT)

3

The Long Wait – Phoney War

(September 1939–10th May 1940)

The reservists being of a very high quality. I know as a Troop Leader how much I owe to some of these old soldiers.
Shand[1]

The plans for the despatch of the Force differed in two important respects from those of August 1914. The possibility of attack by sea and air made it necessary to use the Western ports of France instead of the Channel ports, while the total replacement of animals by mechanical vehicles, which had been completed by 1939, presented a new problem in transportation.
Gort[2]

The End of Peace

On 15th March, Hitler announced that Bohemia and Moravia were taken under German protection and Czechoslovakia ceased to exist as an independent state. In the two months which followed, Germany seized Memel, the chief port of Lithuania, denounced her pact of non-aggression with Poland and her Naval Agreement with Great Britain, and signed a 'Pact of Steel' with Italy, which meanwhile had invaded Albania.

In Britain, the growing menace of these events and Hitler's bellicose attitude to Poland led progressively to the adoption of conscription, the calling up of army reservists for training and the partial mobilisation of the Fleet and the Royal Air Force. Germany's next move was to secure its eastern borders by concluding two treaties with Russia which included a secret agreement to divide Poland and left Russia free

---

1   Shand, 'May 1940: A Memory', p.150.
2   Gort, *First Despatch* (25 April 1940), p.5899.

to take Finland. On 25th August, the British Government signed an Anglo-Polish Defence Alliance, promising mutual assistance in the event of aggression. On 1st September, Germany invaded Poland across every accessible frontier without any previous declaration of war and bombed the Polish airfields without warning. Britain at once ordered full mobilisation and sent an ultimatum to Germany, timed to expire on 3rd September. To this, there was no response and at 1100 hrs that morning, the Second World War began.[3]

Poland, in the face of overwhelming odds, was defeated by the end of September and Hitler, in the meantime, began transferring his armies to the west. By the end of November, Allied intelligence estimated that between 97 and 99 divisions were already concentrated on the Western Front, facing Holland, Belgium, Luxembourg, and France. In November there were strong indications that Germany would attack, and as predicted on 5th November Hitler issued orders for an offensive, however, on 7th the attack was postponed. For the BEF this period was seen as the Phoney War, the war that they were waiting for, that did not come. However, for the people of Scandinavia the war was not phoney, and on 9th April Germany seized Denmark and started an invasion of Norway.[4]

Phoney War

On 3rd September, when war was declared, the 12th Lancers were in their peacetime quarters at Warburg Barracks in Aldershot. Shand wrote that the Regiment was fully mobilised with the right number of armoured cars and a rather mixed collection of 'B' vehicles (mostly from civilian sources). The vehicles all arrived complete with chains through the kindness of Sir William Roots, the father of the Technical Adjutant.[5] The Regiment received all the reservists that had been called up from both the 12th Lancers and 11th Hussars, its 'sister-armoured car regiment' which was still in Egypt.[6] Along with the reservists 'large numbers of seemingly ancient officers also arrived in outdated uniforms.' At the same time, the officers' horses, which had been retained post-mechanisation were 'whisked away.'[7] By the end of the day, all the armoured cars were fully loaded and the squadrons dispersed to the farms and villages of Hampshire, in case of a German air attack on Aldershot.[8]

3   L.F. Ellis, *The War in France and Flanders 1939-1940* (1953), p.13.
4   Ellis, *The War in France and Flanders*, pp.32-33.
5   Stewart, *History of the XII Royal Lancers*, p.349.
6   Bryant, *Some Thoughts at Sunset*, p.7.
7   Shand, *Previous Engagements*, p.17.
8   Hunn, Frederick: (Oral history)/Imperial War Museums <iwm.org.uk> (accessed 11/07/22).

A Squadron at Froyle House September 1939. (http://www.froyle.com/>)

The *Regimental History* stated that, consequently, RHQ was able to 'hand-pick' a Regiment of 700 from a large selection of 1200 trained reservists.[9] Hunn remembered that the reservists had all 'served either six or 12 years in either of the regiments… These older experienced men were of great value and, combined with the enthusiasm of the young soldiers, the ingredients were there for the making of a good team.' Shand noted that it was possible to 'hand-pick a Regiment from a large selection and very good it proved to be, with the reservists being of a very high quality. I know as a Troop Leader how much I owe to some of these old soldiers.'[10]

The Regiment expected to be sent to France as part of the BEF, moving there immediately after the outbreak of hostilities. Shand wrote that 'some genius at the War Office decided that the role of armoured cars was now finished and that we should be re-trained to operate with Cruiser tanks (which of course had not yet even been built).' The decision was described by others as both shocking and farcical.[11] The Commanding

9   Stewart, *History of the XII Royal Lancers*, p.348.
10   Shand, 'May 1940: A Memory', p.150.
11   Stewart, *History of the XII Royal Lancers*, p.348.

Officer, Lumsden, was able to handle this setback with his customary skill and some 'procrastination.'[12]

The Regiment embarked for France on 15th October from Southampton, exactly 40 years to the day and from the same barracks from which they had deployed to the Boer War. It was only given one week's notice-to-move, meaning that the Morris armoured car was temporarily saved from oblivion. The fact of the matter was that the order to re-role the Regiment was never rescinded amongst the chaos of war, and they would go on to serve in another four different types of armoured car during the war.[13]

The Regiment had only received its Morris armoured cars that year. Its armament comprised a Bren gun (.303) and a Boyes anti-tank rifle (.55). Shand thought it could 'show quite a turn of speed'. The vehicle had a crew of four and each member carried a .38 revolver. In

Maurice Barker, Andrew Horsburgh-Porter, Pat Summers, and Peter Arkwright at Froyle House September 1939. (<http://www.froyle.com/>)

Pat Summers, Christopher Noel-Buxton, Peter Arkwright, and Maurice Barker at Froyle House September 1939. (<http://www.froyle.com/>)

addition to its main armament, the vehicle was fitted with a smoke projector and the crew carried a Verey (flare) pistol and a few Mills hand grenades.[14]

12   Military Cross awarded during the First World War whilst acting as a Forward Observation Officer (FOO) with the RHA.
13   Stewart, *History of the XII Royal Lancers*, p.349; Maguire states: Morris, Beaverette, Humber MK 1-3, Daimler, and American Staghound.
14   Hunn Diary, p.1.

Morris Turret. (Author's collection)

Shand thought the Morris later became 'stigmatised' as being under-engined, under-armed and under-armoured, but he felt that this was only partly true.[15] As to the vehicle's speed, he had a 'very vivid recollection' of a race against Lieutenant Tim Bishop:

> Some weeks after we had landed, to find out its maximum speed, we managed to seal off some three miles of a straight poplar-lined French road and had whipped up the vehicles to a speed of nearly 60 miles an hour, when the whole thing was, perhaps, fortunately, brought to a halt by a farmer moving his sheep across the course. The two armoured cars had been running neck and neck with about a foot between them and neither driver was prepared to give way.[16]

Another attribute the armoured car had over its predecessors was, in addition to its top speed, that all the armoured cars were fitted with the No. 9 wireless set which Shand said 'gave good communications (although it suffered from severe interference) and could communicate further when used in conjunction with a mast and morse code.[17]

---

15   Shand, *Previous Engagements*, p.20.
16   Shand, 'May 1940: A Memory', p.151.
17   Shand, 5th Division Exercise ACROSPIRE; Battlefield Tour; NW France, and Belgium 1940 (1970), p.71; Hunn, p.1; Falaise, *Through Hell to Dunkirk*, p.1. Wireless set No. 9: Medium range transceiver covering 1,875-5. MHz, AM and CW – 5-Watt telephony, 10-Watt CW. Range 35 miles. Hunn states 5-6 sections in total of about ½" in diameter. You

Shand wrote that the 'embarkation went smoothly' although the advance party, of which he was a member, 'had to endure a period of alcoholic incarceration in a hotel at Southampton after the vehicles had been loaded':

> We arrived at Cherbourg and all the vehicles promptly disappeared to be put on a train, while the Regiment marched on foot some five or six weary miles to the ancient Chateau de Martinvaast, carrying a great deal of personal kit. We stayed a night here and were then entrained the next day for the area of Arras, to become GHQ troops and, in fact, to hang about there until May 1940, during the period of the so-called 'Phoney War.' These six months were not very amusing and were not helped by an exceptionally hard Winter. The stark villages in which we were billeted were set amongst the cemeteries and battlefields of the previous war and the amenities of life were not immediately apparent nor available.[18]

The Regiment's first billets were in the Arras area. RHQ was at Ambrines, with the remaining squadrons in Penin (A), Maizieres (B) and Villers-Sir-Simon [Villiers-Sur-Simon] (C), where they were visited by the Duke of Gloucester on 22nd October.[19] At the end of the month, A Squadron sent one troop of armoured cars to the 13th/18th Hussars for purposes of recognition. It was decided that all the armoured cars would now be marked with white squares and carry Union Flags. On the same day General Friend, OC GHQ Troops, visited the Regiment and walked around RHQ.[20] It was Friend who had commanded the Mobile Force in Egypt, in which B Squadron had served, and the *Regimental History* stated that he was very much considered an 'old friend' of the Regiment.[21] It was possibly during this visit that Lumsden 'badgered' Friend for additional Engineer support, as on the 1st November, Second Lieutenant David Smith visited the Regiment and gave a lecture to the squadrons on explosives and, by the 9th November, he was on the Regimental distribution list for the Regimental Information Summary No. 4.[22]

The Engineers who came under command were a militia regiment of the Royal Monmouthshire Royal Engineers consisting of mostly 'Welsh miners'.[23] Smith, later wrote about his relationship with the Regiment saying:

could only get three up, and it need to be supported by a line. See Hunn, Frederick: (Oral history)/Imperial War Museums <iwm.org.uk> (accessed 11/07/22).
18   Shand, 'May 1940: A Memory', p.151.
19   TNA WO 167/452, 21-22 October 1939.
20   TNA WO 167/452, 31 October 1939.
21   Stewart, *History of the XII Royal Lancers*, p.350.
22   TNA WO 167/452, 1-9 November 1939.
23   Shand, Exercise ACROSPIRE, p.72; Stewart, *History of the XII Royal Lancers*, p.350.

Maintenance - C Squadron armoured car at Villers-Sir-Simon 1939. (IWM-O-617)

Off on patrol - C Squadron armoured car at Villers-Sir-Simon 1939. (*One Young Soldier*)

We didn't know if we could fulfil our task; equally, we did not know if they could fulfil theirs… We went to war taking each other on trust, it took a very short time to establish that the trust was not misplaced. For our part, we felt that to be thrown together with a distinguished cavalry regiment, that we had to keep our end up… and I was first among equals.[24]

On 23rd November, the Regiment moved billets. RHQ was located at Hebuterne, in a butcher's yard, and although their accommodation was as uncomfortable as everyone else's, Thurston said 'it did have some obvious advantages.'[25] This supported the Commanding Officer's statement that 'it takes a fool to be uncomfortable.' Shand said they 'were at least tolerably warm and well-fed, the Regimental cooks greatly benefiting from French influences.' The remaining squadrons were billeted in the local villages of Foncquevillers (A), Puisieux (B) and Manchy [Monchy] (C), see map 4.[26] Shand observed:

A Squadron was billeted in an unattractive village called Foncquevillers, the Mess being in a farmhouse looking out on a steaming midden. Being more mobile than many other formations, we certainly saw something of the country and did a fair amount of exercises with the French DLMs (*Division Légère Mécanique*), with whom we would be closely in touch when hostilities started.[27]

Hunn's recollection of B Squadron's billets at Puisieux was:

The area was littered with old trenches, barbed wire, unexploded shells and debris, all relics of that terrible war. A few war cemeteries were situated in the area. The other squadrons were based in nearby villages. Each Troop was allocated a house in which to live; there was no furniture but an outside tap and lavatory. Barns, sheds, and yards were used to park our vehicles a few yards from the sleeping quarters. I shared a room of about 10 square feet with nine other men (the Troop).[28] Each of us had a straw-filled palliasse and two blankets on which to sleep, and when these were laid out at night the floor would be covered completely. During the day the beds would be folded back to make a seat. Our meals were prepared and cooked in a central cookhouse about 500 yards away. This was to be our home for almost seven months. Each day was taken up with training, each crew member was capable of carrying out the duties of the other.[29]

24   Letter Smith to Charrington dated 12 April 1997.
25   J. Thurston, *Account* (1990), p.2.
26   Shand, 'May 1940: A Memory', p.151 and TNA WO 167/452, 23 November 1939.
27   Shand, 'May 1940: A Memory', p.151.
28   This is presumed to mean 10 feet × 10 feet.
29   Hunn Diary, pp.3-4.

With the Regiment billeted by the local inhabitants, Shand stated that due to the French doctors being mobilised there was 'constant demand on the medical officers serving with the BEF.' He often recounted the story when he and the RMO, Lieutenant 'Stinker' Dowell, were called upon to deliver a baby in the middle of a frosty night. Shand's presence was required because he spoke some French and the *Agent de Liaison* was away in Paris:

> With both apprehension and reluctance, I accompanied him to the patient's house, being informed on the way that it looked like being a difficult delivery. Despite several degrees of frost, I broke into a heavy sweat and was in poorish shape when ushered into the front room of a small cottage occupied, as far as I could see, by about 20 people. This was obviously a public occasion like a royal birth in earlier times. I was greeted warmly and pushed forward, to find poor Stinker also sweating and complaining that he couldn't make the buggers under-stand. (He told me later that he had done no midwifery since qualifying). The expectant mother was lying very calmly on a huge bed flanked by friends and relations. Fortunately, one of these was the very agreeable wife of the farmer in whose house we had our Mess. I gravitated towards her, and after an inter-minable torrent of words, not wholly understood, gathered that the local 'sage-femme' was in attendance but did not like to do anything without the permission of the British accoucheur. I said I was sure that the latter would welcome the help of such an able assistant, told Stinker that he was in real luck, pushed the sage-femme forward and made for the door. Here a mountainous man, the brother of the expectant lady, shook me warmly by the hand, gave me a large glass of brandy, coupled with the words 'Nous attendons,' and then leant against the longed-for exit. Fortunately, the wait was not long and there were few problems as the lady had previously had several children. More brandy, "Bruce, what do you say for push?" poussez, Stinker, ghastly noises, slaps and Heaven knows what, and finally the famous bleat from the child, much emotion and many embraces all around. At one moment I found myself about to kiss Stinker.[30]

Their presence in the local villages also reminded them that the BEF had been there some 25 years earlier. Even though only the Commanding Officer and Captain Godfrey Macmenemy, the Padre, had served during the First World War, as Hunn noted the war still cast a long shadow, and on 11th November the Regiment laid a wreath at the village war memorial.[31] For the Padre, who had been a pilot in the RFC, the memories were much closer to home. At one point at Hebuterne, where he was billeted, he could see from his bedroom window where he had been wounded many years before.[32]

30   Shand, *Previous Encounters*, pp.27-28; *The Delhi Spearman* (2014), p.27.
31   TNA WO 167/452, 11 November 1939.
32   Stewart, *History of the XII Royal Lancers*, p.349.

That winter was the coldest recorded for many years and it made conditions difficult and uncomfortable. This was compounded by there being no specific issue of Winter clothing for the Regiment nor was there any anti-freeze for the vehicles. To prevent the engines from freezing the armoured cars had to be run for 10 minutes every two hours, 24 hours a day, with each crew member taking turns, in addition to their normal guard duties.[33] During this period Shand caught flu which developed into mild pleurisy. The RMO recommended that he be sent to Cannes to recuperate where the weather was warmer. Shand left on New Year's Day and returned to Foncquevillers the day before his squadron deployed on the second of the scares.[34]

Despite the challenges faced, Lumsden remarked that 'to be bored is a sign of inefficiency and incompetence' and, notwithstanding the restrictions on crossing borders, a shortage of fuel, and restrictions on the use of the wireless, the Regiment 'worked hard continuously through the Winter.' Lumsden increased the amount of wireless training, some thought to the point of excess.[35] The Regimental War Diary noted that in February 1940:

> Frost and thaw precautions have held up training to a great extent. The importance of continuing training to maintain efficiency in all trades, particularly wireless, was clearly brought out during this month when training conditions were bad. Continuous wireless training is essential… Driver Operators completed their course, and the result was satisfactory: out of 64 who sat, 45 passed. It is hoped that there will be an increase in the establishment when all who passed are mustered.[36]

Much imagination was used when conducting these exercises which always seemed to coincide with Paris race days or be situated around golf courses. When not exercising, the Regiment played football against other units which it normally 'handsomely defeated.'[37] It also took the opportunity to 'experiment with ground-to-air communications.' For those fortunate enough to be in the experiment, there was an opportunity to fly around Aberville in a Blenheim bomber.[38] The Regiment also produced its own concert party to provide entertainment in addition to that provided by West End Theatre Companies which would provide shows for the troops in Arras or Amiens. There were also inter-Regimental social and training visits when Messes met and dined, and they became familiar with each other's equipment.[39] In the New Year,

33   Hunn Diary, p.4.
34   Shand, *Previous Encounters*, pp.29-30.
35   Shand, Exercise ACROSPIRE, p.72; R.C. Maguire, *Account* (HHQ), p.1; Also see CAB 106/220, *Bartholomew Committee Final Report* (1940), regarding wireless restrictions.
36   TNA WO 167/452, February 1940.
37   A.J. Clark-Kennedy; 'Record of Service of the Regiment During the War; France 1940' in *The Journal of The XII Lancers* (1946), p.6.
38   Thurston, *Account*, p.2.
39   TNA WO 167/454, 15/19H, War Diary.

there was also an opportunity for the officers and a few NCOs to visit the battlefield of Moy where they were joined by General Richard Howard-Vyse who had been the Brigade Major in 1914 and who had witnessed the Regiment's last mounted cavalry charge.[40] For others, however, the highlight of the week was the shower run to the public baths in Albert.[41]

Once BEF leave started in late 1939, it presented the opportunity to reconstitute the Regimental Band. Most of the Band were already serving with the Regiment in other capacities, so all that was required was to reunite them with their instruments 'for martial music to enliven the drab villages of Pas de Calais.' This was achieved by the instruments being brought back by officers and soldiers returning from leave. Shand was in charge of one of these consignments. While on leave, he became very drunk in London, extended his leave by a day and flew back to Paris 24 hours later. In the process, he completely forgot the instruments that he was supposed to have collected. Upon his return to Foncquevillers he received a well-deserved 'stinging' telling-off from Lumsden who confined him to Foncquevillers 'indefinitely' with no social calls on other regiments, visits to Arras and 'other privations.'[42]

This routine of hard work and play ensured that the Regiment's morale remained high while other units of the BEF 'suffered from staleness and lethargy.'[43] It was noted by the French *Agent de Liaison* that:

> Every one of us knew the role we were to play. We rehearsed it on maps, with sandboxes and on the terrain where we fought sham battles with the Divisional cavalry regiments. This was as a direct result of the Commanding Officer keeping us on our toes, resulting in the men and machines being superbly fit and ready for immediate action when the moment came.[44]

Shand wrote that 'the Allied strategy, such as it was, was bedevilled by the strict neutrality maintained by the Belgians and the somewhat naive belief that the frontier with France was a perfectly adequate extension of the Maginot Line.' However, there were plans to advance beyond it and make contact with the German forces once the fighting started.[45] The BEF was positioned on the left of the French First Army with the task of advancing to the River Dyle (east of Brussels) and holding the enemy forces. The Dyle valley had been deliberately flooded to act as an anti-tank obstacle.[46]

40 TNA WO 167/452, 11 January 1940; Clark-Kennedy, 'Record of Service', p.6. Battlefield study conducted by General Vyse, a former 5th (Independent) Cavalry Brigade Major in 1914.
41 Hunn, Frederick: (Oral history)/Imperial War Museums <iwm.org.uk> (accessed 11/07/22).
42 Shand, Previous Encounters, pp.33-34.
43 Clark-Kennedy, 'Record of Service', p.6.
44 Falaise, *Through Hell to Dunkirk*, p.9.
45 Shand, 'May 1940: A Memory', p.151.
46 TNA WO 167/452, 11 May 1939.

Throughout the winter, there were three 'scares,' which resulted in the Regiment moving up to the frontier at Lannoy. These were on 15th November, 13th of January, and from 12th-17th April when the Regiment was placed on two hours' notice to move but on each occasion, the crisis did not develop, and each time the Regiment would return to its billets.[47] Shand wrote that on the second of the scares they were billeted near Roubaix. The Mess was 'in a turreted villa of unbelievable hideousness. However, at least it was warm, a great blessing in that very cold Winter.' While they were there the Padre preached a sermon of such power (be strong and of good courage) that a couple of troopers and one young officer were obliged to retire from the congregation.[48]

On each occasion, the Regiment's contribution was modified. By January 1940, the 12th Lancers Operations Instructions No. 5 and 6 were finally referred to as Plan D (Dyle Plan).[49] However, notwithstanding the detail and the name change, the role of the Regiment never changed. Shand said 'in all of these, the role of the 12th Lancers was to act as advance reconnaissance to the BEF, with a pretty wide front of some 30 miles.'[50]

Before the scares, Intelligence Summary No. 1 issued on 3rd November articulated the situation as it was understood. It stated that 'information about Belgian roads is very scarce, but generally speaking, the main roads are mostly tarmac or fairly good *pavé* without metalled edges, but 'the local roads are usually bad *pavé* with an edge of mud and road metal... Both French and Flemish are spoken and are the official languages, but French is regarded as the chief of these. English is also widely understood, as a result of the Great War.' The direction was also given to what was expected from the Regiment when it came to reconnaissance and the information required:

> Too much stress cannot be laid upon the necessity of getting back any information obtained as quickly as possible so that it can be of use to the Commander. The main headings under which information is required are:
>
> i)   Movement of enemy armoured formations.
> ii)   Enemy formations.
> iii) Movement of Allied Troops.
> iv)   Movement of Refugees.
> v)   Enemy Aeroplanes.
> vi)   Topographical information.
> vii) Suitable sites for small demolitions.
>
> •   The detailed information required includes the suitability or otherwise of ground for the passage and manoeuvre of vehicles. Information is required

---

47   Stewart, *History of the XII Royal Lancers*, pp.350-351.
48   Shand, *Previous Encounters*, p.30.
49   TNA WO 167/452, see Intelligence Summary No.10.
50   Shand, 'May 1940: A Memory', p.151.

regarding natural obstacles, and where the best opportunities exist for crossing them; also, artificial obstacles, roadblocks, bottlenecks, and locations of anti-tank guns and mines.

- Every possible step must be taken to collect information from the local civilian population and from anyone likely to help in such matters, e.g., local squires, farm employees, gamekeepers, road makers, roadmen etc.
- Every effort must be made to distinguish and identify the enemy with whom contact is made (Handbook on German Army), and it is particularly important to obtain if possible enemy weapons, equipment, buttons, or distinctive tunic markings, caps, badges, etc. off dead or captured enemy soldiers.
- All documents and scraps of paper, even though they appear to be unimportant, should be regarded as likely sources of information. Letters, telegrams, etc. found in captured post and telegraph offices may contain the most valuable information.
- Maps and other important documents should be taken off prisoners before they have had time to deface or destroy them.[51]

During the scare in January, orders were given to increase the number of patrols, so the squadrons used the three vehicles in SHQ and reduced the troops to two cars.[52] This inevitably meant that the Squadron Leaders would also be out patrolling, and the Regiment would become familiar with the ground it would later have to withdraw across.[53] Second Lieutenant John Clark-Kennedy thought that the scares were engineered by the Germans to 'test the BEF's reaction to the threat of Belgium's invasion.'[54]

On 24th April, after the last of the scares, Lumsden went on leave back to England, having been appointed G1 Second Army. Major Geoff Clifton-Brown was appointed as the new Commanding Officer but immediately went on compassionate leave. So, Major Gemmell assumed command of the Regiment in the absence of Major Smith who was also on leave.[55]

The last entries in the War Diary for the period 27th-30th April were as follows:

Conference at GHQ, AFV on re-organisation. Guy Cars are being earmarked for the Regiment and it is likely the Regiment will re-organise on the basis of Light Armoured Cars (Wheeled)... Troop Training, Wireless Training continues.[56]

51 TNA WO 167/452, Information in the Intelligence Summary No. 1, 3 November 1939.
52 Clark-Kennedy, 'Record of Service', p.6. Smith recorded four in his diary, p.1. See also, *Previous Encounters*, p.37.
53 Shand, *Previous Engagements*, p.37.
54 Clark-Kennedy, 'Record of Service', p.6.
55 TNA WO 167/452, 26 April 1940.
56 TNA WO 167/452, 27-30 April 1940.

4

The Dyle

(10th–14th May 1940)

Friday 10th May

(Day One)

It was ascertained that 12th Lancers could be ready to cross the frontier at 1300 hrs, and accordingly, I laid down this time as zero hour… [they] reached the Dyle unopposed at 2230 hrs.

Gort[1]

Plan D. J. 1 today. Zero hour 1300 hours. 12th Lancers may cross before zero. Wireless silence cancelled after crossing frontier. Command Post opens 1300 hrs. Air recces may commence forthwith.[2]

The stillness of the spring evening was rudely broken just before daybreak on 10th May when German aircraft roared over the city of Arras and bombed the neighbouring airfields. The raid was part of a general and widespread attack by the Luftwaffe on the Allies' airfields, railways, headquarters and key supply points to cripple their air forces and disrupt communications. This was the opening move of their western campaign and it did relatively little military damage to the British installations and did not affect their plans. However, it was a noisy 'call to battle.'

Shortly afterwards, at approximately 0545 hrs, a message from the French Headquarters was received at General Headquarters (GHQ) ordering a complete *Alerte 1, 2 and 3*. Approximately 30 minutes later a further message came through the Swayne Mission (British Military Mission to the French *Grand Quartier Général* (GQG)) to say that orders had been issued by the Supreme Command for the

---

1   Gort, *Second Despatch*, p.5910.
2   Ellis, *The War in France and Flanders*, p.35.

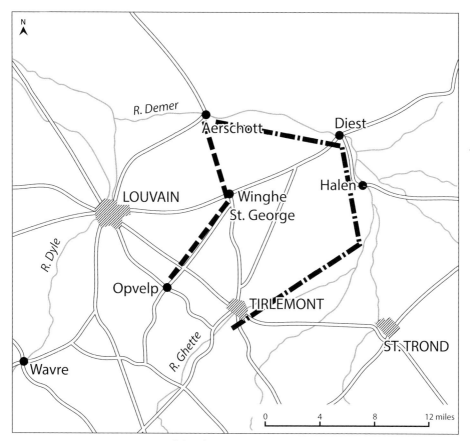

Map A 10–14 May 1940.

immediate execution of Plan D.[3] Gort wrote in his *Despatches* 'it was ascertained that 12th Lancers could be ready to cross the frontier at 1300 hrs and accordingly I laid down this time as zero hour.'[4]

At 0630 hrs, the Regiment (with the Commanding Officer, Quartermaster and Medical Officer still on leave in Britain) was placed on six hours-notice to move. At 0930 hrs, it received orders to move and cross the Belgian frontier at 1300 hrs.[5] The officers had slept soundly as neither Lieutenants Bruce Shand, Tim Bishop nor Basil Hall had been awoken by the heavy air attacks on Arras which other members of

3   Ellis, *The War in France and Flanders*, p.35.
4   Gort, *Second Despatch*, p.5910.
5   TNA WO 167/452: 12/L and TNA WO 167/778: 101st RMRE 10 May 1940.

the Regiment heard as they lay in their billets.[6] For Shand, the 'first intimation' of alarm came through the BBC wireless news bulletin, having been informed by his servant, Trooper Smallridge, but at that stage no orders had been given so he walked up to the Mess for breakfast.[7] Hall overheard someone passing by his window saying that they had heard on the seven o'clock news that Holland and Belgium had been invaded. On hearing the news, he 'got dressed and attended Horsbrugh-Porter's conference.'[8] Bishop also heard the news from his servant, Trooper Rowlands, who said "I think there will be a jildi move, Sir, Jerry's invaded Holland."[9] Lumsden, like his officers in France, had only heard the news of the German advance that morning, but in London.[10] By 0800 hrs, Second Lieutenant David Smith was put on six hours-notice to move and then orders came in quick succession and his detachment of Engineers was ordered to rendezvous with the 12th Lancers at the bandstand in Lannoy at 1300 hrs.[11]

Lannoy Bandstand. (Author's collection)

6   Clark-Kennedy, 'Record of Service', p.6; Hunn Diary, 10 May 1940, p.6.
7   Shand, *Previous Encounters*, p.41.
8   Hall Diary, p.1.
9   Bishop, *One Young Soldier*, p.47.
10   Stewart, *History of the XII Royal Lancers*, p.351.
11   TNA WO 167/778: 10 May 1940.

Clearly, the German invasion had caught the Allies and the Regiment by surprise. Key personnel were still on leave and many of the planned preliminary road moves had not taken place, which in turn would delay the moves of I and II Corps.[12] The 15th/19th Hussars estimated that the 12th Lancers had left one hour before their own departure time.[13] Equally clear from Gort's *Despatch*, was that the role of the 12th Lancers was critical to his plan.

Shand wrote that before the Regiment departed, maps of Belgium, along with the 'extra impedimenta of war' were issued. This included 'rolls of barbed wire, small Union Jacks (to wave at unsure Allies), self-destructive and smoke bombs (containing mysterious chemicals), and to 'crown it all, pigeons (in neat baskets) just in case the wireless failed.'[14] In addition to the Regimental establishment, Major John Erne had joined the Regiment on 15th April from the North Irish Horse on a month's attachment to get some 'practical experience' before returning to command his own Regiment, which was in the process of being 'resuscitated.'[15] Lumsden attached Erne to A Squadron and Horsbrugh-Porter decided to take him as his Squadron second-in-command, a post held by Shand since the move of Captain Willis to C Squadron. Shand returned to his troop which meant the newly arrived Hall was now surplus to establishment and he was duly appointed as the A Squadron Transport Officer. Hall's first task was to load the Squadron's 30 cwt lorry with extra petrol, ready to refuel the Squadron later at Toufflers, before their crossing into Belgium (see Map 5).[16]

With the Commanding Officer still absent, the Regiment deployed under the command of Clifton-Brown and moved off from Hebuterne at 1020 hrs. By 1130, Shand had arrived in Lannoy (Toufflers), where he and Bishop shared a lunch of bread, ham and a bottle of Moet & Chandon, while they sat under the shelter of some high trees.[17] By midday, the whole of A Squadron was complete, and by 1250 hrs, the rest of the Regiment had arrived, having refuelled.[18] During the journey to the border, Shand wrote that they had had 'hardly time to think' and during the 'lovely fresh morning' he noticed how the French peasants were 'busy and undisturbed' as they worked on their farms.[19] The journey of Smith's Engineers to Lannoy was uneventful and, after refuelling the detachment, they met the 12th Lancers at 1245 hrs, where they were immediately broken down into sections. Lance Sergeant Earl was attached

12 Gort, *Second Despatch*, p.5910.
13 TNA WO 167/454: 10 May 1940.
14 Shand, 'May 1940: A Memory', p.151.
15 Falaise, *Through Hell to Dunkirk*, p.2; Shand, *Previous Engagements*, p.35; Hall Diary, p.1 and TNA WO 167/452, 15 April 1940.
16 Hall Diary, p.1.
17 Toufflers, pseud. Bishop, *One Young Soldier*, p.47, Lannoy, pseud. Shand, *Previous Encounters*, p.42; Falaise, *Through Hell to Dunkirk*, p.17.
18 Hall Diary, p.1.
19 Shand, *Previous Encounters*, p.41.

to B Squadron, Lance Sergeant Johnson to A Squadron and Smith attached himself to C Squadron.[20] However, for B Squadron the journey was not without incident.

At approximately midday, B Squadron Headquarters (SHQ) was parked in a farm-yard between two buildings. It was here that Sergeant Freddie Hunn experienced his first air attack before they had even crossed the border:

> I was standing beside the open door of my vehicle talking on the wireless to the other Troops. Horsbrugh-Porter was some 15 yards away talking to the Second-in-Command (Captain Silky Sparke) and a few other Troop members. On looking skyward, I saw two planes which appeared to be one chasing the other, then the leading plane dropped what looked like a beer crate. Turning to the others I shouted, "that plane has just dropped something." Then I watched as the crate descended, followed by a huge explosion showering mud, rubble, dirt, and dust all around. Turning to my comrades, I stated the obvious, "It's a bomb." But they were not to be seen; on hearing the scream as the bomb fell, they had dived for cover. But with the earphones clamped over my ears all I heard was the talking and crackle from the wireless.[21]

Even though Gort had permitted the 12th Lancers to cross the border before 1300 hrs, the Lancers were made to wait. At 1300 hrs exactly, the barriers were 'politely lifted' by the guards and customs officials and the Regiment advanced into Belgium to the sound of Corporal Sims sounding the 'charge' as each troop went past.[22] The order of march was A Squadron at 1300 hrs, B Squadron 1315 hrs, C Squadron 1325 hrs, Regimental Headquarters at 1330 hrs and B Echelon transport at 1340 hrs.

Shand's troop was the lead troop of the Regiment and he had his route (Tournai – Ath – Enghien – Wavre – Grez Doiceau) 'well-memorised.'[23] He remarked that the first town they passed through was Tournai where they were received with 'wild acclaim' and as a victorious army.[24] The population threw flowers at the passing vehicles and made the 'most flattering remarks about the British Army, 'to such a degree that the whole enterprise began to have an air of a musical comedy, an illusion that was only to last for a day.' Shand wrote that it was the 'most perfect afternoon' and the countryside looked 'wonderfully green, with early flowers in profusion, until Trooper Griffiths brought him up short and pointed to the 15-20 German bombers flying westwards.'[25]

By 1427 hrs, the Regiment's first bound (Leuze – Renaix – Audenarde [Oudenaarde]) was reported clear. The second bound (Enghien – Ninove – Alost) was reported clear

20   TNA WO 167/778: 10 May 1940.
21   Hunn Diary, 10 May 1940, pp.6-7.
22   Bishop, *One Young Soldier*, p.47; Shand, 'May 1940', p.151.
23   Shand, *Previous Encounters*, p.42.
24   Shand, 'May 1940: A Memory', p.151.
25   Shand, *Previous Encounters*, p.42.

at 1540 hrs.[26] It was near Enghien when Clark-Kennedy and 2 Troop B Squadron first saw action. Although he never kept a diary Clark-Kennedy once recalled that:

> The only excitement was near Enghien when my troop, being in a clump of trees for the statutory 10 minutes halt, observed a Dornier two-engine bomber pass over us very low going east, obviously returning from a bombing raid. Our Bren gun was already mounted for action and we opened fire as it passed over. No visible result except that its tail gunner fired back at us! Lucky only near misses! This was our first action in World War II.[27]

When the Regiment reached Brussels, it was 'accorded a remarkably good reception,' possibly resulting from being the first troops to enter the city.[28] Hall, in A Squadron's fighting lorry, remembered the terrific reception. That said, he then became completely lost. He found that shouting "a Wavre?" above the cheering was unsatisfactory, so 'co-opted' a civilian to lead him through the city. Hall's problem was now how to 'disguise the exact place' they were actually going to. He eventually 'shook off' his guide in the Champs de Manoeuvres.'[29] Clark-Kennedy said that B Squadron was given a 'tumultuous reception' and was led through the city by a 'friendly taxi driver.'[30] Hunn, also in B Squadron, remembered that, as they passed through, they were 'considerably slowed down' by the crowds which 'lined the route who cheered as they passed by and showered them with flowers and offered them wine.'[31] The local authorities in Brussels had asked that the routes in the vicinity of Brussels be no longer used by the BEF, as it threatened its status as an open city and its use prejudiced its safety. Gort considered the request but since there were no adequate alternatives to the River Dyle, he was 'compelled to adhere to the original plan of using the outskirts.'[32]

By 1800 hrs, the final objective, the line covering Wavre–Louvain, was reached. The position was some eight miles east of the Dyle and they were ordered to hold it until relieved by the Divisional cavalry regiments.[33] A Squadron arrived at Grez Doiceau, where the chosen location was a château to the east of the town situated in the middle of a wooded park (see Map 7). The Squadron was located 'part down a lane and part on the main road.'[34] Here the Regiment was provided with a hot meal

26   Bishop, *One Young Soldier,* p.47.
27   *An Officer and a Gentlemen* <https://www.carsphairn.org/CarsphairnArchive/files/original/c9db07c01e683d6261b500c81fd24c7f.pdf> (accessed 11/12/2022).
28   Clark-Kennedy, 'Record of Service', p.7.
29   Hall Diary, 10 May 1940, p.2.
30   *An Officer and a Gentlemen* <https://www.carsphairn.org/CarsphairnArchive/files/original/c9db07c01e683d6261b500c81fd24c7f.pdf > (accessed 11/12/2022).
31   Hunn Diary, 10 May 1940, p.6.
32   Gort, *First Despatch,* p.5911.
33   Gort, *First Despatch,* p.5909.
34   Hall Diary, 10 May 1940, p.2.

of stew and Bishop watched the tanks of the *DLM's* heading towards the front, which 'heightened' their already high morale.[35]

En route, Shand stopped by a lake in the Forêt de Soignies where he met two American girls who gave him chocolate and *marrons glacés.* The girls told Shand that they had been skiing earlier in the year and had been advised by the Consulate to leave. He thought they seemed 'hardly aware that hostilities had started.' Shand's enduring memory of the last leg of the journey had been the Belgian Army 'which seemed to be going in all directions,' with their vehicles and horses adorned with large bunches of white lilac. It remained 'one of his most powerful memories of that May.'[36] From Shand's multiple narratives it would appear his own journey was free from mechanical problems, although that was not the case for all the armoured cars.

During the road move, 10 × wheel assemblies turned to 'jelly' owing to overheating and they made two long stops to try and cool the tyres down. Troops stopped by the side of the road and used buckets of water from streams in an attempt to lower the temperature.[37] The Regiment went to war with only 15 spare tyres, and this initial shortage rendered 10 armoured cars unserviceable.[38] At one point, B Squadron removed all four tyres from a serviceable armoured car to keep the Squadron moving and the car was recovered later. This problem with the tyres was unique to the advance and did not happen again. It did not interfere appreciably with the rate of advance. The War Diary recorded that 'thanks to special efforts made by Q Maintenance at GHQ, further spares arrived the next day.' It is of note that the Morris was not fitted with a spare wheel.[39] During the advance, it had already become apparent that straight main roads and important railway centres were areas to be avoided when German bombers were overhead and laden. The quick recognition of this lesson and good air discipline undoubtedly prevented many casualties during the following days.

By the evening, after a journey of some 60-70 miles, A Squadron was in position and Shand was sent out to the town of Jodoigne [Djodogne] on the River Ghette, beyond the Dyle, (see Map 6) in search of information. Shand observed:

> This was not easy to find as there were few Belgian troops in this vicinity and the only ones I contacted were [veterans] of some sort of military alms-houses, by their appearance almost veterans of Waterloo, which was only a few miles away. All I could collect were rumours of fighting near Liege, but I did become aware of one problem that was going to haunt Troop and Squadron Leaders whilst we were in Belgium.[40]

35   Bishop, *One Young Soldier,* p.47.
36   Shand, *Previous Encounters,* p.43.
37   Hunn Diary, 10 May 1940, p.6.
38   Clark-Kennedy, 'Record of Service', p.7; TNA WO 167/452, 10 May 1940.
39   Hunn – Morpeth interview.
40   Shand, 'May 1940: A Memory', p.152.

As a result of the strict adherence by the Belgians to their status of neutrality, which resulted in no previous reconnaissances into Flanders, this was the first time the Regiment had tried to use French maps in Belgium and realised that the people of Belgium did not speak French:

> I think we all entered the country under the impression that everyone spoke French. This was not the case and the Flamands were very Flemish indeed. Most of the signposts were in the latter language and all the place names on our maps were in French; there often being a considerable difference between the two spellings. For instance, three important places where A Squadron were very much involved at this time were Louvain, Tirlemont and St. Trond, in French spelling. In Flemish, they are Leuven, Tienen and St. Truidern. Now, no doubt, as we are into Europe, these matters are child's play, but they certainly were not then.[41]

Bishop also remarked that his maps were all 1918 vintage which was 'adequate out in the country but divorced from reality in towns and suburbs.'[42] Horsbrugh-Porter said that 'at times they had to use Michelin maps which they bought locally,' a somewhat ironic situation since the BEF had faced the same problem in 1914.[43]

Later that evening, having gained what information he could, Shand took up position on the ridge overlooking Jodoigne and the Ghette. Once in place, he was visited by Horsbrugh-Porter who informed Shand that they 'should be able to link up with the French early in the morning' and he spent a 'comparatively undisturbed night,' despite the sounds of bombing in the distance to the east.[44]

Having been delayed by the crowds in Brussels, B Squadron eventually reached the Dyle in the evening and then advanced to the river Chetti south of Diest. It was between the area of Diest and Tirlemont that the Squadron had its first action when a patrol of horsed cavalry was encountered and destroyed. Hunn wrote:

> A beautiful black horse came into the possession of the Squadron. There was considerable discussion over the wireless as to how the animal could be transported back for use in the Regimental Stables at the end of hostilities. This highlighted the fact that at this stage of the war the full seriousness of the situation had not been grasped. The peacetime cavalry officer lives for his equestrian activities and the capture of the horse was most important. It was also assumed that the war would be over in a matter of weeks and the horse would be a welcome addition to the stables.[45]

---

41 Shand, 'May 1940: A Memory', p.152.
42 Bishop, *One Young Soldier*, p.55.
43 Horsbrugh-Porter-Morpeth interview; E.W. Sheppard, *The Ninth Queen's Royal Lancers (1939), 1715-1936*, p.234.
44 Shand, 'May 1940: A Memory', p.152.
45 Hunn Diary, 10 May 1940, p.7.

Clark-Kennedy recalled that he had several encounters with horsed cavalry patrols. As a cavalryman at heart, his concern was always for the horses:

> Though tanks, armoured cars, and masses of motorcyclists much more usual. In my troop's case my unrehearsed and unauthorised fire order included, I am glad to recall, "Fire high! Aim for the men, not the horses!"[46]

While the Regiment was crossing the Belgian border, Major Ian Smith and Lieutenant Alan Windeler reported to GHQ Advance Operations at Wahagnies with their No.3 wireless set and car. Smith and Windeler were to remain at GHQ throughout the campaign passing on the Regiment's information directly to the Commander-in-Chief (C-in-C).[47] The Army had tried to withdraw the Regiment's No. 3 wireless sets just before embarkation but being famous for their long-range communications they were retained and loaded as water carts. Shand wrote that this proved to be a crucial decision as 'without them, the Regiment would have been in a great deal of trouble' as no other wireless would have been suitable.[48] Captain Kennard agreed stating that, 'this set proved invaluable throughout the fighting which followed, and no less powerful set would have been of any use.'[49] The ranges the set could achieve were remarkable and in 1932 the 12th Lancers and 11th Hussars exchanged Christmas messages between England and Cairo.[50] In addition to their wirelesses, the Regiment also carried pigeons as an alternative should the wireless fail.

The pigeons were collected by Signalman Crebbin. A French speaker, he was sent to the house of Monsieur Dainhault, who lived in Lille, and who had kindly placed his loft of racing pigeons at the disposal of the Regiment. The idea was that if the pigeons were released and returned home, there was a telephone in his loft so that any messages brought in by his birds could be transmitted by telephone direct to GHQ.[51] To which Shand remarked there must be some sort of 'avian intelligence centre.'[52] The luckless birds saw a lot of travelling and action during the first few days before they were eventually released. This was done as soon as it was realised that their 'home' (Lille) had been overrun by the Germans and they were of no further use to the Squadron. However, up until that point, the initial issue was two birds to

46   *An Officer and a Gentlemen* <https://www.carsphairn.org/CarsphairnArchive/files/original/c9db07c01e683d6261b500c81fd24c7f.pdf> (accessed 11/12/22).
47   Clark-Kennedy, 'Record of Service', p.7.
48   Shand, Exercise ACROSPIRE, p.71; TNA WO 167/452, 10 May 1940. A wireless Set was a mobile transmitter/receiver developed in 1934. Use: medium-range communication between Corps and Division and Line of Communication. Frequency range 1.3-3.4MHz. Output 400W. Range (roof aerial) 25 miles voice and 50 miles morse.
49   TNA WO 167/452: 10 May 1940.
50   Shand, *Previous Engagements*, p.17.
51   TNA WO 167/452: 10 May 1940.
52   Shand, *Previous Engagements*, p.39.

each troop and six to SHQ.[53] Fortunately, the wirelesses worked without intermission or interruption throughout the early operations so it was never necessary to use the subsidiary method for transmitting messages. Some years later Shand attributed the reason for carrying pigeons down to the 'high authority being still rather suspicious of the wireless.'[54]

Later that evening, the three Divisional reconnaissance regiments reached the Dyle. By 2000 hrs, the 13th/18th Hussars occupied a position from Pecrot Chausée to Corbeek Dyle. The 4th/7th Dragoon Guards were on their right in a similar line covering the 2nd Division occupying a line on the Dyle from Warne to Ormendal, a frontage of 8000 yards, arriving at 1930 hrs, without incident. The 15th/19th Hussars were on the extreme left covering the 3rd Division, arriving at Louvain at approximately 2230 hrs, placing a troop from an anti-aircraft battery with Bofors guns to defend the bridge at Pecq, which was situated behind the Regiment.[55]

It was not until all the Divisional cavalry regiments were in position that the Commanding Officer of the 12th Lancers rejoined the Regiment from leave in England having flown back. He arrived at RHQ at 2355 hrs, having 'dashed back' from leave that evening and taking a taxi from Calais.[56] Shand thought that the reason Lumsden was away in England was that his period of Regimental command had come to an end, and he was waiting for a new appointment but 'happily' for the Regiment he worked his way back.[57]

Saturday 11th May

(Day Two)

I could not help feeling it strange that the first dead one saw were women and children, but I was beginning to realise that my ideas of war were a trifle old-fashioned; the truth upset my knightly preconceptions.'
Shand[58]

During the night, the Divisional cavalry regiments had begun to take over the area of the line. Early in the morning, the squadrons sent out patrols to make contact with their

---

53   Stewart, *History of the XII Royal Lancers*, p.351 and TNA WO 167/452: Operation Order No. 6, January 1940.
54   Shand, Exercise ACROSPIRE, p.71.
55   TNA WO 167/454: 10 May 1940; C.H. Miller, *History of The 13th/18th Royal Hussars (Queen Mary's Own) 1922-1947* (1949), p.39; G. Courage, *The History of 15th/19th The King's Royal Hussars 1939-1945* (1949), p.17; J.M. Brereton, *The History of the 4th/7th Royal Dragoon Guards 1685-1980* (1982), pp.367-368. There are no official War Diaries for the 13/18H or 4/7DG for May 1940.
56   Blaxland, *Destination Dunkirk*, p.73; Corps Recce Study Day, 'Salvation of the BEF 10-31 May 1940', p.19; Shand, *Previous Encounters*, p.44.
57   Shand, 'May 1940: A Memory', p.151.
58   Shand, *Previous Encounters*, pp.44-45.

adjacent British and French counterparts. A patrol from B Squadron under Second Lieutenant Peter Miller-Mundy accompanied by Guy de Barbarin, the Squadron's French *Agent de Liaison*, made contact with the French *3ème DLM* in Tirlemont in the early hours. C Squadron sent out a patrol to try to find the French *1ème DLM* on their left who were reported to be in the area Herenthals–Westerloo–Lierre, and also make contact with the 15th/19th Hussars, in the area of Louvain. The two squadrons of Hussars made contact with the Regiment at Bautersem and Winghe St. George.[59]

A Squadron made contact with the 4th/7th Dragoon Guards in the area of Wavre. They reported that the 12th Cuirassiers had passed through the area at approximately 2000 hrs the previous evening. Horsburgh-Porter sent Shand and Bishop to make contact with the *3ème DLM*. What he actually said was that they were to go and "find out what the bastards are up to." Horsburgh-Porter was described as the 'epitome of a free-range officer' with a 'volcanic temper and brusque language.'[60] Shand made contact with the General Commanding the 7th Belgium Division and the *3ème DLM* at St. Trond where he witnessed a somewhat 'hectic' engagement with German armour trying to enter the other side of the town. Fortunately, these tanks did not push westwards towards Tirlemont, where A Squadron was in position.[61] Bishop had an entirely different experience:

> I found their HQ and more or less breezed in to see the General, meaning absolutely no disrespect but, I dare say, rather thinking of him as just a friendly old Frog. He was the reverse of friendly. I had to alter my approach. Here was a very pompous man indeed. Be that as it may, it resulted in my getting all the information I needed immediately as, in the adjoining room, into which I was vocally catapulted, were his staff. They had not witnessed our meeting. Maps were laid out under my nose, and I was quickly told everything I had come to find out. I did not think the General would appreciate my saying goodbye, so returned at once to the Squadron with a marked map and we moved on up to Tirlemont.[62]

Bishop returned to SHQ in Tirlemont to pass on his information. On arrival, Horsbrugh-Porter sent him into the town to get some fresh loaves. In answer to his inquiries, a pretty little girl of about 10 years old was detailed by her nodding smiling parents to guide him:

> To cut out the necessity for words, she very sensibly took my hand in hers and led me back past my cars and the grinning faces in their turrets. I was willingly

59   TNA WO 167/454, 11 May 1940.
60   Bishop, *One Young Soldier*, p.46; Shand, *Previous Engagements*, p.32 and Corps Recce Study Day, 'Salvation of the BEF 10-31 May 1940', p.15.
61   Clark-Kennedy, 'Record of Service', pp.7-8; Shand, *Previous Encounters*, p.42 and Shand, 'May 1940: A Memory', p.152.
62   Bishop, *One Young Soldier*, p.48.

presented with bread; payment was refused, and it was altogether the most charming bit of shopping I had ever known. As we were walking back, however, planes flew in low over the roofs. I saw people coming out of their houses, shading their eyes as they looked up. The planes were hidden by other houses. It seemed they were fighters who had started shooting up the landing ground. Hurray for the boys in blue, we said and then saw the big black crosses on their sides as they zoomed over the chimneys. This was the first of a hundred such moments of disillusionment to come. These boys belonged to the Luftwaffe, and, for at least a fortnight, they always did. We were heading for St. Trond and [Horsbrugh-Porter] yelled at me to get all the cars out of the town. I returned my adorable companion to her puzzled parents and ran back to my car. As we took the St. Trond road, however, we at once met a formation of Germans bombers flying straight down the line of the road as it were to meet us, bombing as they came. The fact that they were not specifically aiming at us made not a ha'porth worth of difference. They were bombing the road, accurately, and we were on it. Moreover, owing to deep roadside ditches, we were unable to get off it.[63]

During the bombing of Tirlemont, Bishop's gunner and wireless operator watched in silence except for the word "Bastards!" occasionally (and almost disbelievingly) which they whispered from time to time. They knew the town to be clear of troops, but Bishop contemplated what had happened to his 'little friend' and her proud parents and what of the obliging kindly baker? Bishop recorded the aftermath of the bombing:

> Much of the place had already been reduced to a burning shambles. But we had to go on, and as we did so I noticed that what seemed to be bundles of laundry had been thrown into the roadside ditches. Then I saw, with a crawling horror, legs and arms sticking out of the clothes and suddenly a green, upturned face. Dead men are bad enough; these were mostly women. The picnic period was over.[64]

When Shand witnessed the same sights on the road to St. Trond he wrote 'I could not help feeling it strange that the first dead one saw were women and children, but I was beginning to realise that my ideas of war were a trifle old-fashioned; the truth upset my knightly preconceptions.' Having had his personal values challenged, momentarily, Shand 'cherished the possibility' that his troop went further east than any other unit of the BEF.[65]

At 0750 hrs, RHQ moved to Weert St. Georges [Sint Joris Weert] as telephone communication had previously been arranged between the village and Brussels, and

63 Bishop, *One Young Soldier*, p.49.
64 Bishop, *One Young Soldier*, p.49.
65 Shand, *Previous Encounters*, pp.44-45.

then to Advance GHQ at Wahagnies (H6720). However, the telephone system was not a success as communications were very slow and liable to many interruptions. The communications issues were attributed to it being in a valley and the electric power wires were still live making it very bad for wireless reception. Therefore, at 1220 hrs, RHQ was moved back to the northern edge of the Forêt de Meerdael, where it was easy to conceal the RHQ including the B Echelon lorries. The co-location of the echelon and RHQ was ideal when it became necessary to call forward petrol, supplies, and spare wheel assemblies: it also had a charging lorry with spare wireless batteries. During the day a message was received that German parachutists had been dropped at a village approximately two miles from RHQ, but after several patrols were sent out nothing was found.[66]

During the morning, the Divisional cavalry regiments had made contact with each other and were now covering the front of the BEF from Wavre to Louvain. This was reported to GHQ and authority was requested for the 12th Lancers to move to its secondary tasks:

(a)   To cover the left of the French *3ème DLM*, which was supposed to have its left at Tirlemont, by observing the crossings over Ghette to include Diest.
(b)   Observe crossings over the River Demer from Diest to Aerschott
(c)   Make contact with any Belgian troops or formations which might be in this area and report on their dispositions.

However, it is clear that the squadrons had already started some of their secondary tasks once they had moved into position the night before as they had already made contact with the *DLMs*, and Shand's position at Jodoigne overlooked the Ghette, a position he had maintained overnight.[67]

At 1415 hrs, permission was obtained for the Regiment to move eastwards. By 1600 hrs, troops were in observation on the general line Tirlemont – Ghette – Diest – Aerschott. This subsequent move resulted in having to re-establish communications with their flanking units. A Squadron on the right was in touch with the *3ème DLM* and relieved one troop of B Squadron which concentrated on the centre from Tirlemont to Diest (not including the two towns), with C Squadron on their left from Diest to Aerschott, (including the towns). Second Lieutenant Edward (Ned) Mann, in searching for the *1ème DLM*, made contact with the Belgian formation holding the Albert Canal in the area of Gheel (K18). It was during these moves that the importance of keeping the vehicles well dispersed at all times, particularly when moving down main straight roads, was well borne out as the Germans had complete air superiority in the area. A Squadron was heavily bombed in the area of Tirlemont which received the concentrated attention of the Germans, the railway and main roads being

66   Hall Diary, 11 May 1940, p.2.
67   Shand, *Previous Engagements*, p.44.

their particular objectives. The wireless sets in two armoured cars were put out of action through the valves being broken by the concussion of the bombs but, apart from a scratch or two, the crews miraculously escaped. Shand noted it was the refugees who suffered the most as they still 'thronged the sides of the road.'[68]

The two vehicles in question belonged to Shand and Bishop. Shand was very conscious of the 'tinny protection' of the Morris armoured car especially when another wireless set was knocked out, leaving him 'incommunicado.'[69] Bishop had the same problem and had lost his antenna and was not in communications which he thought was 'the *raison d'être*' of an armoured car. This necessitated Bishop swapping armoured cars and working with a new crew. Trooper Cupples was now his driver, replacing Trooper Lloyd. Bishop wrote 'since every man in the Squadron was first class and everybody knew everyone, it made little difference if any.'[70] The loss of wireless communications necessitated Shand sending a despatch rider (DR) back to SHQ. Trooper Sparkes, who had been a reservist, 'set off with great aplomb' with the message and, within an hour, was back with orders for them to return to Tirlemont.[71] Without having a troop DR to send back to RHQ, Shand would never have received the order to withdraw as the pigeons were only suitable for sending messages, not receiving them. Eventually, Shand and Bishop arrived back in time for 'more bombing' but managed to get the wireless fixed (something the operators were trained to do).[72]

During the day, B and C Squadrons managed to locate the Belgian troops as directed in their secondary tasks in the area of the Ghette, but what they saw was a 'depressing spectacle' of the Belgian Army passing through their front. They were tired, dirty, unshaven, and were mostly marching, though not in their correct formations, and already gave the impression of a defeated Army.[73] Shand noted that as they passed 'none of them seemed anxious to stop or give any coherent information.'[74] What the Regiment was witnessing would help inform Lumsden as to the operational effectiveness of the Belgian Army, and their ability to fulfil their part in the coalition in the coming days.

That evening, it became apparent that the plans of the *3ème DLM* and the Belgian Mechanised Cavalry Division on the Ghette did not completely dovetail. By 2130 hrs, A Squadron had confirmed the existence of a four-mile gap astride the main road, St. Trond – Tirlemont in the area Haekendover – Elixen. As neither of the Allies was at first prepared to alter their dispositions, A Squadron was detailed to cover the gap, and Lumsden was instructed to use his 'most persuasive endeavours to induce either or both of the Allies to close the gap, which was a very real danger to all three partners.'

68   Shand, *Previous Engagements*, p.44.
69   Clark-Kennedy, 'Record of Service', p.7.
70   Bishop, *One Young Soldier*, p.49.
71   Shand, 'May 1940: A Memory', p.152.
72   Jones-Hunn interview.
73   Clark-Kennedy, 'Record of Service', p.7.
74   Shand, *Previous Engagements*, p.44.

Horsbrugh-Porter was 'ordered to employ his well-known blandishments to further good purpose and induce one or either, or both' of the Allies to take over this imperative task.[75] Eventually, all the bridges were successfully blown by 1750 hrs, although it was still only A Squadron in position, and it was fortunate that the Germans did not push on through their position as it was only the water defences that provided any strength to their position.[76]

At 1830 hrs, two miles from Jodoigne, it was purely by chance that Henry de la Falaise [A Squadron's *Agent de Liaison*], who had left Paris the night before, caught up with the Regiment by 'some adroit lorry hopping.'[77] It was here he found the two cars of Shand's troop parked under a clump of trees on the right-hand side of the road. Falaise was greeted by Shand's broad grin, but 'hardly recognised the usually spick-and-span Shand under the dirt and stubble of beard.' Shand briefed Falaise on the day's proceedings and told him that they had just stopped in a quiet spot to try and fix his wireless and the troop were all 'still badly shaken up.' They were joined by Sergeant Ditton who had just returned from patrol and had his car blown off the track by a dive-bomber. He also reported problems with his wireless and thought he could not receive although could still transmit.[78] Shand assigned Falaise to Ditton's armoured car and asked him to go forward to the French Armoured Brigade on their right and liaise. Falaise found the command post of a Brigade of Cuirassiers, in the small village of Petit Orp. He discussed the situation with the Colonel who commanded it and it was agreed that the best thing for the Squadron to do was to keep watch south of the Tirlemont – St. Trond road as the French troops were on the Tirlemont – Hannut road between Goetsenhoven and Opheilissen [Opheylissem]. Falaise wrote that it was the opinion of the French staff officers that the Germans were trying to repeat exactly their manoeuvre of 1914 in Belgium by pushing their light armoured forces, as they did then with their cavalry, through the Hannut gap and then marching north towards Tirlemont, Diest and Antwerp. They thought that the following day would be a hard and decisive fight. All these names on the map brought back Falaise's memories of the battles fought in August 1914.[79]

It was nearly dark when Falaise and Sergeant Ditton returned to Shand's location. Falaise made his report back to SHQ by wireless hoping that they had received his message, as they could still only transmit. The three armoured cars took up a concealed position in a small wood a mile west of Jodoigne. It was while the crews were making tea and having a 'light supper' of biscuit and bully beef that a DR from

75   Lumsden's diary in Stewart, *History of the XII Royal Lancers*, p.351.
76   Clark-Kennedy, 'Record of Service', p.8.
77   Shand, *Previous Encounters*, p.43.
78   Ditton had previously served with the 11th Hussars. Bryant, 'Some Thoughts at Sunset', p.9. Ditton returned to England after approximately four days later suffering an 'immovable stoppage of the bowels.' He was replaced by Sergeant Lewis. See Shand, *Previous Encounters*, pp.35-36.
79   Falaise, *Through Hell to Dunkirk*, p.20.

SHQ brought orders to move back to SHQ, north of Hoegarden [Hoegaarden], three miles south of Tirlemont, thus indicating their message had been received. Shand was only back at SHQ long enough to get his remaining set repaired before he was sent out to re-establish contact with *3ème DLM*, where he stayed until the following morning.[80]

Shand sent Falaise forward again with Ditton so he could speak French if challenged by French or Belgian troops since they would be 'unfamiliar' with the silhouette of the British armoured car. The vehicles had no real identifying marks on them except for a white square on both sides of the rim of the turret and a small British flag which was to be pulled out and 'waved in time of need.' Falaise thought this 'would hardly be satisfactory at night.'[81] When they reached Jodoigne, they found that the road was so filled with refugees that they could hardly move forward. Falaise observed:

> Carefully, we move on through the flow of fleeing humanity: old men pushing small carts filled with their families' hastily-gathered belongings; women wrapped in shawls and loaded with bundles, dragging children of all ages behind them; tired, wild-eyed children; others are urging goats and cows before them. Every now and again they start to run. I can hear frantic screams when bombs plaster the road ahead. We have to stop while this flowing human tide brushes by us, bumping into the armoured car as it stumbles along, accompanied by the crash of nearby explosions and the bleating and mooing of the terrified farm beasts. We have been on our way now for nearly an hour and have covered only about eight miles when we pass through the village of Lumay and are free of the refugee column.[82]

It was 2245 hrs before they reached their destination where they halted alongside a small villa a mile east of the deserted village of Hoegarden. On the other side of the road were the metal-fenced walls of a large factory. Ditton's car faced west toward the railroad tracks and the river, with Shand's car concealed to their rear in the village. The troop's position was covering the crossroad to Outgarden [Outgaarden], 50 yards away. Falaise noted:

> There is a strange silence around me. Not a real silence, since I can hear in the distance the crackling of burning timber and can see smoke and flames rise over the horizon under the starlit sky; yet the silence exists. It is due to the complete absence of human sounds. I can hear that the houses are empty around me, that there are no cattle breathing heavily in the stables, that no life is left in this village, where not even a dog barks… exhausted, Sergeant Ditton, who has been

---

80   Shand, *Previous Encounters*, p.45.
81   Falaise, *Through Hell to Dunkirk*, p.20.
82   Falaise, *Through Hell to Dunkirk*, p.21.

on his feet for 48-hours, is lost to the world. He is fast asleep, all crumpled up in a heap at the bottom of the car and wedged somehow between all the parapher- nalia which clutters it, his head on an ammunition case. Every time I move, I have to be careful not to kick him in the face as I stand up in the turret keeping watch. The fires ahead die down, but now parachute flares are dropping all over the countryside, lighting up the horizon with blue-white halos in the direction of the St. Trond road. On my left, and in the distance, comes the intermittent muffled rattle of machine gun fire and frequent loud explosions which seem to proceed from Tirlemont shake the windows of the houses around me.[83]

Meanwhile, Falaise and Ditton would not have been aware that during the day the aerodrome at Geetbetz was also heavily bombed and much cratered. There had been a number of aircraft there but the Belgian pilots appeared unable to take off in the aircraft which was available and so the machines were in due course destroyed by bombing, and the pilots left by car. From what Lumsden had seen during the day having made a tour of the front, he thought that 'the Belgians did not offer as much resistance as they could have done.' That evening the Germans closed up on the line along the whole front.[84] Hall, who had become separated from his kit during the day, spent an 'unpleasant, horribly cold,' sleepless night huddled under a single blanket. All through the night, there were solitary rifle shots and an occasional burst of machine gun fire.[85]

Sunday 12th May

(Day Three)

The armoured car was in a very good position and completely in control of the bridge crossing... quite a few German advanced scouts must have found that out too, for the half-destroyed bridge was strewn with their corpses.
Bishop[86]

At 0130 hrs, Falaise was beginning to feel chilly and sleepy; his feet were numb from standing so long in the turret. To his relief, Ditton was stirring and said he was feeling 'much better' after his two-hour nap. Falaise jumped out of the car and walked to the railroad tracks where he found one of the Regiment's DRs on duty, straddling his motorcycle. He crossed the tracks and reached a small bridge with a sign on it saying 'Ghette.' He slid down the steep embankment and washed his head and face. Although the water was icy cold, it did not succeed in making him feel any less sleepy. He returned to the armoured car and curled up in the bottom of it in much the same

---

83   Falaise, *Through Hell to Dunkirk*, p.22.
84   Clark-Kennedy, 'Record of Service', p.8.
85   Hall Diary, 11 May 1940, pp.2-3.
86   Bishop, *One Young Soldier*, p.32.

position as that assumed earlier by Ditton and promptly passed out. At 0300 hrs, the whine of the wireless generator woke him up after only 30 minutes. He was now feeling cold and stiff but after a biscuit and a piece of chocolate he felt 'somewhat warmer.' Burns, the wireless operator, who had spent part of the night fixing the set, made contact with SHQ, his 'patience being rewarded at last.'[87]

A message came through from SHQ informing Falaise to try to establish contact with the 'French armoured car unit of the *3ème DLM* Regimental Headquarters on their left. Horsbrugh-Porter wanted to know the exact positions held by the French Cuirassiers, as it was feared that the Germans might be pushing on to Tirlemont after going through Hannut which they seemed to have captured. Falaise was also to tell the Cuirassiers that the 4th/7th Dragoon Guards were on their way up to reinforce them and should be available at noon.[88]

On finding their HQ, Falaise established that the two squadrons of Panhards had spent a relatively quiet night watching the roads east of the high ground between the Tirlemont – St. Trond road and Landen. He arrived back at Shand's location in Hoegarden at 0530 hrs, whereupon he was given orders 'to proceed at once to SHQ in Meldert.' Falaise found SHQ located at the farthest end of Meldert, close to the churchyard. Horsbrugh-Porter and Erne were both sitting on the ground with their backs to the wall of a house near the forward link armoured car which was concealed in a shed. Falaise noticed how 48 hours without sleep was showing 'clearly on their drawn faces and in their bloodshot eyes.' Falaise gave them all the information he had collected so far. Horsburgh-Porter immediately phoned it through to RHQ. Falaise then sat down to a breakfast of hot tea and boiled eggs that Trooper Machin, Horsburgh-Porter's 'clever and resourceful batman, had mysteriously conjured up.'[89]

At 0845 hrs, the Regiment suffered its first serious casualties when Lance Corporal Francis Averill was killed and Trooper Date wounded. These two men were with the forward transport lorries in the Forêt De Meerdael when some parachutists were reported to have landed nearby. In the search, they met some of their Allies who were similarly employed and unfortunately shot first. There is no doubt that several parachutists were dropped in the area at various times and it is difficult on such occasions, when two or three different bodies of men go in search of the Germans, to avoid regrettable incidents such as this. At approximately 0900 hrs, the news was received that A Squadron had rescued two British airmen who had bailed out when their plane was shot down and landed between the French and the Germans. One of the grateful flyers was Squadron Leader Tomlinson, who, before he was sent to the rear, was given a sandwich and a glass of beer. He told A Squadron that 'he and his pilots had shot down more than 13 German planes in two days.'[90]

---

87   Falaise, *Through Hell to Dunkirk*, p.23.
88   Bishop, *One Young Soldier*, p.24.
89   Bishop, *One Young Soldier*, p.27.
90   Bishop, *One Young Soldier*, p.29.

At 0900 hrs, Lumsden telephoned A Squadron SHQ saying that he was 'worried' over a report to the effect that German tanks were 'swarming' over the countryside between Hannut, Jodoigne, and Tirlemont. Falaise was tasked to find out if this was true and, if so, ask the Cuirassiers what line they intend to hold on to in case they should be forced to retreat. He was also to tell them that the 4th/7th Dragoon Guards' light tanks were being rushed up in support. As he was leaving, they began to arrive.[91]

At 1055 hrs, the first German tanks were engaged at Dormael (K1549, see Map 9). Some 20 minutes later, A Squadron reported the presence of a considerable number of German tanks in the area of St. Trond. There was still a gap at this time between the French and Belgian Armies which A Squadron was doing its best to cover. It was not until 24 hours had elapsed (since this gap was first discovered) that any attempt was made by the French or Belgians to close it. Even then their efforts were somewhat sporadic and it was indeed fortunate that the main thrust of the German tanks was in a south westerly direction against the *3ème DLM*. So far that morning, A Squadron SHQ had learned that one of Shand's cars was damaged, Arkwright's troop (2) had killed 15 motorcycle scouts and destroyed a German armoured car at point-blank range and Roddick's troop (3), which at one point was surrounded, had managed to slip away unscathed.[92]

Later in the afternoon, A Squadron passed Falaise in a cloud of dust. Arkwright shouted, "that they were off to hold a small bridge on the Ghette, north of Tirlemont." Shand and his troop 'sped by shortly after, followed by Roddick's troop, and they all disappeared down the road to Bunsbeek, enveloped by dust.'[93] Smith and his Engineers had been sent out during the afternoon to persuade the Belgians to blow the bridges over the Ghette. Smith thought that the Belgians had 'no settled plan for belts of demolitions' but by 1730 hrs this was accomplished.[94]

The Germans were by this time in contact with the Belgians along the whole line of the river. When Lumsden visited the front to 'inspect the inundations and demolitions' it was obvious that with good troops, this portion of the front could be held for several days. The German infantry was seen to be posted at most of the crossings and 'incautious movements' promptly drew fire in their direction. Anti-tank guns could be seen being moved up under cover of the crossings and a few casualties were inflicted on either side.[95]

During his tour of the front, Lumsden met 'a very interesting Belgian Commandant' in the area of Driestlinter. He stated that 'they had marched the whole way from Maastricht and as a consequence, he and his men were already feeling rather weary,' but what seemed to upset him most was the fact that two of the bridges at Maastricht had not been blown, owing to the actions of German agents and saboteurs, who had cut all the leads to the demolitions underneath these bridges so that they had 'failed to

91   Bishop, *One Young Soldier*, p.28.
92   Bishop, *One Young Soldier*, p.29.
93   Bishop, *One Young Soldier*, p.30.
94   TNA WO 167/778: 12 May 1940.
95   TNA WO 167/45: 12 May 1940.

go up.' He further stated that 'the Burgomaster in Maastricht had met the advancing Germans in German uniform, and that it was obvious that the Germans realised that they would be able to cross the Meuse in this area.' Lumsden thought this Belgian major was 'a first-class officer' who had already appreciated the devastating effect that the German fifth-columnists would exert in his country and its army.[96]

When moving through this area, observers from the Regiment thought it interesting to note the number of anti-tank guns, in fact, guns of all sorts, which were constantly on the move, when one would have expected them to be in position and dug-in. The impression created was that, despite their having a front line and a reserve line held by some five Divisions of Belgians, there was no real intention to fight and inflict casualties on the Germans. It was also noticed what a marked heartening effect the presence of a few British troops had on the Allies and similarly how depressed they felt when these troops had to move to some other even more important task.[97]

At 1900 hrs, Falaise and Horsbrugh-Porter went to visit their Squadron troop locations. They made their way towards the small road which ran parallel to the Ghette, north east of Tirlemont. Their first stop was at Oplinter where they examined Roddick's position which was guarding a small, destroyed bridge across the river. They then moved on to Drieslinter where they found Arkwright guarding another blown-up bridge. Two miles farther on, they saw Roddick's other two cars and Shand (see Map 8). Falaise thought Shand looked 'very tired.' The last car of Shand's troop was in position half a mile farther on, near the end of the village of Budingen. When Horsbrugh-Porter visited the location, he remarked to Falaise that 'the armoured car was in a very good position and completely in control of the bridge crossing.' He added 'that quite a few German advanced scouts must have found that out too, for the half-destroyed bridge was 'strewn with their corpses.'[98] At one point, Shand found himself arrested by a Belgian colonel who had asked Shand to take his troop through a ford and attack what was believed to be a German battalion, while Shand thought the Belgian colonel 'planned to stand and applaud.' During their conversation shells started to land close to where they were talking which sent the colonel running for cover, and consequently, Shand found himself 'out of arrest.'[99]

Hall's day had been far less exciting. He recorded he had done 'absolutely nothing' with his transport because his vehicles had all been out on task during the day. His transport had been tasked to collect the LAD, deliver fuel and food and eventually, through some misunderstanding, or through lack of orders, his vehicles went back to Ophern. The only task he completed during the day was taking the rescued British airmen back to the 13th/18th Hussars. This resulted in Hall resorting to 'gratuitous criticism.' He thought it was a mistake to bring forward only part of the transport:

96   TNA WO 167/452: 12 May 1940.
97   TNA WO 167/452: 12 May 1940.
98   Bishop, *One Young Soldier*, p.32.
99   Shand, Previous Encounters, p.46.

- It left the Squadron Transport Officers doing nothing most of the day (his request to move either forward or back was refused).
- The spare personnel were not with us, so we had no adequate fighting force.
- Things were constantly being needed for the lorries at the rear which could not be got.
- If a lorry broke down, there was no means of transferring its loads without grossly overloading.
- There was plenty of room to conceal all the lorries in the forest.
- No provision was made for feeding the spare men.
- The exact role of the transport wireless was never clearly defined. Though it proved of immense value in saving our lives in one case, and in communicating in emergencies direct to the Squadron.[100]

Without his transport, Hall spent the majority of his day at SHQ's location. By 2045 hrs, Horsbrugh-Porter and Falaise had returned to SHQ's location in St. Martins. Everyone was tired and hungry so Falaise set out to find a place where they could cook some kind of a meal and eat it in peace. Eventually, having been turned down by half a dozen householders' and 'more or less forcing' his way into the last house, he made 'a bargain' with the owner for the use of half the stove and the unoccupied dining room. By 2200 hrs, they had a hot dinner of eggs and tin beef and after eating they lay on the hard tiled floor trying to catch up on sleep. At midnight, Horsbrugh-Porter woke Falaise and told him Lumsden needed more information from the battery of Belgian guns just on the outskirts of the village. On finding the HQ he was informed 'that the Belgian positions on the road to St. Trond were holding fast, but that the Germans had occupied Goetsenhoven and the airfield near it.' The *DLM* and the British armoured cavalry, though outnumbered by the German panzer divisions, seemed to be holding for the time being a position forming a rough semi-circle between Tirlemont and Jodoigne.[101]

Shand observed 'that evening was not a night for sleeping as the sky was full of planes' and that heavy firing continued. There were rumours from the Belgians saying that the Germans were crossing the river in collapsible boats in large numbers. This resulted in Shand having to visit four different Belgian HQs which he found a 'hair-raising' experience as only a few of their sentries could speak French and they were 'very quick on the trigger.'[102] Despite Hall's 'gratuitous criticism,' and not doing a lot, he did record in his diary that he 'had a good night's sleep.'[103]

100 Hall Diary, 12 May 1940, p.3.
101 Bishop, *One Young Soldier*, p.33.
102 Shand, Previous Encounters, p.46.
103 Hall Diary, 12 May 1940, p.3.

Monday 13th May

(Day Four)
There appeared to me to be little danger, but nevertheless, I ordered 12th Lancers to watch the situation, assisted, if need be, by Divisional cavalry regiments.
Gort[104]

The 15th/19th Hussars War Diary records that Lumsden arrived at their RHQ 'for consultation' with the Commanding Officer and at Lumsden's 'suggestion and in default of other orders the following plan was evolved':

> Lumsden would withdraw his troops from their present advanced positions and would dispose of one squadron in front of 15th/19th Hussars, one squadron on the left to the north of the Diest–Louvain road. RHQ 12th Lancers would be established on the high ground south of Holsbeck. It was arranged that when the retirement took place the 12th Lancers would use the bridges to the north of Louvain. These positions, it was hoped, would be taken up by about 0100 hrs on 14th May.[105]

The Regiment was still in close contact with the *3ème DLM* on its right, now being engaged by a number of German armoured cars and tanks, closely supported by motorcyclists, particularly in the area of Dormael. The Belgians were still holding the line of the Ghette, supported by B and C Squadrons and with all the bridges on this front long since blown.

A Squadron was also heavily involved in supporting the Belgians and managed to identify the German units from two of the German dead, who were from the 17th Regiment.[106] The Squadron had remained overnight on its bridges overlooking the Ghette, but they were running short on fuel and ammunition. Lumsden went out to visit the A Squadron locations. It is unclear at exactly what time this took place, but Shand wrote that Lumsden 'materialised out of the morning mist' and told him they were being outflanked in that sector and that they should be withdrawing that night.[107]

At A Squadron's SHQ location, breakfast of hot tea and eggs was prepared by Machin for Horsbrugh-Porter and Falaise. It was early in the morning and dawn was only just breaking as a somewhat 'bleary-eyed' Erne joined them for breakfast having been on watch since 0200 hrs. At dawn, Hall's missing lorries turned up, only to be told by Lieutenant Butler (Technical Adjutant) that Lumsden was not happy with the

104 Gort, *Second Despatch*, p.5910.
105 TNA WO 167/454: 13 May 1940.
106 Clark-Kennedy, 'Record of Service', p.8.
107 Shand, 'May 1940: A Memory', p.153.

transport and felt that they were not doing any work. Hall in his diary uses the words 'fury' and 'enraged' to explain how he felt, adding that he had been asking for something to do for the last two days. Hall took his lorry and went back to A Squadron ready to start refuelling the troops.[108]

Falaise was washing and shaving under the farmyard pump when Horsbrugh-Porter, who had returned from RHQ 15th/19th Hussars, called him over and said that Shand and Arkwright had requested a resupply. With the exception of Horsbrugh-Porter, he was the only other person who knew exactly where they were located. Falaise had asked him to take the fighting lorry (with Hall) and resupply the armoured cars. Horsbrugh-Porter was concerned as to how close Falaise could get his lorry as it would be in full view of the Germans but told him that he would leave it to him to 'be the judge as to how far' he could go.[109]

At 0600 hrs, Falaise reached Roddick's position in Oplinter. After the troop had filled up, he then moved onto Drieslinter where they were 'greeted by a continuous crackle of rifle fire coming from across the small river.' Despite the fire, Falaise continued his move along the road to get behind the cover of a house in the village. Once undercover, Falaise checked his load to see if there was 'any harm done' but fortunately only one fuel can had been punctured. Falaise left the lorry behind the house and went on foot to where he had last seen Arkwright's troop the night before. After 15 minutes of unfruitful searching, Falaise continued his journey to Shand's location at Budingen without further incident. Once he had arrived, he hid the lorry in a small farmyard and unloaded the fuel and ammunition. When Falaise saw Shand, he noted that he had had a tough night and was 'haggard.' Falaise thought that Shand had not slept a wink as his position was exposed and had clearly been unable to relax for a moment. Just as he was about to leave, Shand's location was attacked by three Junkers which machine gunned the location from a height of approximately 600 feet. After taking cover in a pigsty, Falaise made his way back to Drieslinter. He made the journey to the village in 'record time' and hid the lorry under a tree and camouflaged it with branches.[110]

Once the lorry was under cover, Falaise commandeered a Belgian motorcyclist and they made their way towards the river to try and find Arkwright's troop. Finally, he saw them on a small dirt road near a shack behind a tiny blown-up road bridge at the narrowest part of the stream, north east of the village. The Germans were behind a line of trees approximately 150 yards away. They appeared to have had some machine guns in a one-storey house which was barely visible around the bend of the road. On the way, he found three wrecked German motorcycles and six dead bodies sprawled in the mud 30 yards ahead of Arkwright's advanced car. When he arrived at the troop location he was greeted by Arkwright. Falaise wrote:

108 Hall Diary, 13 May 1940, p.3.
109 Falaise, *Through Hell to Dunkirk*, p.35; TNA WO 167/454 stated that Horsbrugh-Porter had been there at 0400.
110 Falaise, *Through Hell to Dunkirk*, p.36.

Smiling and gay as always, Peter welcomes me to his dilapidated lodgings as graciously as a country squire receiving a weekend guest. Even his nearby Boche neighbours have not prevented him from having his morning shave. He is puffing away at the little pipe I gave him one day in Arras, a month ago. His No. 1 car is covering the bridge, No. 2 is behind the wall of his shack, and No. 3 is about 100 yards away to the left, commanding the railroad tracks and the railway bridge which has not been blown up. Chicken feathers are scattered all over the ground and an appetising odour of broth emanates from a large iron pot that is sitting on some bricks over burning embers. Peter's troop will not go hungry. Their morale is excellent. Peter has also found some bottles of mineral water which he insists I must take back with me. When I tell him I am running short of our favourite pipe tobacco, he dives inside his armoured car and emerges triumphantly with a pound tin which he also forces on me. I notice then that a fuzzy plush monkey has been fixed on the hood of his car. It perches there solemnly with a silly worried expression on its face. It is a prime mascot for Troop No. 2. As we laugh and joke and walk around in full view of the Germans, I can't help wondering if some Boche beyond the river isn't watching with bewilderment all these touching domestic scenes through his Zeiss glasses.[111]

Hall's comment on the resupply of Shand's and Arkwright's troops was that 'both the troops seemed to be having a very good time,' and that the Belgians were cheerfully inefficient.[112] While A Squadron was being resupplied, at approximately 0850 hrs, German infantry supported by machine guns attacked in the area of Wommersom – Haelen – Geethetz and a few Germans succeeded in crossing the floods. Motorcyclists were also engaged in the area of Diest at 1023 hrs. Hunn described C Squadron's action, recording that the German's forward patrols were of motorcycles and sidecars consisting of three men who would race to the river bank. This was usually met by 'intense' machine gun fire and the noise of the guns from both sides was 'deafening,' and it was the 'Germans who suffered great casualties.'[113]

At approximately 1150 hrs, Second Lieutenant Henderson captured a German horse in the area of Haelen. This horse was marked on the off-hind with the number 35/104 and had been the mount of a trooper in a cavalry patrol which waded and swam across the river and floods in this area. The Belgians supported by Miller-Mundy wiped out this patrol, which was some 15-20 strong, and the horse went spare, to be captured by 3 Troop. There was much discussion over the wireless about it and how it could be transported back to England and the Regimental Stables. Hunn saw these conversations as a reflection that they had not 'grasped' the seriousness of the situation… and gave the impression that they still believed the war would be over in a matter

111 Falaise, *Through Hell to Dunkirk*, pp.36-37.
112 Hall Diary, 13 May 1940, p.3.
113 Hunn Diary, 13 May 1940, p.7.

of weeks.[114] Hunn also wrote that the bridges over the Diest were destroyed once all the Allied forces were withdrawn, although this would not have appeared to be the case.[115] At Diest, one of C Squadron's locations, Lieutenant Tatton Brinton used his command of the French language to get the nervous Belgian commander to blow his bridges. The resulting demolition resulted 'in a sharp rap over the knuckles' from GHQ as it was reported that there were still two Belgian Divisions on the far side. In truth, that might have been the case, but the first units to arrive at the blown bridge were a large number of German motorcycles. This action like the others, prevented the Regiment's line being penetrated.[116]

Before hostilities, very careful arrangements had been made to train the wireless detachment to co-operate with the RAF in the hope that the Regiment would be able to listen into the BEF's strategical reconnaissances. This would have been invaluable at the time, when the Regiment was trying to determine whether the main German thrust would be north or south of the Albert Canal. Up to midday on that date, no air information whatsoever had been received, and in fact no air information was at any time received, either by this means or from the formations the Regiment served.[117] At 1300 hrs, Horsbrugh-Porter went to visit the Belgian Battery Commander who was firing at a long line of German lorries coming up the road leading to Goetsenhoven. Notwithstanding the Belgian commander's enthusiasm, the news from the south was bad as the German tanks had 'rammed a hole' through the *DLM's* defence around Jandraine. Horsbrugh-Porter was concerned that his position was in danger of being cut-off from Louvain, so went off to the bank of the Ghette to see what was happening.[118]

When he arrived, he found Oplinter was quiet, so continued to Drieslinter where he walked to Arkwright's position. When he arrived, Arkwright's troop and a Belgian patrol were being heavily engaged from a house across the river. Falaise observed:

> We hug the hedges and dodging from tree to tree reach the armoured cars. Two wounded soldiers of the Belgian patrol are lying in the field across the stream. A German machine gun is making it difficult to rescue them. Peter, rifle in hand, is shooting at the bushes about 200 yards away from which the Germans fire is coming. Bullets are spattering against the shack behind which we stand. The major and I grab two rifles and run to take cover behind what remains of the bridge stone parapet. On our right, a Belgian officer is blasting away at the small house with an anti-tank gun. Another group of Belgians, squatting behind a heavy machine gun on our left, fire short bursts in the direction of the railroad

114 Hunn Diary, 13 May 1940, p.7.
115 Hunn Diary, 13 May 1940, p.7.
116 Stewart, *History of the XII Royal Lancers,* p.353.
117 TNA WO 167/453: 12 May 140.
118 Shand states that Horsbrugh-Porter was accompanied by Lumsden, See Shand, *Previous Encounters*, p.46.

tracks. Four men, two Belgians and two volunteers from Peter's group succeed in crossing the deep gully under the blown-up bridge and worm their way up to the wounded men. Moving cautiously along the hedge which hides them from the Germans, they dart across the field and drag the men to the safety of a ditch. Then, inch by inch, yard by yard, they crawl back to us, dragging the two unconscious bodies while bullets whistle overhead and toss up tufts of grass around them. Twenty minutes after they have left, we help them up the gully and carry the wounded to a Belgian field ambulance which has driven up behind Peter's armoured car. Both men are hit in the belly. They look as if they were dead.[119]

At 1530 hrs, the firing subsided, so Horsbrugh-Porter decided to move off and visit Shand's troop. When he arrived at Budingen they found the armoured cars in the same positions as the day before. Falaise thought:

Bruce looks completely exhausted. He has had no sleep for 66 hours. His face is grey with caked sweat and dust, his eyelids heavy and swollen. His men are no better off than he. They have not been as lucky as Peter's troop, having no place in which they can rest and eat. The major, after looking them over and talking to Bruce, does not think he can leave the troop there much longer. I make Bruce drink some good wine which I always carry with me and force him to eat some biscuits and chocolate. This bucks him up a bit. After a few minutes, we leave them to their lonely and dangerous task and turn the car toward Tirlemont. As we are nearing Drieslinter at full speed, a motorbike lying in the middle of the road forces us to stop. Getting out of the car to drag it out of the way, we catch sight of its driver, a Belgian cavalryman, lying on his belly in a field of clover on the side of the road. When he sees us, he points upward and back of us. We promptly turned around and at once understand why he had abandoned his motorcycle.
   Screeching down from the sky, five Stukas are diving straight at us. Three leaps carry me to the middle of the field. I nose-dive into the green clover. I flatten down, my heart thumping like a bass drum – 1, 2, 3, 4, 5, 6 bombs hurtle down, screaming. A deafening noise. Smoke. Blinding flashes. The earth rocks under me. Then the roar of the planes passes, and I stagger to my feet feeling rather sick. Fifty yards away to my left I am happy to see Andrew waving to me. Fred, our driver, scrambles out of the ditch. The Belgian soldier walks slowly back to his motorcycle. The Junkers have missed the road; all the bombs have fallen quite near but on the other side of it. The smoking craters are in a straight line about 20 yards apart. We reach the car and find that the left door is damaged. It won't shut, but somehow, we fix it. Andrew, after taking one look at Fred, who is too

119 Falaise, *Through Hell to Dunkirk*, p.38.

shaky to be of any use, gets into the driver's seat. We hurry to Oplinter where we pay a visit to the Belgian Colonel at his HQ.[120]

The Belgian Colonel confirmed that the *DLM* had been forced to abandon its position which it had held in the morning south of Tirlemont. This meant that the Germans might now be able to push up from the south to gain access to the Tirlemont–Louvain road, which would cut-off A Squadron's positions. Horsbrugh-Porter wasted no time in getting back to St. Martins so he could report by wireless to Lumsden what he had found out. The Battery Commander told Horsbrugh-Porter that he had been ordered to cover the retreat of the troops defending Tirlemont by laying a heavy barrage ahead of them. The evacuation would start at dusk and should move rapidly. Erne informed the Colonel that the Squadron would protect him with a troop of armoured cars:

> Young Andrew's troop is to have this job and it takes up its position a few hundred yards ahead of the different gun emplacements on the narrow country road which winds down toward Tirlemont. Bruce and Peter call up to say that the Belgian troops around them are withdrawing. They want to know what to do. They are told by the major to stick it out until further orders.[121]

At 1339 hrs, information was received that German tanks were moving west in the area of Beverloo (K2480). At 1645 hrs, Haelen was heavily bombarded by artillery and it seemed that an attack would shortly develop in the area. At about 1950 hrs, three troops of German motorcyclists attacked but were easily repulsed in the area of Orsmael (K1249). The Regiment's casualties to date had been three armoured cars lost through bombing and shellfire. At 2000 hrs, Horsbrugh-Porter's information regarding a Belgian withdrawal was confirmed and the news was received that the Belgians intended to withdraw at 0300 hrs the following morning.[122]

At the same time as the Belgium withdrawal had been confirmed, Falaise was dining at A Squadron's SHQ location on a 'mighty banquet' of hot soup, bread, and butter, and three soft-boiled eggs each! Horsbrugh-Porter advised everyone to 'snatch' a few minutes sleep as he thought they would have a busy night ahead. Two and a half hours later Horsbrugh-Porter woke everyone up and told them that RHQ had informed him they were to 'start the withdrawal at 2300 hrs.' Falaise went outside and climbed a hill to get a better view, where he also could hear the rattle of machine guns down on the Ghette. He noted that 'Budingen appeared to be on fire and that Bruce and Peter were still down there. Silhouetted against the scarlet horizon 100 yards ahead' he could see 'one of young Andrew's cars, watching and waiting.' Falaise was informed by Horsbrugh-Porter that he had ordered both troops on the Ghette

120 Falaise, *Through Hell to Dunkirk*, p.39.
121 Falaise, *Through Hell to Dunkirk*, pp.38-40.
122 TNA WO 167/452: 13 May 1940.

to withdraw much to his relief. The Squadron's rendezvous was to be at Lovenjoel on the Louvain road, so when they got the order to move Shand and Arkwright's two troops joined up and travelled together.[123] When they arrived, they were greeted by an 'appalling sight'. According to Falaise:

> German bombers have reduced this wide and lovely road, lined with tall trees, to havoc and desolation. Trucks, large passenger buses, and private cars, some still on fire, are strewn over it. One huge holiday bus has been blown up beside a wrecked house, its front wheels resting on what remains of the roof. It is still flaming like a gigantic pyre, casting a red glow on the pools of blood and the mutilated bodies which are lying about it. We make slow headway, avoiding the bomb craters and obstacles in our path. To the left of the road on the railroad tracks, a train is ablaze, lighting up the countryside. Finally, we reach the hamlet of Lovenjoel, which consists of about a dozen houses among tall trees on both sides of the road.[124]

Shand again recorded the difficulty in using the French maps when all the signposts were in Flemish. This was made even more of a nightmare by the 'insidious sleeplessness' that he had to fight against all the time. Shand wrote that his troop 'were wonderful' and that they never complained and received 'with the utmost equanimity the completely unreserved maledictions.' The total journey was only 20 miles, but Shand felt they travelled double that distance, making detours to avoid roadblocks using secondary roads. The roads were still packed with refugees, flocks of sheep and herds of cattle as well as 'heterogeneous elements' of the Belgian Army which were all being subjected to bombs and flares.[125] It was nearly dawn before they reached the rendezvous and took up a new position south east of Louvain.[126]

Meanwhile, Hall was making his way back to RHQ with one of his lorries which he had had to patch up after it was overloaded with the Regiment's entire ration allocation. By his own admittance, he had been very lucky, as had he arrived a minute later he would have missed them as 'somewhat stupidly' he had not switched on his wireless and was unaware of the order to withdraw. Once found, he joined them for the move. For anyone who had travelled over this area, the pitfalls became well known, especially when it came to travelling the same roads at night without lights, although it was still possible to avoid them. For the drivers of other vehicles, it was not so easy and the rear-link wireless set, which was a No.3 set on a Leyland chassis, was unfortunately driven into a deep bomb crater, from which it was impossible to recover it.[127] It was a 'faithful old servant' of the Regiment, in that it had twice been to Egypt

123 Shand, *Previous Encounters*, p.46.
124 Falaise, *Through Hell to Dunkirk*, pp.41-42.
125 Shand, 'May 1940: A Memory', p.153.
126 Shand, *Previous Encounters*, pp.46-47.
127 Hall Diary, 13 May 1940, p.4.

with them and was some eight years old, but still in excellent condition. The Adjutant wrote:

> We parted with this old friend very sadly and it was not until 0730 hrs when a spare No.3 set mounted on a Guy lorry, which fortunately had been standing by with B Echelon could be brought up, that communication with GHQ could be restored.[128]

The Guy lorry, which was used belonged to Crudden, was one of A Squadron's vehicles which was part of Hall's echelon.[129] This delay meant that there was a period of approximately six hours when the Regiment was out of wireless contact with GHQ, but communications were eventually restored.

In anticipation of the Belgian withdrawal, the Regiment began its own withdrawal at 0100 hrs, (which was a little later than expected), by which time the Belgian artillery was already on the move and was seriously blocking all the roads.[130] The squadrons fell back to the general line Opvelp (J9350) – Winghe St. Georges [Sint Joris Winge] (J9960) – Aerschot [Aarschot] (J96). The withdrawal of the Belgians through the Engineer eyes of Smith was the first time that the prepared demolitions had not been covered by fire, which meant that the Germans were now able to use with 'impunity' whatever method they chose to overcome the obstacles created.[131]

Tuesday 14th May

(Day Five)

The Admiralty have made an Order requesting all owners of self-propelled pleasure craft between 30' and 100' in length to send all particulars to the Admiralty within 14 days from today if they have not already been offered or requisitioned.
BBC

[Lumsden] 'told Horsbrugh-Porter to use his own judgement, but to keep in mind that if we linger too long, we may be cut-off from the only bridge to Louvain.'
Falaise[132]

By 0330 hrs, A Squadron was on the move again towards Loo on the donkey-back ridge between the main roads between Louvain–Diest and Louvain–Tirlemont. Falaise recorded that Erne, who had had a good sleep, was either totally unaware of the corpse that had companioned them in the cellar or else was 'prevented by British

128 TNA WO 167/452: 14 May 1940.
129 Hall Diary, 13 May 1940, p.4.
130 Clark-Kennedy, 'Record of Service', p.8.
131 TNA WO 167/778, 13 May 1940.
132 Falaise, *Through Hell to Dunkirk*, p.48.

reticence from mentioning it.' They both remained silent as they rode through the night standing up in the turret between the Bren and Boyes guns.[133]

Bishop had been in position since 0300 hrs, in front of Louvain, having taken over command of Roddick's troop.[134] The troop had remained behind at Oplinter to cover the withdrawal of the Belgian artillery. It had gone well and they had only lost one gun. The commanding officer thanked Lumsden and Roddick for the difficult task they had taken on. When Roddick finally arrived at SHQ, he reported that his gunner had been wounded in the operation. Horsbrugh-Porter ordered Erne's gunner to take his place and Falaise became a temporary substitute for Erne's gunner in the rear-link car.[135]

Bishop wrote that they were 'weary but needle-sharp' from the sense of danger. The three cars watched the dawn break, fine and dry once light, and they noticed they were surrounded by smashed civilian cars. As the dawn light picked them out, it also picked out their dead occupants, sitting up as if ready to be driven away. One woman wore a fur coat which did nothing at all to 'cheer him up.'[136]

Finally, Falaise reached Loo at 0400 hrs and Shand's and Arkwright's troops moved off towards an advanced position near Lubeek. Meanwhile, the 'ever-resourceful' Machin forced his way into a boarded-up and empty *estaminet* which was to be used as SHQ's location. After exploring several hay lofts, Machin returned with his steel helmet filled with eggs. Hot water was soon boiling and a breakfast of eggs and tea was provided. Falaise tried to compel young Roddick to eat a little, but he was so tired that he could not keep his eyes open, and his head kept falling on the table. Finally, Roddick went to sleep with his face in the eggs.[137]

At 0530, A Squadron SHQ was woken by the sounds of German Stuka bombers and Heinkels sweeping over their location as they bombed Louvain. They quickly mounted some of the Bren guns on wooden posts and blazed away at the Stukas as they went by. Falaise observed:

Either they don't see our armoured cars and trucks, which are very well camouflaged and covered with straw to make them look like haystacks, or their mission is to bomb Louvain only. Anyway, they leave us alone and disdainfully ignore our Bren guns which are harmlessly popping at them. After watching this spectacle for a while, I return to the estaminet where I find a sewing basket left by the fleeing owners. Helping myself to needle and thread, I sit in a corner and consolidate a few of my loose buttons while waiting for orders.[138]

133 Falaise, *Through Hell to Dunkirk*, p.43.
134 Falaise attributes this wrongly to Bishop just returning from leave.
135 Falaise, *Through Hell to Dunkirk*, p.43.
136 Bishop, *One Young Soldier*, p.50.
137 Falaise, *Through Hell to Dunkirk*, p.45.
138 Falaise, *Through Hell to Dunkirk*, p.46.

After the bombing stopped, Horsbrugh-Porter and Falaise went off in the staff car immediately on a reconnaissance towards Lubeek. Horsbrugh-Porter told Falaise that he was 'not quite satisfied with the positions that Shand's and Arkwright's troops had taken, and Bishop was also believed to be in a 'bad spot.' However, as they left, Fred the driver seemed more concerned with the German aircraft than with his driving. Horsbrugh-Porter decided to take over the wheel and ordered Fred to the back seat where he could watch the planes to his heart's content through the rear window:

> Every few hundred yards we pass light tanks of the 13th/18th Hussars hidden behind hedges and stacks of wheat. Horsbrugh-Porter drives on unmindful of the threatening Heinkels, some of which are so low that we can see the short flame-bursts of their machine guns as they dive toward us. I am so nervous that I keep my hand on the door handle ready to jump out. As for poor Fred, he is green in the face. But, Horsbrugh-Porter, who I have discovered does not know the meaning of the word fear, merely grins, and drives on with that mad look in his eye that I know so well by now, and I don't like it much when I happen to be in a position to be concerned with its consequences.[139]

After some difficulty, Horsbrugh-Porter saw 'the soft soil fresh tracks of the distinctive tread of the armoured cars and in the distance the dust raised by a column of German armoured vehicles which were advancing toward Lubeek from Attenrode.' Eventually, Horsbrugh-Porter found Bishop's location and new instructions were given. According to Falaise:

> They are now all holding good, well-concealed positions on high ground from which they can watch and report the German's advance. Bishop believes that they will make contact with the Germans within a half hour at most. We turn the staff car back towards Loo and reach it by 0830 hrs.[140]

By 0930 hrs, the Regiment was in position on their new line. Plans were made by Lumsden in collaboration with Lieutenant Colonel Stirling of the 13th/18th Hussars and Lieutenant Colonel Frazer of the 15th/19th Hussars to co-ordinate the defence of the front thus presenting an intact front to cover the Dyle position. To conform with the plan, the 12th Lancers moved to the north of the road Louvain–Diest to cover the left flank of the 15th/19th Hussars. Demolitions of all sorts were prepared and made on the roads between Ghette and Dyle to delay the German's advance, particularly on the line of the *De Cointet* Anti-Tank obstacle, which the Belgians had erected east of the Dyle to cover Louvain to Wavre. During the morning the German infantry moved up to this position, and Aerschot was again heavily bombed.

139 Falaise, *Through Hell to Dunkirk*, p.47.
140 Falaise, *Through Hell to Dunkirk*, p.47.

At approximately 1000 hrs, Bishop was joined by three Bren Gun Carriers from the 13th/18th Hussars commanded by Derrick Martin who had been sent to support him. Over the wireless, he could hear the troops to either side of his position reporting the German advance. Some German motorcyclists were on the move and when he checked the map reference Bishop found that they were already behind him. Bishop recorded that:

> There were the sounds of explosions to our rear, each of which sounded to me very like the bridge across which we were eventually to withdraw being sent sky-high. Hours after the last of the 'braves Belges' had retired through my position (at 60 mph and pointing back, shouting "Les Allemands!! Un kilomètre par là!!" no Allemands appeared. But eventually, a posse of motorcycles came into sight some 600 yards distant. I was waiting until they came closer when Derrick's guns opened up with a roar that made me jump. The men and their machines just subsided in a heap in the middle of the road and lay there, some still astride their motorcycles. For half an hour, I think about as bad a half-hour as ever I spent, I searched through my binoculars the road and the flat, grim countryside for their chums. But the whole treeless, unfenced, characterless, hideous wilderness was devoid of life. In front, Tirlemont with its nice people burned on in the hands of the Germans and explosions continued to rend the air from Louvain. I wished I knew what they were destroying back there. As an answer to my several reports, all I ever got from the operator back at HQ was laconic "OK." Perhaps it was comfortingly phlegmatic and when my turn came, I am sure I sounded just as inhuman and unhelpful.[141]

At 1000 hrs, Bishop reported on the wireless that he had just had a skirmish with some advance elements and was holding out. The firing of all his and the 13th/18th Hussars' guns at once seemed to have surprised the German column further back as it stopped and appeared to be trying to turn around to reach shelter or to await reinforcements. He stated that he had 'seen no tanks yet and one of his men' was wounded. A little later, Bishop reported that the Germans had passed through Korbeek and were now less than three miles from Louvain. Shand's wireless was out of action, so he sent one of his DR's to report it. Then, at 1200 hrs precisely, Horsbrugh-Porter's voice came through the earphones. He told Bishop to withdraw and come straight through Louvain to SHQ at Beverloo. Bishop wrote that 'relief outdoing shame,' and informed Derrick as the passed through his carriers. 'He waved cheerfully and Bishop 'never saw him again.'[142] Shand's position likewise was relieved, however by the 15th/19th Hussars. On his way back Shand's troop 'was singled out for a strafing attack from

---

141 Bishop, *One Young Soldier*, p.51.
142 Bishop, *One Young Soldier*, p.51.

a German fighter.' Shand wrote that fortunately, it was not using armour-piercing bullets and they 'only collected a few honourable dents on the plating.'[143]

At 1250 hrs, Stirling reported that he was being heavily attacked and would have to withdraw. This was only after Horsbrugh-Porter tried to persuade him 'to stay a while longer, but orders were orders,' and he was unsuccessful. Finally, Horsbrugh-Porter stormed out of their HQ grumbling that, "the 12th Lancers will jolly well show these blankety-blank Hussars that they are not afraid of the adjectived Huns."[144] One by one under Horsbrugh-Porter's 'stony glare,' the light cavalry's tanks rumbled by leaving the village on their way toward Louvain and relative safety.

By midday, A Squadron was alone on the narrow Loo ridge. Shand was in retreat towards his SHQ and Falaise could see his dust in the distance. Arkwright, who had been practically surrounded, was fighting his way back and Bishop had moved to a new position from where he could see a great number of German tanks entering Lovenjoel, where the Squadron had been only a few hours before.[145] Hunn noted that the speed of the German advance was 'unbelievable' and their advance could not be halted. Eventually stronger forces crossed using boats, pontoons, and rafts, under the cover of darkness and artillery fire.[146]

Lumsden eventually ordered the Regiment to withdraw west of the Dyle to cover the left flank of the 15th/19th Hussars. Lumsden informed A Squadron that B Squadron, on their left in a position similar to theirs on the parallel ridge which lay between the Louvain – Diest and the Louvain – Arrashot roads, was withdrawing towards Louvain. Lumsden told:

> Horsbrugh-Porter to use his own judgement, but to keep in mind that if we linger too long, we may be cut-off from the only bridge to Louvain. Horsbrugh-Porter stubbornly decides to hang on a little longer but orders the advanced troops to start falling back toward Loo. Erne says nothing, just looks at me. And Machin slyly suggests that we may still have sauerkraut for dinner.[147]

Officers were immediately sent off to ensure that the bridges over this river, which were in most cases being prepared for demolition and guarded by the Belgian Army, should not be blown until the Regiment had crossed over safely. This proved to be a very sensible precaution as the retired General who was responsible for the demolitions north of Louvain was somewhat overkeen to see his bridges safely demolished. When he had been assured that the Germans were still some distance away and that he would be given ample time to complete his demolitions after the Regiment had safely crossed, he co-operated most helpfully.

143 Shand, *Previous Encounters*, p.47.
144 Falaise, *Through Hell to Dunkirk*, p.48.
145 Falaise, *Through Hell to Dunkirk*, p.48.
146 Hunn Diary, 14 May 1940, p.7.
147 Falaise, *Through Hell to Dunkirk*, p.48.

The timing as to when to blow the bridges was critical and officers were sent to each location to ensure they were not blown until all troops had crossed. This was marred by the fact that once the bridges were blown it was reported that two troops of B Squadron were still to the east of the river. However, some clear speaking on the wireless established that it was an error in map reading and they had in fact crossed the river. Hunn stated it was a coding and decoding error. However, it prompted a discussion as to what vehicle crews should do if they did find themselves cut-off and it was decided that they should destroy the vehicles and swim to safety. Browne-Clayton was so relieved to hear that all his troops were safe that instead of 'administering the necessary reproof he dispensed six bottles of looted beer instead.'[148] Hunn attributed the mistake to being a result of extreme fatigue from being in contact with the Germans for four days and nights without sleep.[149] Eventually, Horsbrugh-Porter managed to gather the Squadron in Loo and sent Arkwright and his troop down the hill toward the Louvain Bridge on the Diest road, with orders to report if the road was clear. Arkwright duly reported that he had seen some German motorcycle scouts and had fired on them. Horsbrugh-Porter directed him to proceed to the bridge at once and to warn the engineers there not to blow it up until the Squadron had crossed.[150]

At 1400 hrs, A Squadron set off with Shand's troop leading, followed by Bishop and then SHQ Troop with Horsbrugh-Porter, Roddick, the fighting lorry, and the staff car. Erne's armoured car brought up the rear with Falaise still acting as the gunner. Falaise swung the turret around to face the rear. Shand wrote:

> Poor John [Clark-Kennedy] had been stung on the eyelid by a wasp and was suffering agonies… we moved off through Louvain to cross the Dyle. To reach the bridge of boats we had to go by the most circuitous route and I was terrified that I should lead the whole squadron into a dead end. We arrived there eventually and found the river bank manned by the Grenadiers, all looking immaculate. I shouted out to a friend of mine and wondered why he was so slow in recognising me until I realised that we were all covered with dirt, unshaven and looking like nothing on earth. We crossed the bridge of boats (all the others had been blown).[151]

On their way, they pass 'the crumpled bodies' of the German motorcyclists killed by Arkwright's gunner sprawling in the dust near the crossroad. German bombers were still 'diving and zooming' up again over the bridge they had to cross. Falaise thought they seemed 'to have decided to destroy it and cut us off and was not 'happy over the situation.' However, since there was nothing that could be done about it, he decided,

148 Stewart, *History of the XII Royal Lancers,* p.353.
149 Hunn Diary, 14 May 1940, p.7.
150 Falaise, *Through Hell to Dunkirk,* p.49.
151 Shand, *Previous Encounters,* p.47.

to stand up and try to hide his feelings while the armoured car sped on. By 1430 hrs, the whole squadron had crossed the bridge.[152] As his troop went over, Bishop observed:

> We all felt a lot happier for seeing the Guards there. They were the first British troops, bar Derrick's men, that we had yet seen. Furthermore, they were, of course, cool, calm, and collected. They looked at us without interest. They might have been waiting to line some royal route through London instead of a foreign river line shortly to be stormed by relentless Germans which they knew to be vastly superior in numbers and armaments, if in nothing else.[153]

Falaise thought the Guards on the bridge looked 'well-armed and determined, and it was good to see them.' Horsbrugh-Porter asked Erne and Falaise to stay behind near the bridge until it was blown and then to rejoin the Squadron at Ophem near Brussels. All the houses beside the Dyle were banked with sandbags and bristling with light and heavy machine guns. Two well-camouflaged and well-protected anti-tank guns were set up on the right and left sides of the street at the bridgehead. 'Unmindful of the bombing,' a young officer from the Guards dashed across the street to bring them bottles of beer and lemonade. Falaise wrote that it was 'very welcome; that their throats were parched,' as they had nothing to eat since 0500 hrs that morning. The officer told them 'that since this morning more than 60 men had been killed by the bombing.' The same question was on everybody's lips: 'Where are our planes? What are they doing? Why are they not sent here to protect us'? Falaise observed:

> Lord Freddy Cambridge, the cousin of the King, and my friend... sends a messenger to Erne and me with a bottle of old brandy and a funny note explaining why he is too busy now to help us drink it. We scribble a few words of thanks and best wishes and are about to despatch it when the rattle of two heavy machine guns breaking into action near us sends everyone helter-skelter to their battle stations. At the same moment, the bridge is blown up with a terrific blast, right under the wheels of a platoon of German motorcyclists who are sent flying skyward. The explosion is so loud and shattering that it knocks me down to the bottom of the car. Erne's pipe flies out of his mouth. Scrambling to our feet, we pull Lord Freddy's messenger up onto the car and speed off to a safer spot around the next corner while bricks, stones and scraps of iron come crashing down on the paved street all around us. It was exactly 1600 hrs when the bridge blew up. Now that it is gone, our job is finished, and we drive off through the ruins of Louvain with a feeling of relief. The fighting is up to the infantry now and we of the 12th Lancers are heading for food, sleep, and maybe a much-needed bath![154]

---

152 Falaise, *Through Hell to Dunkirk*, p.49.
153 Bishop, *One Young Soldier*, p.51.
154 Falaise, *Through Hell to Dunkirk*, p.50.

The services of Smith and his sappers were again required to complete the destruction of two bridges which were only partly destroyed on the first attempt and also to destroy a wooden bridge which had been overlooked. His day did not go without incident and while travelling along the Tirlemont–Louvain road which had come in for 'very rough treatment':

> Lance Sergeant Johnson and his party were travelling along the road with their truck of explosives during the heaviest part of the attack. A bomb scored a direct hit on the road in front of the truck and in trying to avoid the crater the truck became firmly wedged in the railway track which runs beside the road. Driver Waller was wounded in the ear by a piece of shrapnel, but in spite of the bombing, Johnson persuaded the crew of a Belgian tank to use their vehicle to get the truck back onto the road. This was successfully accomplished and this action by Johnson and the coolness of Waller enabled the truck to be got safely away. It seems unlikely that Johnson told the crew of the Belgian tank that his truck contained 1 ton of explosives.[155]

Hall was sent to the bridge at Haecht to relieve the Squadron Second-in-Command. When he arrived, he saw a troop of the Skins [sic] and B and C Squadrons, followed by RHQ, cross the bridge before it was closed with a 'big gate affair'. According to Hall:

> An unhappy cyclist left on the wrong side climbed over quite easily though. Then went towards Louvain to see the bridge go up. Had Scott's petrol lorry with me; met John Clark-Kennedy and persuaded him with some difficulty not to re-cross the river The bridge went up when I was still in the open; seeing the stones fly up I jumped into a barn when the whole roof seemed to fall around me. I have rarely been quite so dirty which is saying quite a lot! Then we returned to Ophem.[156]

In a masterpiece of understatement, the War Diary states that 'after a few alarms and excursions,' the Regiment withdrew complete and intact to Ophem (J7154), where everyone had their first good night's rest since the war started.[157] Erne and Falaise finally caught up with the rest of the Regiment. Falaise noted that all the squadron's armoured cars and the trucks from the transport echelon were waiting for them at Ophem. They were hidden under the 'thick foliage of the beautiful trees in the park of a chateau belonging to the Comte de Grune. The house was large, modern, and well-furnished:

---

155 TNA WO 167/778: 14 May 1940.
156 Hall Diary, 14 May 1940, p.4.
157 TNA WO 167/452: 14 May 1940.

I am much too tired to appreciate these luxurious surroundings and I just manage to climb up the stairs to a tiny room on the second floor which has been assigned to me. There I find Stevens, my batman, who has prepared a wonderful-looking bed for me on a narrow couch. The last time I saw Stevens was a week ago when he helped me pack my things to go to Paris on leave. Much has happened since then! He is a regular Army soldier and a pukka batman with a dry sense of humour and the rare knack of knowing when to remain silent. He helps me to undress and to pull off the heavy cavalry boots which have been on my swollen feet and tired legs for four days and nights, ever since last Saturday morning. Deftly he unpacks my light kit while I fall into a deep and much-needed sleep. I wake up at 2000 hrs and join the others in the dining room. We are all in pyjamas and still so exhausted that we just sit there and munch our food in a sort of daze without saying a word. It feels good though to sit at a table and have warm soup, roast meat, and vegetables. Best of all, God only knows why none of us is missing. After coffee, we all return to our bedrooms for more sleep. Right now, our only ambition is to sleep, to sleep long and hard. Just sleep for hours.[158]

Bishop noted that on reaching Ophern that they were so tired that some of them 'were beginning to say things backwards,' he also, 'found that people's outlines seemed to have white edges and misty haloes,' and he did not remember going to bed.[159] However, Shand did:

We all went to sleep… after a wonderful meal. Tim and I slept in an enormous voluptuous bed in a very attractive little house… We hardly woke when a German aeroplane was shot down and crashed a few hundred yards away.[160]

When Hall returned to Ophern, on passing through a village to the north he noticed that the Belgians were very excited and a moment later there was a shout when Bloom told him he had seen a parachutist in the field to the right. It is unclear if these were parachutists or the crew from the downed aircraft. Hall wrote that:

Rather than turn back we took the next turning to get behind him. The moment we stopped the whole of the crews of the Bug and petrol lorry ran towards the man or rather men, firing from the shoulder, leaving me doing a sort of Plaza Toro. With stout, rugged common sense I had the Bren; I cannot shoot with a pistol. Unhappily it had no bipod, and I couldn't bring it into action.[161] However, when we were about 200 yards away, Scott, who had just climbed on top of his

158 Falaise, *Through Hell to Dunkirk,* p.50.
159 Bishop, *One Young Soldier,* p.51.
160 Shand, *Previous Encounters,* p.48.
161 'Bug' was the vehicle nickname.

lorry, shot one through the thigh and the other put up his hands. When we got there the unwounded man burst into floods of tears. About a hundred Belgians came up at the same moment, so we let them have him. We saw another running like a hare half a mile away but by then I had had enough and returned to the cars.[162]

This was the first of the Regiment's tasks completed. In the process it had lost three armoured cars due to bombing and shelling, with very few casualties. The Regiment now withdrew and looked forward to its first full night of rest since the Germans had invaded. Clark-Kennedy thought the reason that the whole Regiment was very tired was 'primarily due to the fact that all the troops were employed for the whole five days' and an additional contributing factor had been 'the lack of experience in arranging reliefs effectively.'[163]

Wednesday 15th May

(Day Six)
Up north the battle in Holland is over; the Dutch Army has laid down its arms. This complete elimination of our ally in so short a time, five days, fills us with gloom.
Falaise[164]

The much-needed full night's sleep was interrupted at 0430 hrs when the German bombers returned. Falaise was woken by the 'long and steadily increasing roar of engines from what he thought sounded like at least 50 bombers.' This was immediately followed by the sound of the 'short staccato' of Bren guns from underneath his window. Falaise jumped out of bed to find out what was going on, and he could see the tracer being aimed towards the waves of the large black bombers which were flying in 'perfect formation' over the park, apparently headed for Brussels. The aircraft were so low that their black crosses, outlined in white, were plainly visible.[165]

Suddenly, one of the planes broke formation and made a steep left turn This was followed by 'a steady stream of bullets' from the Bren guns. Smoke was seen to be pouring out of it. Falaise saw three of its crew bail out, their parachutes widening into big white mushrooms, while the abandoned plane crashed with a loud explosion on the crest of a hill about a mile away and burst into flames. Horsbrugh-Porter, still in his pyjamas, ordered a sergeant and two men armed with rifles to go to the crash site. In the distance Falaise heard three loud cheers which rose from the park which was 'the boys celebrating their victory,' whereupon everyone in SHQ went back to bed.[166]

162 Hall Diary, 14 May 1940, p.4.
163 Clark-Kennedy, 'Record of Service', p.8.
164 Falaise, *Through Hell to Dunkirk*, p.57.
165 Falaise, *Through Hell to Dunkirk*, p.53.
166 Falaise, *Through Hell to Dunkirk*, p.53.

The War Diary attributed the shooting down of the bomber to B Squadron. It turned out to have been a Heinkel and Clark-Kennedy later named Trooper Watts as the Bren gunner.[167] When the soldiers arrived at the scene of the crash, they found that the crew had all been killed, one of the crew having shot two Belgian soldiers before dying from his own injuries. However, having made the journey the soldiers took the opportunity to rescue 'a few souvenirs from the burning wreckage.'[168] Falaise heard the news of the bomber crew at 0700 hrs when Stevens woke him with a cup of tea and the news that the 'Jerries were dead before they landed, riddled with bullets from a machine gun.' The two stories differ in detail as to how the crew died but die they did. However, it would appear that the most accurate account is Hall's as it was he, still in his pyjamas, who went out with his vehicle to see if there were any prisoners or items of value. Hall noted, however, that 'there wasn't, and the plane and the crew were spread over about two acres.'[169]

A Squadron was given orders to move at 0800 hrs, and Horsbrugh-Porter detailed Falaise and Erne to travel to Lennick St. Kwintens [Quentin] south west of Brussels to prepare the billeting. On the way, Erne told Falaise that A Squadron had been given the honour by General Gort to act as his special guard. Falaise thought this was as a result of the 'squadron's good showing on the Ghette and at Loo, and that for the next 24 hours at least they were to provide for the safety of the C-in-C's advanced HQ against airborne troops and German agents.'[170] Shand was 'heartbroken' when he heard the news they were about to move. They suddenly had to pack everything up just as they were getting ready for a 'gargantuan breakfast.' As it was, his hot coffee scalded his mouth and he mounted his armoured car with a 'large and messy piece of bread and honey.'[171]

When Falaise and Erne arrived in Lennick, it appeared that no one in the town seemed to be aware that Gort had established his headquarters in the small chateau surrounded by trees only 100 yards away from the square.[172] The remainder of the Regiment, B and C Squadrons moved to St. Martin [Lennick St. Martin], and RHQ to the Chateau De Cronburg (see Map 10).[173] Smith and his sappers were also ordered to rejoin RHQ once they had completed their task of destroying the bridges on the Louvain – Ophem road which had been 'overlooked' by the Belgians. Smith and his men, like the rest of the Regiment who were not on guard duties, spent most of the day on vehicle maintenance and generally repacking the trucks.[174]

167 Clark-Kennedy, 'Record of Service', p.8.
168 TNA WO 167/452: 15 May 1940.
169 Hall Diary, 15 May 1940.
170 Falaise, *Through Hell to Dunkirk*, p.54.
171 Shand, *Previous Encounters*, p.48.
172 Falaise, *Through Hell to Dunkirk*, p.54.
173 TNA WO 167/452: 15 May 1940.
174 TNA WO 167/778: 15 May 1940.

In addition to the threat of parachute attack, there was also much concern over communists and other local fifth-columnists. This entailed making a reconnaissance of the area and establishing posts for all-round defence. The purpose was to 'regulate the flow of unlicensed wanderers' which, due to its volume, was difficult to do much about.[175] It had also been established that one local inhabitant (the Burgomaster) was found to be the *Gauleiter-Designate* and someone who the Allies were keen to arrest.[176]

When Falaise and Erne arrived at Lennick it took them approximately three hours to find sheds, barns, and garages in which to hide all the Squadron's armoured cars as well as the trucks and lorries of the transport troop. Once that had been completed, they had to find suitable billets for the men and the officers. They had only just done this when Horsbrugh-Porter and the whole squadron arrived in the village square. Falaise found this a thankless task:

> As usual, they are all dissatisfied and, to finish it off, Horsbrugh-Porter tells me that I have to find a house where the officers can be billeted as he has orders that we must all be together and on constant alert. Little does he know that I have been trying all morning to find such a house and that I have been assured that it is impossible. This is a word that Horsbrugh-Porter doesn't like. So, I shove off again, waved on cheerfully by Shand and Arkwright who are sitting on the pavement of the main square under the blazing sun hoping for a bottle of cold beer and a sandwich. It is past 1300 hrs now and the cup of tea and biscuit which we had at 0700 hrs this morning seem very far away.[177]

On his arrival at Lennick, Hall noted how bad the maps had been on the journey and remarked that they 'were uncannily bad in this area.' Likewise, Falaise had some negative observations, but they concerned the population and not the mapping. He thought the civilians in the town were not particularly helpful. He thought this might have been based on the fact that the news they had heard so far on the wireless had 'been rather on the optimistic side.' So, there was little wonder that the people were 'bewildered' by the Squadron's appearance:

> Faces grey with dust and drawn with fatigue, our uniforms dirty, our armoured cars caked with clay and showing the marks of German bullets. It does not seem possible to them that they are actually seeing men who have just fought the Germans and who have been under fire. They look upon us with curiosity mingled with distrust, regarding us more like intruders who have come to disturb their peaceful habits and deplete their stores than as Allies who are trying to save them from destruction. Some of them, too, have very definite sympathies toward

175 Shand, *Previous Encounters*, p.48.
176 Falaise, *Through Hell to Dunkirk*, p.55.
177 Falaise, *Through Hell to Dunkirk*, pp.54-55.

the invaders. These mostly belong to the Rexist Party, and we have a list of them. They bear watching.[178]

To make life even more difficult, all of the shops and *estaminets* had been closed by the local authorities. Falaise and Machin managed to get into a grocery store through a back entrance which Machin discovered and Falaise cajoled the owner into selling him some food for the officers and men:

> She is tall, buxom, pink-cheeked, and a friendly type of woman. When I tell her about my troubles in finding an empty house, she takes pity on us. She informs me that there is a small villa on the main square which has been abandoned by its proprietor, an old lady, this morning. I go there immediately only to find it locked; its shutters are closed. A neighbour, aroused by my banging on the door, tells me that the keys have been taken by the old lady's nephew who lives in a village seven miles away. I hop into the staff car and return an hour later with the keys. We move in. The house is small and there is only one bedroom on the first floor with a double bed and a mattress. I allocate this room to Horsbrugh-Porter and Erne... At the back of the house, a walled orchard and a small flower garden will provide us with privacy and an agreeable resting place. The major returns from a visit to the Colonel. When he sees the house, he pats me on the back and seems delighted with the arrangements.[179]

When it came to the close protection of GHQ, this did indeed fall to A Squadron. One troop was ordered to place its armoured cars in strategic positions around the main square, hidden in the shade as much as possible. All the other troops were detailed to take 'their turn during the coming night.' Arkwright and his troop took the first watch. The remainder of the Squadron stripped and bathed under a garden pump using a large wooden bucket as a tub. Falaise noted that they 'splashed about minus their clothes while German observation planes circled ominously above them.'[180] That evening, Bishop's troop spent the entire evening in the garden of the Burgomaster who was said 'to be returning at any minute.' Bishop noted that 'wisely he refrained from putting in an appearance,' and he thought this task was quite different from the 'relatively easy-sounding forecast' he was expecting, and Shand wrote that he thought it had been a 'cheerless vigil.'[181]

Falaise and Machin went out again into the village shopping for the officers' dinner. While they were out, they managed to find some cauliflowers, canned peas, and potatoes and a 'few slices of a delicious ham' which the shopkeeper had privately sold

---

178 Falaise, *Through Hell to Dunkirk*, p.55.
179 Falaise, *Through Hell to Dunkirk*, pp.55-56
180 Falaise, *Through Hell to Dunkirk*, p.56.
181 Bishop, *One Young Soldier*, p.52 and Shand, *Previous Encounters*, p.48.

them. She invited Falaise into her living room to hear the new wireless, but he found it difficult to hear as she talked 'continually,' telling him that her husband had been mobilised and that she hoped the war would soon be over as she is already 'beginning to feel lonesome.'[182]

That evening, Lumsden dropped in on A Squadron and told them that GHQ was 'well satisfied' with the 12th Lancers and briefed them on the other squadron's achievements since 11th May. B Squadron had destroyed several German tanks and one troop leader had made a wonderful record extricating his cars from what appeared to be a hopeless position.' Lumsden added that the German aircraft had been pounding the positions along the Dyle through the day and that the Guards had suffered severe losses at Louvain.[183] During the night they were woken again as bombs fell in and around the village with one landing by the railway crossing 300 yards away. Falaise wrote:

> We feel helpless with no other defence than our ineffectual Bren guns and can only hope for the best. By good luck, no bombs are dropped in the direction of the chateau where General Gort is staying. A few minutes later all is quiet again and we return to our hard beds to try to sleep. Arkwright and Shand take a swig from their flasks, I share a bottle of beer with Bishop, and we argue for a while as to what has happened to our anti-aircraft guns. We have neither seen nor heard one since the battle started. One of us suggests that they are probably protecting the higher staff far back in the lines, and there are not enough of them to send up here to protect the men at the front.[184]

Back at RHQ that evening the RMO, Lieutenant Dowell RAMC, and a party of leave personnel rejoined the Regiment. The War Diary noted that 'they had made many persistent efforts to find' them and they were 'delighted to have them back as the Regiment was below strength owing to leave parties.' One individual was Trooper David who on hearing about the invasion of Belgium made 'his own way to Southampton, crossed to France and made his way 'lorry hopping' to the Front carefully avoiding the official channels.' The *Regimental History* drew a comparison to a similar feat carried out by Corporal Davis 25 years earlier and remarking that it 'epitomised the spirit of the Regiment' which was to share in the company of friends in that curious and lively atmosphere of confidence which a good Regiment will inspire.'[185] However, others were not as lucky as David and did not manage to escape the eye of the authorities at the ports. On return from leave the QM, Major Bill Mabbott, was held at Le Havre whilst he was trying to rejoin the Regiment and was put in

---

182 Falaise, *Through Hell to Dunkirk*, p.56.
183 Falaise, *Through Hell to Dunkirk*, p.56.
184 Falaise, *Through Hell to Dunkirk*, p.57.
185 TNA WO 167/452: 15 May 1940 and Stewart, *History of the XII Royal Lancers*, pp.354-355.

command of the Base Troops, which required the RQMS to fill his appointment.[186] That evening RQMS James, who was acting as QM, returned with rations for the Regiment. In addition to the supplies he also had some mail for the Regiment. This was the only mail seen during the brief campaign. The RQMS also told everyone of the horrors he had seen on his journey back where refugees had been deliberately attacked by German planes using both bombs and machine guns which resulted in the deaths of 'at least 40 women and children,' a story which others had already told.[187]

186 Obituary, *The 12L Regimental Journal* (June 1946), p.31.
187 TNA WO 167/452: 15 May 1940 and Clark-Kennedy, 'Record of Service', p.9.

5

Acting as Divisional Cavalry and the Withdrawal

(16th–19th May 1940)

Thursday 16th May

(Day Seven)

The doubts cast by Headquarters, 48th Division on the accuracy of these reports were unreasonable and caused much justifiable annoyance.
Regimental War Diary[1]

The C-in-C sent for Lumsden and expressed his great satisfaction for the good work which the Regiment had accomplished during the first day's fighting. It soon became evident that the alarmist reports of the previous night were, correct and that the Senegalese Division on the right of the 2nd Division had been driven in and 'compelled to retire.' As a result, later in the day, the Regiment was placed under command of the 48th Division, in the divisional cavalry role to help them in their withdrawal.[2]

Falaise walked around the village with Machin to look for fresh bread as 'the dawn patrol' of more than 60 Heinkels and Junkers flew overhead. Falaise found fresh bread which was still hot and had only just been taken out of the oven. The baker was willing to sell it to him, but only at a high price. On his walk back to the lodgings, Falaise met HRH the Duke of Gloucester. He thought Prince Harry was in the best of moods despite having the house he was in bombed during the night. Falaise thought he looked like a 'real soldier' and when he saw him, he understood why he was 'so much liked and admired' by the army. Falaise returned to the troop leaders where he provided them with a breakfast of warm bread and claret.[3]

1   TNA WO 167/45: 16 May 1940.
2   Clark-Kennedy, 'Record of Service', p.8.
3   Falaise, *Through Hell to Dunkirk*, p.59.

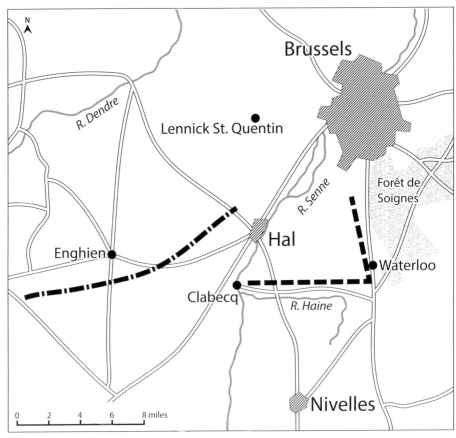

Map B 16-18 May 1940.

After their breakfast at 0500 hrs, A Squadron was sent out to support the infantry in the area of Braine le Château, south east of Halle [Hal]. The Squadron was strung out along the railway covering a front of about 10 miles as far as Waterloo. Shand thought this was too much to be watched over by three troops. Shand's bridge was in Haine and was a large road bridge over the railway crossing.[4] Bishop at his location 'wondered, perhaps a mite sardonically, if the real reason was that there was no one else to do it,' as between them he and Shand had been 'given between no less than six bridges to cover.'[5] At 0600 hrs, the rest of the Regiment was put on one hour's notice-to-move.

4   Shand, *Previous Engagements*, p.48.
5   Bishop, *One Young Soldier*, p.52.

At 0800 hrs, Falaise was summoned to GHQ by DR which caused much excitement and speculation, and everyone was sure that he was about to attend some historic conference between General Gort and some high French general, perhaps General Gamelin. On his arrival he was asked if he was the liaison officer from A Squadron 12th Lancers and, having established who he was, he saw Gort and his staff leave GHQ by car to have a conference with the Generals commanding I Corps and II Corps. It was only after they had left that the real reason for Falaise's presence became clear.

The task he was given lasted about an hour. It transpired that the owner of the chateau 'disliked' having a staff of British officers in his house so he proceeded, or rather Madame did, to inaugurate a blockade of a special kind on the British guests. In protest, she removed all the pots and pans from the kitchen and locked the door leading to the coal cellar. Having resolved the situation, Falaise was thanked 'profusely' as the direct consequence of the owner's actions had meant that the General's French chef was unable to cook any sort of meal! Hence the hurried call for his services, as the C-in-C had had no breakfast. Falaise thought the situation could have been resolved had the staff simply told the owner who their guest was but, for reasons of security, 'that was entirely out of the question.' When Falaise left, the chateau and the coal cellar was wide open; the pots and pans were back in the kitchen, each on its own hook; the French chef was beaming; Madame had dried her tears and was smiling happily once again and, most important of all, GHQ was to have some lunch![6]

By 1100 hrs, Lumsden had been informed that I Corps had withdrawn behind the River Lesne and the French to the right of the Regiment had fallen back as a result of the Germans forcing their way across the Meuse and the fall of Namur. The concern was that if the advance was not checked the Germans would reach the main Brussels – Charleroi road. While they waited, the Echelon left and collocated with RHQ and the officers sat down to a 'snack and a bottle of beer.'[7]

At 1500 hrs, Lumsden attended a conference at 48th Division HQ and the Regiment was ordered to move at 1700 hrs and rendezvous at Rhode St. George, where Lumsden was given the role of protecting the right flank of the 48th Division, on the general line of the *De Cointet* Anti-Tank obstacle, which stretched from the south west corner of the Forêt De Soignes – Cross-roads (J6558) – Braine L'Alleud – River Le Hain – Clabecq, where he was to make contact with the French (see Map 12).[8] To assist Lumsden in this task he was given command of 4 Gloucesters who arrived late that night having marched some 35 miles in the 24 hours and who would complete 53 miles before the next 24 hours had passed. Lumsden was also given a section of 'I' tanks which were in the area, and during the night another battalion of the 48th Division came to his assistance at the south west corner of the Bois De Hal.

6   Falaise, *Through Hell to Dunkirk*, p.60.
7   Falaise, *Through Hell to Dunkirk*, p.61.
8   Falaise states 1630 hrs. See Falaise, *Through Hell to Dunkirk*, p.61.

Lieutenant Colonel Martin RA, with his Regiment of Field Artillery and part of a battalion of infantry under his command, was also operating in the area. As a result of Martin and Lumsden being old friends, there was no difficulty in co-ordinating the satisfactory defence of this very wide front and ensuring the safe withdrawal of the 48th Division. However, it was never intended to conduct anything more than a delaying action as the whole of the BEF was withdrawing to the east of the River Escaut.[9] Once the Regiment started to move, RHQ moved to a big house near Groenenberg where it was joined by the Echelon which pulled-in under the trees.[10] Soon after the Regiment was in position, it was apparent that the Germans were collecting in the southern corner of the Forêt de Soignes. After dark, the Regiment withdrew to the line of the Brussels – Braine – L'Alleud railway but unfortunately not before one armoured car from B Squadron had been lost to mines on the field of Waterloo.[11]

That afternoon, Horsbrugh-Porter told Falaise that since the Germans had crossed the River Senette, and the Brussels–Charleroi Canal, he thought 'they would be used in support of the French and most likely fight all night.' In the distance, they could see Messerschmitts flying around unchallenged looking for targets which was 'tremendously disheartening' as they wondered what had happened to the Air Force. Falaise travelled on the roof of Erne's armoured car and when they reached Rhode St. George, Falaise was 'amused' by the names painted on the British tanks coming in the opposite direction, Gamelin, Garbo and Gorgonzola.[12] Moments later, five Stuka's bombed the Squadron, as the tanks continued to roll through, and as the bombs landed the armoured cars 'rocked like dinghies.' Fortunately, none of the Squadron's armoured cars were hit, so they moved out of the village onto a small dirt road which led away from the now-burning village.[13]

At approximately 1600 hrs, the two sections of Royal Engineers under command of the sergeants arrived at Shand's and Bishop's locations with orders to blow the bridges as the German advance was soon to be expected (see Map 11). So, during the remaining daylight, the bridges were prepared for demolition. At Bishop's bridge, the biggest, the 'heroic' Sergeant Earl had to swarm down one of the camouflage nets like a surprised lover leaving a bedroom window.[14] At Shand's bridge, he described Johnson as having the 'agility of a monkey as he swung about on a rope above a 30-foot drop, knocking holes in the masonry.' When Shand's bridge was ready to be blown, Braine was still full of people and transport.

Shand wrote:

9   Stewart, *History of the XII Royal Lancers*, p.355.
10   Hall Diary, 16 May 1940.
11   Stewart, *History of the XII Royal Lancers*, p.355.
12   Falaise, *Through Hell to Dunkirk*, p.61.
13   Falaise, *Through Hell to Dunkirk*, p.61.
14   Bishop, *One Young Soldier*, p.52.

A seemingly endless column of lorries passing over the bridge, while French gunners and cavalry were now added to the diverse elements in the streets. I felt rather desperate about the whole thing. Even shouting 'Je ferai sauter le pont en trois minutes exactement' ['I'll blow up the bridge in exactly three minutes'] had singularly little effect and I reflected that the French had much of that phlegm which they so frequently attributed to the British. The jam only began to shift when we started to lead out individual horses which we despatched up the road with a good 'belt,' irrespective of their riders' wishes. The troop enjoyed this enormously and Griffiths, who had been my groom before the war, showed splendid impartiality, at one moment accelerating the departure of a speechless major and the next that of a whole gun team. In this manner, we succeeded in clearing the town of Braine in about 40 minutes. The bridge was at last clear of traffic and the fuse was lit. I had a gripping fear that vehicles would arrive on it at the crucial moment, but it went up without loss of life. Unfortunately, the explosion only cratered the road, and it was still possible to cross over. Johnson started to put in more charges, but I received orders to retire north west of Braine onto some high ground on the main Halle road and I gathered that we had to cover the withdrawal of the infantry.[15]

It was after dark by the time Smith and his party made contact with the 12th Lancers and a company of Gloucesters near Waterloo. When he arrived, it was decided that the large road bridge over the Brussels – Braine – L'Alleud railway should be destroyed. However, upon closer inspection of the bridge, it showed that it was too 'formidable a task for a party of three.' Therefore, it was decided to crater the road on the bridge approach. According to Smith:

The camouflet equipment was pressed into action but the flash caused by the firing of the camouflet charge had the very unexpected result of drawing German fire from the railway line. This was rather disturbing, but arrangements were made to deal with this new situation and a Carrier Platoon was brought back for the protection of the party. The charges were laid without further interruption and the fuse fitted with a percussion igniter so that the 12th Lancers troop who would be the last people to cross the bridge could fire the charge as they withdrew… When it came to using the rapid cratering device, something Smith had never used in anger… only speed mattered. He wrote that we worked out a method of using it which broke almost every rule for safety using explosives ever devised.[16]

15   Shand, *Previous Engagements*, pp.48-49.
16   TNA WO 167/778: 16 May 1940 and Smith to Charrington correspondence dated 12 April 1997.

Not all the action was taking part on the bridges and, during the afternoon, two saboteurs were caught with rifles and were handed over to the local police, who summarily shot them. RHQ, which was at the northern edge of the wood (at J6143), was bombed by three squadrons of Germans planes, each 27 strong, but fortunately owing to being well-dispersed, suffered no casualties. The tactics employed, which were by now recognised as being their normal method for bombing attacks, was that a spotter aircraft came over first.[17]

After Shand left Braine, he was joined by Bishop in his new location with a 'make-shift troop' of two SHQ cars where the Royal Engineers laid a 'modest minefield in the pavé to their front.'[18] They were informed that the Germans 'might arrive at any minute' and a very silent night 'descended upon' them until a mine was hit. Bishop wrote that it went up 'unexpectedly and prematurely with a gigantic spout of flame, a red glow that lit the sky and a blast that knocked their 'hats crooked.'[19] Shand wrote that at approximately 2100 hrs:

> We heard what we thought was motor traffic coming up the hill out of Braine and a few minutes later the land mine exploded with what seemed a world-shattering detonation and then someone gave a shout. In the momentary glare we had been able to see a vehicle or two and promptly opened fire on them, evidently with great effect as they appeared to stop without any retaliation, and after a few minutes of the rather frenzied conference moved down the road in our cars, very gingerly, to investigate. I did not like it at all, nor did Tim. We thought some very unpleasant trap lay ahead. I kept drinking from my water bottle, which I believe is a sure sign of fear.
>
> On the far side of the mine's crater was a dark shape. Then we heard a rustling noise at the side of the road. I switched my torch in that direction and saw emerge from the ditch two figures with their hands up. As they approached, I saw they were a French colonel and his driver. It was a rather disastrous anti-climax. I endeavoured to apologise but the colonel took it very well considering that his car was riddled with bullets which he and his companion had only evaded by abandoning ship in the nick of time. His unfortunate despatch rider who was preceding him had been blown up by the mine. We found his body later and felt very bad about it. I sent the colonel and his man back to SHQ and then talked to Andrew on the wireless. He said that very high authority was still of the opinion that the Germans would be upon us shortly. I ventured to take a contrary view and said, I was convinced that a considerable part of the French Army lay between us and the Germans. He was inclined to agree with me, and I was proved correct in about half an hour when a procession of French transport

17   TNA WO 167/778, 16 May 1940.
18   Shand, 'May 1940: A Memory', p.153.
19   Bishop, *One Young Soldier*, p.52.

started passing. Most of it belonged to one of the *Divisions Marocaines* and was drawn by grey horses which I thought looked a trifle out of date. They took most of the night to pass and it was dawn before the road was free for the Germans. It was still free when we withdrew to Halle in the morning.[20]

As the Moroccans marched 'unconcernedly over the crater,' seemingly neither interested in the Lancers nor the Germans, Bishop contemplated how 'Wellington's transport must have travelled the same road at that same pace 125 years before. With the smell of sweating horses, fresh droppings, and the fact that no one was talking, they could have been the ghosts of Waterloo.'[21] Hunn also had the same thoughts as he tried to 'imagine the same area… when the men of the 12th Lancers [Light Dragoons] fought under the command of Wellington.'[22] Once the Moroccans had passed and they were certain the 'next guests' would be the Germans, the Royal Engineers sergeant 'blew the bridge.'[23]

During the night, no Germans were encountered by C Squadron on their very wide front. To overcome the shortage of numbers and to give the impression that the troops were a larger force they 'resorted to the old ruse' of patrolling with one troop 'to give the impression of strength.'[24] By dawn, C Squadron could see through their binoculars some 600 yards away the Germans scanning the Regiment's positions. During the rest of the night, the German patrols remained active to the west of Braine, and an infantry attack was made along several points, particularly on the right, in front of A Squadron, this was the only time during the fighting that the Regiment experienced a determined attack at night. By dawn there was not one demolition on the front which had not been either fired or prepared for firing by Smith and his troop.[25]

The reports that the Germans were pressing hard in this area were rather scoffed at by Headquarters, 48th Division, but it was obvious from the large forces which were seen the following morning attacking from the direction of Waterloo. If the German patrols had not been severely dealt with the night before, the situation would have been more serious. The Regiment had already been complimented on the excellence and accuracy of their reports both by GHQ and II Corps, and the doubts cast by Headquarters, 48th Division on the accuracy of these reports were unreasonable and 'caused much justifiable annoyance.' The Regiment was to hold its positions overnight until 1030 hrs the following morning.[26]

---

20   Shand, *Previous Engagements*, pp.49-50.
21   It is possible that these were the Senegalese troops referred to in t TNA WO 167/452 or vice versa.
22   Hunn Diary, p.8.
23   Bishop, *One Young Soldier*, pp.52-53.
24   Clark-Kennedy, 'Record of Service', p.9
25   TNA WO 167/778: 16 May 1940.
26   Stewart, *History of the XII Royal Lancers*, p.356.

Friday 17th May

(Day Eight)

Well, it wasn't your fault. No one could know it wasn't a Boche... Anyway, the man who fired that shot was a good marksman. My poor countryman certainly never knew what hit him.

Falaise[27]

The Regimental war diarist recorded that:

> During the early hours of the morning, German reconnaissance elements tested the front at various points such as Waterloo, Braine L'Alleud and Braine le Chateau, all of which were met by our fire and obviously discouraged his further efforts until he was able to make a proper attack. There was a considerable amount of movement in the area of Waterloo and in the southern portion of the Forêt de Soignes. The Germans had collected a force in this area the previous evening and it was anticipated that his major effort would be from this direction.[28]

A Squadron's SHQ was established about 200 yards from the top of the hill on the reverse slope towards Eschenbeek [Essenbeek]. The fighting lorry and the staff car were hidden on the extreme side of the road against the walls of a farm and turned toward Halle. Erne's armoured car was positioned under a slender tree on a track leading toward the Sart Wood. Horsbrugh-Porter's armoured car was parked a little further away on a cart road behind a short hedge. The third car of the troop was sent to reinforce Shand's position in Braine le Chateau as there were three small bridges and a larger one to guard. Horsbrugh-Porter was not at all satisfied with the Squadron's current position as they did not have a 'commanding view over the valley; and if a German patrol succeeded in getting through at Braine, it would be on top of them before they could do anything about it. Furthermore, the night was pitch dark, and the stars and the moon are hidden by thick clouds making visibility very poor. So, Horsbrugh-Porter sent Falaise to the top of the hill with a party of men on foot. The party consisted of Machin, the driver of the staff car, and three other men from the reserve in the fighting lorry, a Boyes anti-tank rifle and a Bren gun.

On top of the hill, they dug two shallow emplacements for the guns on the right and left of the road. The hill rose about 300 feet above Braine and the valley toward Clabeck [Clabecq]. From their location, they were able to command the road ahead and had a clear field of fire of at least 300 yards. Falaise was confident that their location was well-concealed and if called into action it would buy enough time for the troops behind them to get into fighting formation. In the distance, they could hear

27   Falaise, *Through Hell to Dunkirk*, p.76.
28   TNA WO 167/452: 17 May 1940.

machine gun fire, which seemed to come from Arkwright's troop on the left of the valley. In the far distance, the sky was still red, and at times Falaise could see 'small lights flickering on the opposite ridge.'[29]

After an hour, Horsbrugh-Porter adjusted Falaise's position a quarter of a mile down the road to a group of houses on the crossroads to Lembeek and to Sart Wood. The armoured cars of SHQ Troop, the staff car and the fighting lorry all congregated on the crossroads. The new position was just half a mile short of Braine and on the midpoint of the hill. Falaise thought it 'a much better site' as it afforded shelter, concealment for the armoured cars and two roads for retreat.[30]

At the crossroads, some of the houses were still occupied, so Falaise was sent to warn them to stay inside their homes regardless of whatever happened. Having visited all the farms and passed on the instruction, when he got to the last house, he found the door open:

All is pitch dark inside except for a streak of pale light under a door at the end of a hall. I push it open and enter a small room. In the semi-darkness, a rather attractive-looking girl jumps out of bed with a scream when she sees me. She is in such a fright that she does not seem to notice that she is half-naked. She runs to a crib, which I hadn't noticed, in the corner of the room and picks up a small baby who starts to cry. I apologise for my intrusion and tell her not to be afraid. When I say she must remain in her house, she begs me to let her leave with her small child and her old father, and putting the screaming baby on the bed, she even goes so far as to fall on her knees in front of me. As she clings to my hand, I notice that she is so beside herself with fear that she is trembling all over like a frightened animal. Only her hair, which is long, dark, and rather beautiful, hides her bosom. Her nightgown has fallen off her shoulder a fact of which she seems completely unaware. I try my best to calm her, but this isn't easy with the baby howling on one side, and the rattle of machine guns on the other. I ask her where her father is, and she tells me between her sobs that she has fixed a room for him in the cellar so he will be safe from the bombs. So, I tell her to put some clothes on and I proceed to the cellar to have a talk with the old man. He is semi-invalid and is very sensible about his present plight, agreeing that there is no possible chance to escape now. When the girl finally comes down, sobbing quietly, with her baby at her breast, we both convince her that she must remain. As I take my leave, the grateful old man tells me that I will find a pail of fresh warm milk in the cowshed and that I may take it along. I walk into the warmth of the shed where I see three cows lying in the sweet-smelling straw peacefully chewing their cuds. I find the milk and carry it to the armoured cars where Horsbrugh-Porter, Erne, and the men receive it with joy. I drink two bowls of it myself and

29 Falaise, *Through Hell to Dunkirk*, p.70.
30 Falaise, *Through Hell to Dunkirk*, pp.69-70.

it makes me feel warm and comfortable. Our last sandwich was eaten over 12 hours ago.[31]

At 0230 hrs, Erne was told over the wireless the welcome news that a company of infantry and an anti-tank company were being sent up from Halle to reinforce the Squadron. Arkwright's troop reported that they had been under fire and consequently had to adjust their positions. Shand's troop indicated that they could hear engines on the hill beyond the river and saw flashes, but that the Germans had not attempted to get near their bridges.

The bridges remained the focus of the Regiment. The ones to their front needed defending and the ones to their rear needed securing for their withdrawal. A formation of German bombers flew very low, heading for Halle. Horsbrugh-Porter thought they were on their way to destroy the bridges over the Charleroi – Brussels Canal, which was the Squadron's only line of retreat. He sent Falaise 'across the canal with the staff car... the fighting lorry and the two DRs with instructions to find a sheltered spot on the Halle – Edingen road and to wait there for further orders.'[32]

Falaise arrived at their new location on the Edingen road at approximately 0315 hrs. He parked the convoy under some thick trees and sent one of the DRs back to Horsbrugh-Porter with the grid reference for his location. The night was very chilly and there was no traffic. All they could hear were 'the low rumblings' in the distance coming from the area of Mons and Charleroi. Falaise decided to curl up in the back of the staff car and join Machin and the driver who was already snoring in the front seat.[33]

After approximately an hour, Falaise was woken by young Roddick who was sent back in his armoured car to find Falaise's location. Roddick had arrived just as the sun was rising and Falaise got out of the staff car to talk with him. On getting out of the staff car, Falaise noticed the bodies of two Belgian motorcyclists lying on the road near their machine about 30 feet ahead and to the left of the road. Their bodies were riddled with bullets, and since he had not noticed them when they had arrived, he presumed 'they must have been machine gunned by a German plane' while they were sleeping. When he met Roddick, he thought him 'pallid from lack of rest, but cheery' as he conveyed Horsbrugh-Porter's message. "Things are getting lively down by the river and Horsbrugh-Porter is lonesome without you," he said smiling.[34]

Roddick had also arrived with Smith and the Royal Engineers lorry and Roddick's instructions were to stay with Falaise 'and wait for further orders.' As dawn broke Falaise's ever-growing packet of vehicles was now parked on the roadside in broad daylight. Thinking that this was not 'healthy,' Falaise went to look for a better location, finding one approximately a mile up the road under some trees in an orchard.

31   Falaise, *Through Hell to Dunkirk*, pp.70-71.
32   Falaise, *Through Hell to Dunkirk*, p.70.
33   Falaise, *Through Hell to Dunkirk*, p.72.
34   Falaise, *Through Hell to Dunkirk*, p.72.

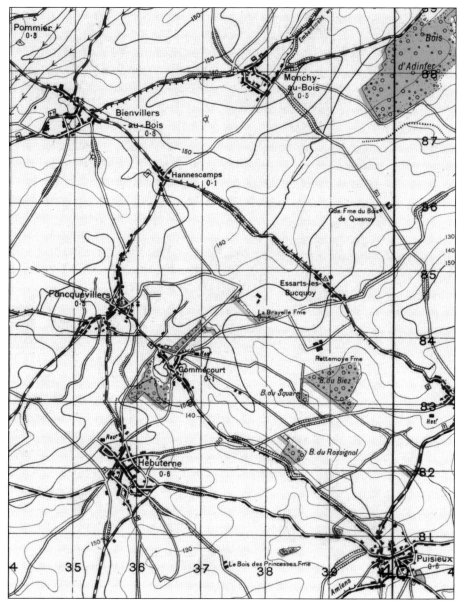

4 23rd November 1939: Regimental Billets. (Beaumetz Sheet 85)

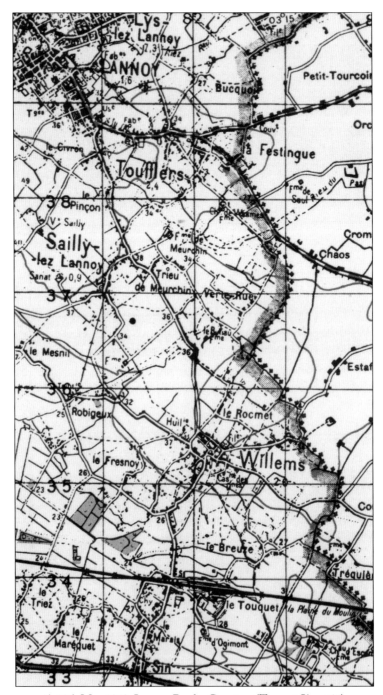

5 10th May 1940: Lannoy Border Crossing. (Tournai Sheet 64)

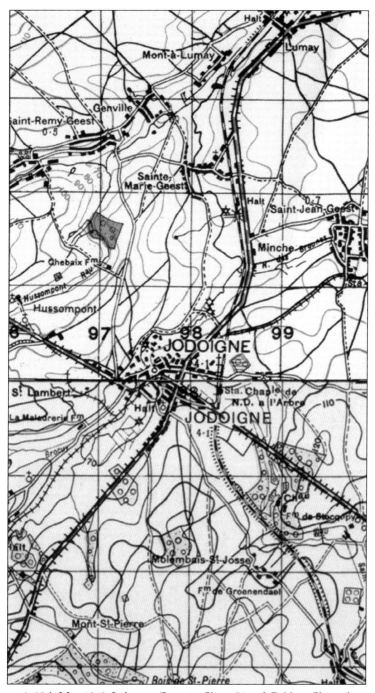

6 10th May 1940: Jodoigne. (Louvain Sheet 56 and Gebloux Sheet 6)

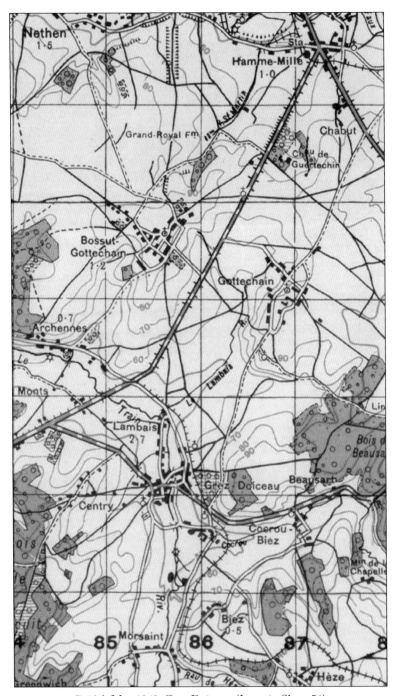

7 10th May 1940: Grez Doiceau. (Louvain Sheet 56)

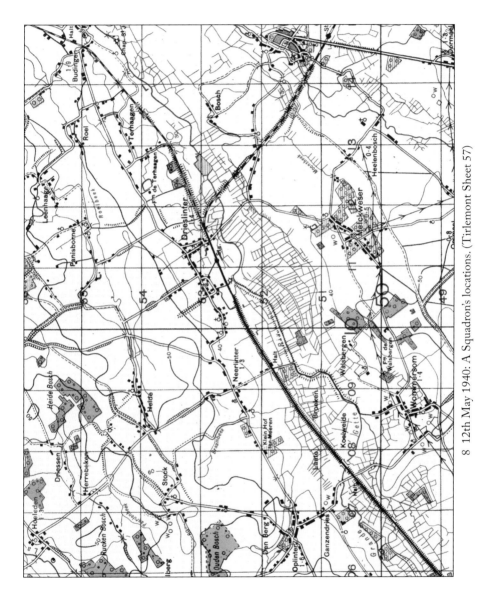

8 12th May 1940: A Squadron's locations. (Tirlemont Sheet 57)

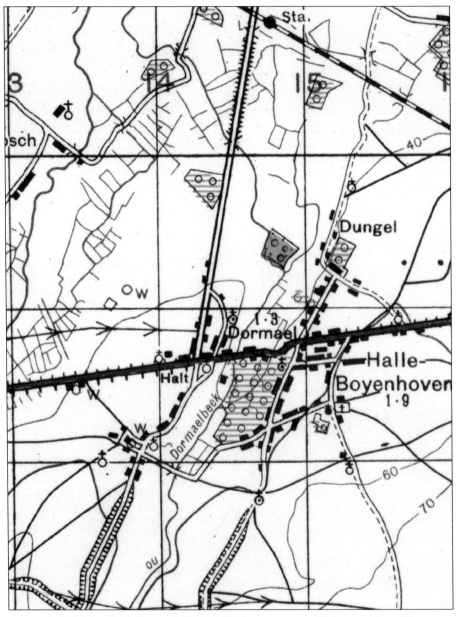

9 12th May 1940: Dormael (K1549), Tank engagement. (Tirlemont Sheet 57)

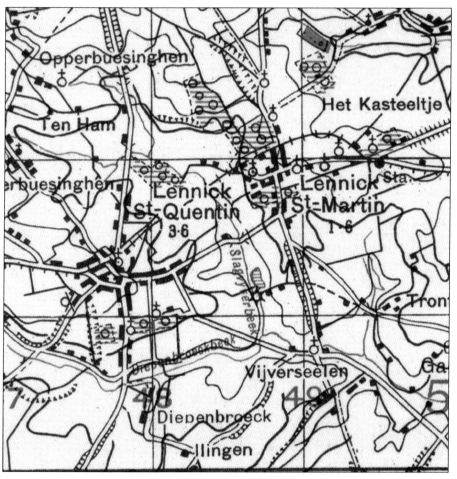

10 15th May 1940: Lennick St. Quentin (GHQ). (Brussels Sheet 55)

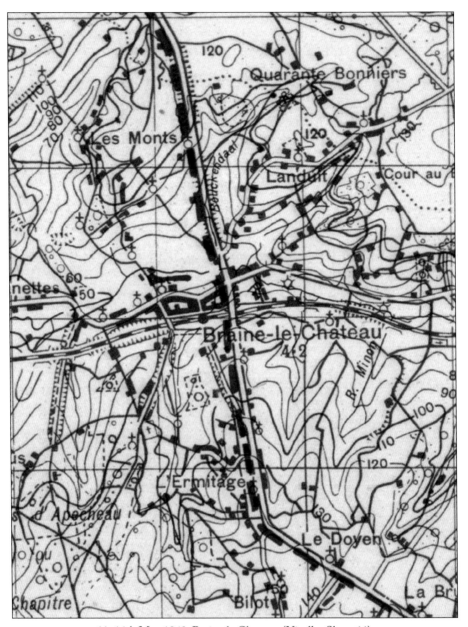

11 16th May 1940: Braine le Chateau. (Nivelles Sheet 66)

12 16th May 1940: Braine and Clabecq. (Nivelles Sheet 660)

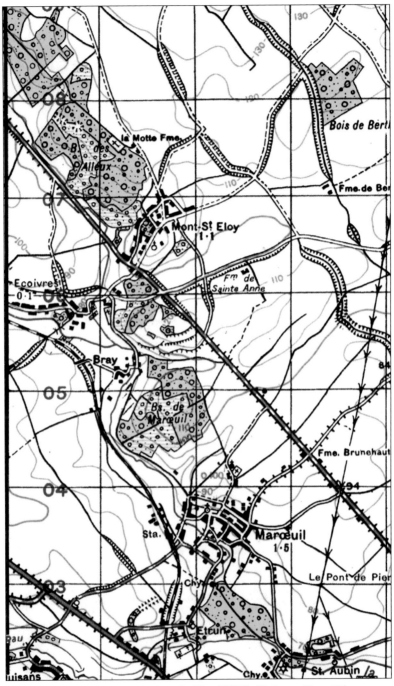

13 22nd May 1940: Mont St. Eloi (RHQ). (Aubigny Sheet 73)

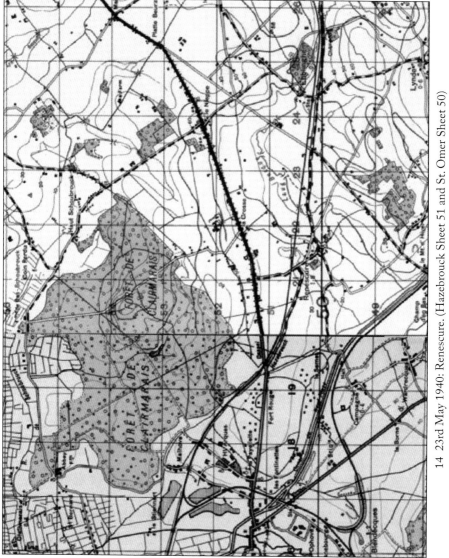

14 23rd May 1940: Renescure. (Hazebrouck Sheet 51 and St. Omer Sheet 50)

15 26th May 1940: Ypres. (Ypres Sheet 41 and Tourcoing Sheet 52)

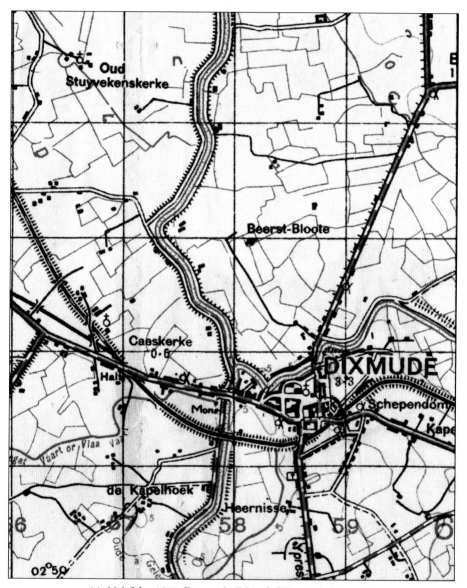

16 28th May 1940: Dixmuide (Mann). (Dixmuide Sheet 30)

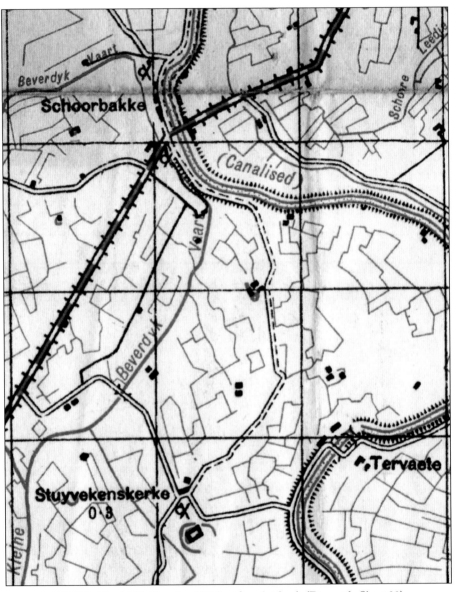

17 28th May 1940: Shand and Bishop (two bridges). (Dixmuide Sheet 30)

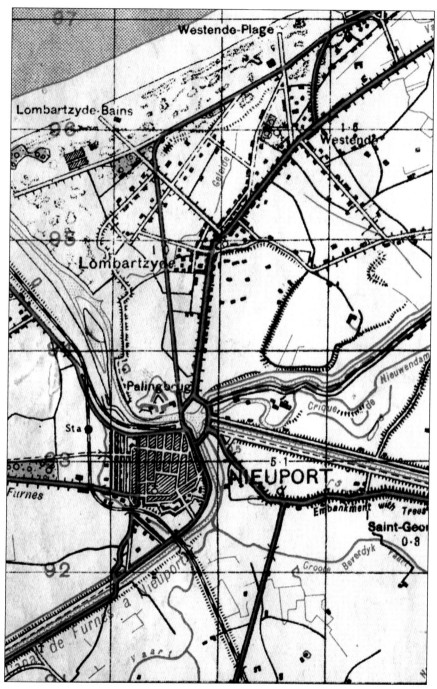

18 28th May 1940: Nieuport (Miller-Mundy) Bridge. (Dixmuide Sheet 30)

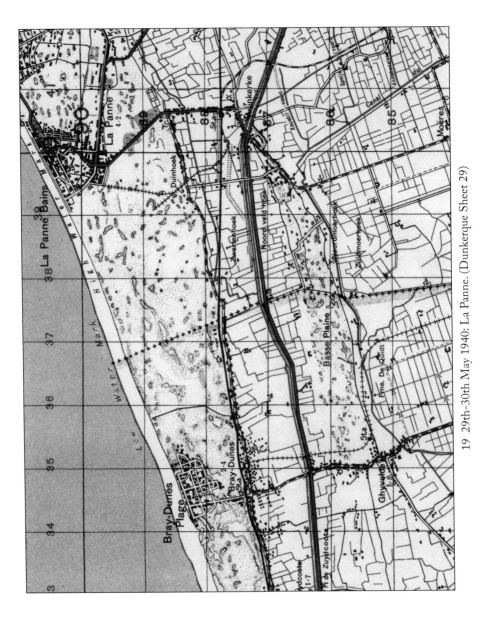

19 29th–30th May 1940: La Panne. (Dunkerque Sheet 29)

Falaise visited the farmhouse nearby which had been totally destroyed. Amongst the carnage of baby clothes and dead livestock, Falaise found an abandoned black car. The front axle was broken so they decided 'to salvage' its batteries for Horsbrugh-Porter's armoured car which needed a new set badly.[35]

Eventually, the packet moved towards Halle, with Roddick's armoured car leading. At the bottom of the hill, as they turned into the main street of Halle, they could see the effects of the bombing attacks. The houses to the right and left had been turned into heaps of rubble and the streets and pavements were obstructed by the wreckage of all kinds and descriptions. Some houses were still smouldering. Just as they came to the street which led to the bridge, they saw three Heinkel bombers 'streaking' towards the town from the east. The armoured car in front forged ahead and Falaise instructed his driver to "follow at 50 yards and not to stop for anything":

> Just then the first bombs come screeching down all around the bridge, which is about 200 yards ahead of us, splashing up tall geysers of muddy water from the canal. If we can get across before the bombers have time to wheel around and come back for the next attack, we are safe. At 50 miles an hour, through the black smoke and the dust raised by the high explosives, our wheels bouncing over the fallen bricks and timber, we follow the armoured car in a mad dash towards and over the bridge and we make it! The canal is at least 300 yards of us, and we are practically up the hill and out of Halle when, through the rear window, I see the bombers launch their second attack on the bridge. In the car no one has said a word. Now, as I look at Machin and the driver, I notice that they are deathly pale. I know that I must be too.[36]

Falaise and Smith joined Horsbrugh-Porter and SHQ at their new location in a deserted farmyard on the left of the road on the far side of the village of Eschenbeek. The set of batteries were 'much appreciated' and were immediately installed in the forward-link armoured car, the wireless of which was getting faint. Horsbrugh-Porter explained the situation that the 'British infantry and an anti-tank company, which had come up during the night, were holding the heights above Braine. The front line was now about half a mile away, and the armoured cars were on the hill with the infantry.[37]

Bishop was in position when the anti-tank guns arrived:

> As dawn broke, the anti-tank guns of the Warwickshire Regiment were leaving us again and we were told that we were to cover their withdrawal! Throughout the morning we stayed on that river line while Halle was continuously dive-bombed

35   Falaise, *Through Hell to Dunkirk*, p.73.
36   Falaise, *Through Hell to Dunkirk*, p.73.
37   Falaise, *Through Hell to Dunkirk*, p.73.

to our immediate rear and the sound of bridges being blown behind as once again regularly split the air. Cows trotted past us along the middle of the road, mooing, milk squirting from their swinging and swollen udders. Angora rabbits skipped out of their way, wondering where to go. A lost dog ran by, ignoring us as it was too frightened to allow kindness. A hastily abandoned house reminded one of a sort of dry-land Marie Celeste. An unfinished meal was still on the table, curtains fluttered out of the open windows, doors were unlocked, and a fire was dying in the kitchen grate. It was a civilisation on the run, and I liked none of it.[38]

A Squadron's SHQ is joined by the HQ of the supporting anti-tanks and is quickly overflown by low-flying German bombers. There is again conversation and comment regarding the perceived absence of the RAF:

Everyone is beginning to feel uneasy and even mortified about the unexpected and total absence of British or French planes. Since the start of the German offensive, German aircraft have had the sky all to themselves. This makes it easy for them to fly in perfect formation and stunt over our heads as if in a peacetime air show. They have been practically unmolested. Furthermore, Allied anti-aircraft batteries are conspicuous by their absence. Where they are, no one knows, but one thing is certain: they are not protecting us. The effect is far from happy![39]

They were all aware that Louvain had fallen, and the Dyle position had collapsed. The Germans were reported to be pushing forward on the heels of the retreating British forces on their left and were on the outskirts of Brussels. To the Squadron's right was a Panzer Division which had reached Soignies and was moving towards Edingen. When looking at the map, it was apparent that A Squadron was in 'great danger of being cut-off from the rear.' Falaise looked up from the map at Horsbrugh-Porter and wrote that 'reading my thoughts,' he 'smiles sadly and silently nods his head. One thing was for certain. If they succeed in destroying the bridge behind us, we are caught like rats in a trap.'[40]

   After breakfast of tea and egg sandwiches, which Falaise and Machin had provided for everyone in the headquarters, including the anti-tank gunners, a DR arrived from Shand's troop. The request was for assistance with a wounded French soldier who had just 'stumbled' into their outpost. Falaise was sent in the staff car to assist. Falaise left the car at the infantry company headquarters and went to look for Shand's location

38   Bishop, *Some Young Soldier*, p.53.
39   Falaise, *Through Hell to Dunkirk*, p.74.
40   Falaise, *Through Hell to Dunkirk*, p.75.

which was behind a small farmhouse. On his arrival, Shand informed him "I am sorry, Henry," he murmurs, "it is too late" …

> I look at the blood-caked uniform and the grey face of the dead man and notice from his collar tabs that he belonged to a colonial regiment. I take his identification disk and papers, write his name and number on a piece of paper and place this in an empty bottle which has been found in the house. A shallow grave is dug, and the body is placed in it. I put the bottle in the grave. Bare-headed, we say a silent prayer, and then we fill the hole with earth. All this is done very rapidly because we are being sniped at. After the little ceremony is over, we run back to the shelter of the wall and, with shaky hands, light cigarettes.[41]

Falaise noticed that Shand looked 'extremely tired; having had no sleep nor food since yesterday.'

> *As we smoke in silence for a while, I look at his unshaven face, so covered with* dust that his eyelashes are white, the puffed lids over his weary and bloodshot eyes and his soiled uniform. I can hardly believe that this is the same Shand I used to know, rosy-cheeked, bright-eyed, and immaculate. After a bit, he says, "I want to show you something. Something happened last night, something terrible, and I think you ought to know about it." He leads the way around the house and down the road which runs to the bridge at Braine… Tight-lipped, without bending an inch of his six feet, Shand walks on as if he has neither heard nor cared. At the bend of the road, 100 yards farther on, I see a military car lying turned over on its side in the ditch. Shand stops short and, with a nod and a look, asks me to go see what is inside. It is a French staff car, a Citroen. I notice then that there is a large bullet hole in the centre of the windshield just opposite the spot where the driver's head should be. Looking inside the car, I see the body of a French artillery officer. His head has been literally exploded by the bullet from the Boyes gun, his helmet is crushed, and his brains spattered over the upholstery. I suddenly feel very hot and uncomfortable, and I can't utter a sound. Taking a deep breath, I turn around and face Shand. He is sitting in the ditch now, watching me. I can see how upset he is. I go and sit beside him, and we stay there without speaking. After a while, all I can find to say is, "well, it wasn't your fault. No one could know it wasn't a Boche." Then, as he doesn't answer, I add, feeling that I must say something more: "Anyway, the man who fired that shot was a good marksman. My poor countryman certainly never knew what hit him."[42]

---

41 Falaise, *Through Hell to Dunkirk*, p.75.
42 Falaise, *Through Hell to Dunkirk*, p.76.

Ten minutes later, Falaise was back at SHQ at Eschenbeek. There he was told that the Germans had reached the Waterloo – Brussels main road, occupied Sart le Comte, and that Arkwright's troop had fallen back. Horsbrugh-Porter lent Falaise his binoculars and, after climbing a ladder, he could see the dust raised by the German armoured cars on the road to St. Genese. Roddick and Arkwright's armoured cars were on the high ground to the left of SHQ and were engaging the Germans. From SHQ's location, they could hear their machine guns and every now and again the 'sharp crack' of a Boyes rifle.[43]

At 1030 hrs, a DR arrived from RHQ with a new set of orders. It stated that the infantry which was holding the line with the Regiment was about to start retiring immediately behind the Halle Canal. The plan was that they would withdraw one platoon at a time and 'dribble down' the road toward the bridge. Horsbrugh-Porter calculated that it would take at least two hours before the move was completed. It was understood that the anti-tanks were to support the Regiment until 1200 hrs. The first to withdraw was the Gloucesters and the force under Martin was got away, then the section of 'I' tanks, and when they were clear, the Regiment started to withdraw.[44]

While Horsbrugh-Porter and the artillery colonel discussed the possible merits, shortcomings, and danger of this retreat in broad daylight, their conversation was 'abruptly cut short by a swarm of Junkers which come roaring straight down the road in threes, their machine guns blazing.' A few moments later the ground rocked as the bombs exploded around the bridge at Halle, an attack which lasted for approximately 15 minutes. Shand reported by wireless that "bombs had fallen in his vicinity," but reported "no casualties." He also reported that "the infantry has started to withdraw" and he 'thought that some of them must have been caught by the blast of bullets and bombs.' Soon the first platoon passed the front gate of SHQ's location. Many of the soldiers were wounded and Falaise thought 'they all seem very tired.'[45]

After the attack, he took the opportunity to spend some time alone and slept in an orchard. When he returned to the farmyard, he found the artillery colonel giving orders for the withdrawal of his anti-tank guns at midday. He also found Horsbrugh-Porter and Erne standing near the armoured cars looking 'very glum.' They had their earphones on and were listening to the report from the troops:

Arkwright and young Roddick are doing very well on the left, although one car has been hit and two men have been wounded. As for Shand and Bishop, they report that they have fired at German patrols which have succeeded in filtering into Braine. Also, that a German armoured vehicle, either a light tank or an armoured car, which came half-way down the hill leading to Braine and, seeing that the bridge was half-blown up and not wide enough, or being afraid that it

43   Falaise, *Through Hell to Dunkirk*, p.77.
44   TNA WO 167/452: 17 May 1940.
45   Falaise, *Through Hell to Dunkirk*, p.78.

might conceal a buried land-mine, backed up and disappeared over the crest. From all this, it appears that, for the moment at least, only infantry threatens the Braine – Halle road on which we are, and that our worst danger lies on our left. There, Arkwright's troop must try to keep the German mechanised forces off the dirt road which would lead them to the Halle Canal and eventually, if they turned south after reaching it, to the bridge itself, thus cutting us off. The anti-tanks are withdrawing. Their colonel and his officers bid us farewell and good luck and leave for Halle. We are alone now. An ominous and extraordinary silence has suddenly fallen over the countryside. It is hard to believe that even at this moment crack German troops are crawling silently through the woods toward the crest of the hill.[46]

The War Diary noted that:

There was the usual trouble over securing a bridge for our withdrawal, but we had by this time learnt most of the difficulties attendant on withdrawal over a river line, and officers had been sent back to reconnoitre the crossings and ensure some bridges were left intact for our withdrawal. The was a good deal of congestion on the main roads and as was to be expected, a good deal of German bombing, but the Regiment was by now quite used to such attacks and was so accustomed to keeping well spread out, that they suffered no casualties.[47]

Thirty minutes later, Lumsden called and reminded Horsbrugh-Porter that the bridge at Halle was the only one left; and warned him 'to make sure that no anxious Royal Engineer blows it up thinking there are no more Allied troops remaining on this side of the canal.' Horsbrugh-Porter acknowledged the message and said, "I'll send Henry to investigate and tell them about us." Immediately Falaise was dispatched back to the canal bridge:

The bridge has taken on a very warlike aspect since I saw it early this morning, but it is still standing. By some strange freak of luck, the bombs seem to have hit everything around but left it unscathed. To the right and left, the canal waters are filled with sunken barges. All the houses in the neighbourhood on both banks have caved in under the blasts of high explosives. On the other side of the canal, the small square across the bridge has been hastily fortified. Machine gun nests, made of sandbags and large paving stones, have been erected and through a hole in the only remaining wall of an estaminet an anti-tank gun points its long, thin, black muzzle. Dozens of British soldiers are hurrying about, bringing sandbags and stones to reinforce the positions, digging more pits, and carrying

46   Falaise, *Through Hell to Dunkirk*, pp.78-79.
47   TNA WO 167/452, 17 May 1940.

ammunition boxes. Around the bridge itself, Royal Engineers are busy laying land-mines. The central part of the bridge has been torn up in several places and the holes are full of dynamite. All that is required now to blow it sky-high is for someone to push a small button. Leaving the car in a concealed spot a short distance from the canal, I walk over the bridge looking for the officer in charge. The men all glance up sharply as I step cautiously around the mines. My uniform and French tank corps helmet, which is different from the infantry helmet to which they are accustomed, make me a stranger. I show my credentials and identity card and deliver my message, explaining to the officers who have gathered around me that our squadron is still holding the line of hills east of the canal and that the only pressure we have had so far is from German tanks or armoured cars on our left. We look at our maps and see that there is a bridge at Huinzingen [Huizingen], a mile north of here. When, and if, the German columns reach it and find that it is destroyed, they will have the choice of either turning left and trying this bridge or going north over the one at Lot. They all seem grateful for this information and, when I leave them, it is with the promise that they will not blow the bridge until every one of us has crossed over. Just as I am about to return to the car, I see Edouard, my French colleague at RHQ, coming towards me. He has been sent here by our Colonel to make doubly sure that the bridge will be kept open.[48]

Falaise returned to SHQ where they were still waiting for the order to withdraw. There was an air of restlessness. The usually calm Erne was beginning to show signs of strain and Falaise thought the 'silence was ominous.' This might be because the Germans were moving through the Sart wood, between Shand and Arkwright's troops, unseen by them, and the fact they were in armoured cars meant they could only move on roads, not in woods. Falaise thought the situation was a 'hopeless guard, and there was nothing to do except wait for orders.'[49]

The Germans came at 1415 hrs. Horsbrugh-Porter pulled 'off his earphones with a jerk' and told everyone to "get ready to leave." Falaise was the first to leave in the staff car and he went off to collect the fighting lorry and the Royal Engineers light truck which he had left earlier in the morning in the orchard on the Halle – Edingen road, with orders to join SHQ at Brucom [Brukom], one mile west of the canal. When Falaise found the two lorries they had been 'blissfully unaware of the German advance' and they had used their time well, having 'washed, shaved, and made minor repairs on the vehicles.' But when he showed them on his map that the German tanks were 'barely a mile away,' they were on the road within 15 minutes. The journey to Brukom was difficult. The road they had to use was subjected to air-attack by Stukas, so Falaise sought an alternative route, which meant the journey took more than an

48   Falaise, *Through Hell to Dunkirk*, p.80.
49   Falaise, *Through Hell to Dunkirk*, p.81

hour to reach the crossroad near Brukom. When he arrived, he found a DR who told him that 'the Squadron had gone by' and Horsbrugh-Porter was expecting them at Lennick St. Kwintens.[50]

When Bishop and Shand were given the order to move and cross the bridge at Halle, they believed that they were the last Allied troops to cross the bridge. Bishop wrote that they drove 'so fast that Bruce's hat blew off, a Herbert Johnson number from Bond Street' as they were not wearing their tin hats.' However, they were going too fast and they 'did not stop to retrieve it.'[51]

It was 24 hours since they were last in Lennick but there had been significant changes. Most of the inhabitants had fled, hastily closing up their homes and shops. The cafés were locked; the little house on the square, where SHQ had billeted the previous day was shut. Falaise wrote as they sat on the pavement:

> They watched the long lines of swanky civilian cars speeding west filled with wealthy Bruxellois and overladen with luggage. A driver stops to ask me the way to Edingen and tells me that the Germans are expected to enter the capital tonight. This is terrible news, and hunger, thirst and despair are my only companions as I sit here on the pavement gazing blankly into space. Horsbrugh-Porter has gone off to RHQ to get orders, Shand, Arkwright and Bishop, sitting on the pavement with their backs to a wall, are sound asleep, their heads drooping on their chests. It is very hot in this dusty square. My body feels anumb [sic] and lifeless. I, too, close my eyes.[52]

Shand thought there was an 'air of desertion that hung over the countryside. It was rather sinister.'[53] On Horsbrugh-Porter's return he woke Falaise and told him to go to Herne, a village eight miles south, to secure billets for the Squadron for the night.

It was 1900 hrs when Falaise arrived at Herne to be faced again with empty and locked-up houses. As he walked through the deserted streets, he felt under pressure to find enough accommodation for the men, armoured cars, and trucks. He started to climb over walls and smashed windows and managed to succeed in opening up a few of the abandoned houses and by the time the Squadron arrived he had rooms ready for almost everyone. An hour later, the tired and hungry men were in their billets and the vehicles were safely hidden in barns, sheds, or orchards. SHQs location was in the lodgings of the caretaker of the deserted brewery, where the two armoured cars of SHQ Troop, the staff car, and the weary crews were all collocated. Having now completed his task, Falaise joined SHQ and recorded the scene which met him:

50   Falaise, *Through Hell to Dunkirk*, p.81
51   Bishop, *Some Young Soldier*, p.53.
52   Falaise, *Through Hell to Dunkirk*, p.82
53   Shand, *Previous Encounters*, p.51.

I drag my tired feet into the small dining room which, with two rooms above it and a small kitchen, make up our billet. On the table there is a half-empty whisky bottle; the young subalterns are in convention around it, some on chairs, others on the floor. Erne is snoring in the only armchair. Through the open door, I can see Horsbrugh-Porter in the adjoining kitchen standing naked between two pails of warm water taking what he calls his 'before-dinner bath.' Machin is scrubbing his back while he keeps one eye on the stove where canned sausages, canned soup and canned potatoes are simmering. The young lieutenants, who are silently sipping the whisky, are fighting to keep their eyes open. Arkwright calls me to his side on the floor and hands me a bottle of wine which he has found in a house and kept for my special benefit. The good, heavy Burgundy revives me a little and enables me to stay awake until dinner. When the tasteless food later is brought to the table, we force it down our throats in silence. We are much too tired to talk and, anyway, what would be the use of giving voice to our thoughts? Only one thing is important, to try and keep as fit as possible, a prize-fighter who has but a minute's rest between rounds but in that space saves his breath and recuperates his strength for the next round.[54]

Finally, the Regiment returned to the area of Herinnes (J3843) and Thollenbeek (J3745) in time to get a hot meal prepared by the B Echelon and fresh orders for another night's work.[55] Hall had mistakenly gone to Gammerages [Galmaarden] 'owing to the wrong map reference or something.'[56] At 2115 hrs, the arrival of a DR from RHQ broke the silence. The orders were to get whatever rest they could and be ready to move off at any time after midnight. This meant with 'any luck' they would get approximately two hours of sleep. They all scrambled upstairs and lay down on the bare floor of the unfurnished room. In total there were five of them and they all lay on 'the hard boards side by side. In the next room, Horsbrugh-Porter and Erne shared the only mattress.[57]

By 2330 hrs, the Regiment was again put under command of 48th Division and was ordered to cover their withdrawal. The Regiment had deployed with B Squadron on the right and C Squadron in the centre who were in position covering the approaches to Bassilly (J3237) and Enghien. Smith and his detachment had also been given the same task. By 0600 hrs, A Squadron was in position on the left of C Squadron and the line was complete.[58] The Regiment was now facing south east covering all the exits from Halle.[59] Kennedy subsequently observed:

54   Falaise, *Through Hell to Dunkirk*, p.83
55   Clark-Kennedy, 'Record of Service', p.9.
56   Hall Diary, 17 May 1940, p.5.
57   Falaise, *Through Hell to Dunkirk*, p.84.
58   Clark-Kennedy, 'Record of Service', p.9.
59   Stewart, *History of the XII Royal Lancers*, p.356.

This practice of using the Regiment in the role of a Divisional cavalry regiment was exceedingly hard on all ranks, as the Regiment was not organised for such tasks, and there were insufficient men. In consequence, the same people who were driving, operating, and shooting all day had to remain on the alert all night, as there were no spare crews or personnel to draw on.[60]

Saturday 18th May

(Day Nine)
'Each troop leader was given instructions to withdraw as he sees fit toward the Galmarden rendezvous.'
Falaise[61]

Lumsden arrived at A Squadron SHQ at 0110 hrs and briefed the gathered officers that Brussels, Halle and Soignies had fallen to the Germans and that the BEF was no longer going to attempt to hold the Germans on this line. However, the Regiment was going to stay in position to try and delay the Germans while the infantry retreated to an intermediary position, 10 miles to the west to make a stand on the River Dendre. Falaise wrote 'we are again called upon to fight a rearguard action.'[62]

It was at this moment Falaise looked at Lumsden, and saw his qualities as a leader and commanding officer:

As I look at Lumsden while he talks, I wonder how he manages to appear so fresh when I know that during every minute of the day, he is in constant touch with all his squadrons, personally directing their every move and that at night, while we snatch a few hours' rest, he remains at his task, visiting each Squadron, looking over the officers and men and pepping them up with always the right word of cheer and encouragement. The more I see of him the more I realise what a great leader he really is. I feel that I would do with complete confidence anything he commanded, and I know that every man in the Regiment would do the same.[63]

Prior to Lumsden's departure, he directed Hall to go and wake all the Troop Sergeants and tell them to get ready to move out.[64] Once Lumsden had left, at 0330 hrs, A Squadron filed out through the dark and silent streets of Herne heading east, back towards Halle and the waiting Germans. The countryside was covered with low fog,

60 Clark-Kennedy, 'Record of Service', p.9.
61 Falaise, *Through Hell to Dunkirk*, p.89.
62 Falaise, *Through Hell to Dunkirk*, p.85.
63 Falaise, *Through Hell to Dunkirk*, pp.85-86.
64 Hall Diary, 18 May 1940, p.5.

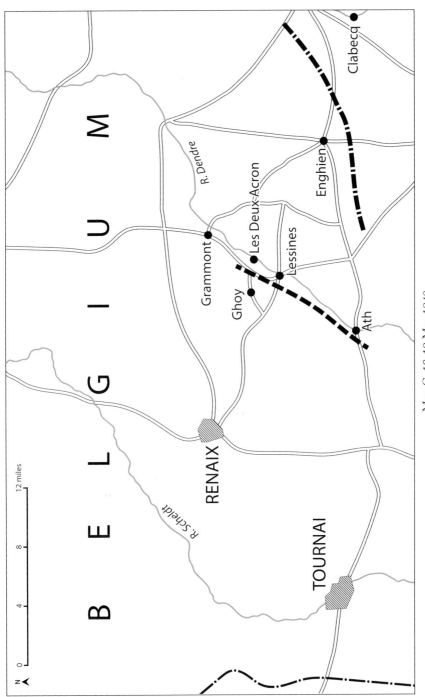

Map C 18-19 May 1940.

the heavy dew was falling, and everything was cold and damp. After travelling for approximately an hour, the Squadron started to move more 'cautiously, halting at intervals, and sending patrols forward.' At dawn, the Squadron stopped just outside a small village about five miles east of Herne. From the high ground, they could see emerging from the fog the tree-tops of the Bois du Strihoux, (a forest lying to the south near Edingen).

Horsbrugh-Porter's orders to his troop leaders were that they were 'to spread fanwise' to cover a five-mile front between Pepingen on the Halle – Ninove road, and Saintes on the Halle – Edingen road. SHQ Troop were to be located near Bogarden [Bogaarden] at the centre of the Squadron's line. The situation was that as far as they knew was the Germans were to the west, south, and south east of the Squadron. Fifteen minutes later, the troops led by Shand, Bishop, Arkwright and Roddick moved off, followed shortly afterwards by the SHQ packet.[65]

By 0515 hrs, SHQ were in location in a large farmhouse on the right side of a dirt road running through the hamlet of Den Dail [Den Dael], approximately two miles from Bogarden. When they arrived, they found a company of Light Infantry was already well-established with their most advanced position being 100 yards forward of their position at a large farmhouse. On the right, beyond the farm building, was a field of growing wheat which was occupied by a platoon of machine gunners. To the left, was an anti-tank gun hidden behind a low wall. It was these men who had been in position all night that the Squadron had come to relieve. Falaise thought the chosen position was perfect as at the corner of the crossroads a few yards from where he was, there was a signpost marked 'Pepingen 3 km. 800,' on the other 'Saintes 3 km. 200.' This put them at the 'centre of the Squadron's battlefront,' exactly as Horsbrugh-Porter had intended.[66]

While the squadrons had been moving into position at 0600 hrs, RHQ moved to its new location at Herrines (J3843).[67] At 0700 hrs, the infantry platoons silently moved out of the village, the whole process taking a little over an hour until the 'sole occupants' of Den Dail was the SHQ with its two armoured cars. Falaise noted that 'true to their British tradition,' the men made tea. Machin found some eggs that they shared and had a hurried breakfast, sitting on the ground in the shadow of the farm buildings. While they waited, they let the starving cattle out of the stables into the fields so they could feed themselves. Above them flew a lone Henschel observation plane but they were confident that they had not been seen, although they knew that the Henschel was known to work with German armoured units.[68]

Arkwright reported that he could see German tanks moving along the Halle – Edingen road. Shand reported that he had opened fire on German vehicles coming up

65   Falaise, *Through Hell to Dunkirk*, p.86.
66   Falaise, *Through Hell to Dunkirk*, p.87.
67   TNA WO 167/452: 18 May 1940.
68   Falaise, *Through Hell to Dunkirk*, p.87.

from Halle on the Ninove road. Ten minutes later, he reported that the vehicles had disappeared. After being in position for five hours, the Squadron sat and waited 'for something which wasn't 'in a hurry to happen.' Falaise thought that the Germans were not 'likely to want to come over this particular spot,' and 'they were 'getting around them to the south.' Arkwright's troop reported that German armoured vehicles were steadily streaming down the road from Halle to Edingen. Shand also saw 'plenty of them' on the Ninove road heading north west, indicating that none were coming their way.[69]

While his Squadron had been engaging the Germans, Hall and his vehicles moved out at 0700 hrs, passing the troops of the 48th Division who were withdrawing. He thought they all looked 'worn out, having had no food for a day or more.' Hall managed to attach himself to the end of the RHQ packet. As they passed through Gammerages, Lessines, and Les Deux Acren on their way to Buissenal the move had been 'terribly slow' due to the numbers of refugees on the roads. Hall's day for the most part had been uneventful but he thought everyone was 'windy' saying that the Germans were only a couple of miles away.[70]

Despite Falaise's earlier opinion, at 1007 hrs Shand reported he had been attacked by three light tanks.[71] The War Diary states that Shand was able to avoid the Germans by making use of his superior speed and Arkwright's troop was at this time heavily engaged with motorcyclists who nearly surrounded him. However, from Falaise's account, it appears that Shand actually engaged the German tanks.[72] From the SHQ location, they could clearly hear the shooting coming from their left. The 'whip-like cracks' of Shand's Boyes anti-tank rifles sounded 'above the 'clatter' of the machine guns. They listened anxiously, and eventually, Shand reported that he had "knocked one tank out of action" and the two others had "turned tail." A few minutes later, Shand reported that he had "gone to the destroyed tank and found its three occupants dead." Arkwright and Roddick also reported 'that the whole countryside ahead of them was swarming with German tanks, armoured cars and motorcycle scouts moving toward their positions.' From Den Dail they could see dark shapes visible moving along the crest, so, Horsbrugh-Porter 'waved SHQ back to their cars and reported the situation to RHQ.'[73]

At 1100 hrs, B Squadron made contact with the rear elements of the French colonial troops withdrawing on the right of the Regiment.[74] The *Regimental History* records that Miller-Mundy 'handled his troop well' when he came under attack while trying to recover one of his armoured cars. The German infantry attack came just at the point the tow rope had been attached.[75] By noon, the Regiment had several men

69   Falaise, *Through Hell to Dunkirk*, p.88.
70   Hall Diary, 18 May 1940, p.5.
71   TNA WO 167/452 records 'two enemy medium tanks were engaged by A Squadron in the area Brages (J4643).
72   TNA WO 167/452: 18 May 1940.
73   Falaise, *Through Hell to Dunkirk*, p.88.
74   TNA WO 167/452: 18 May 1940.
75   Stewart, *History of the XII Royal Lancers*, p.356.

wounded and one car was badly damaged. At this point, Lumsden ordered a general withdrawal to Galmarden [Galmaarden], a village east of the Edingen – Ninove road and six miles from the Dendre. Each troop leader was given instructions to withdraw as he saw fit and make their way towards the Galmarden rendezvous.[76]

As the SHQ packet travelled to Galmarden it was attacked by a single bomber, possibly attracted by the amount of dust that the convoy was raising. Once the dust had settled one armoured car, was on its side in a deep gull This was witnessed by Falaise who wrote:

> Horsbrugh-Porter comes running up and calmly orders all hands to get busy and try to pull the car out of its perilous position. For five minutes, we dig and push while another armoured car skids and tugs at its bogged-down mate. Just as we are about to succeed, and the car is on the verge of being righted, its driver makes a wrong move, and it falls back into a deeper hole. Our work is made more difficult by the constant attention that two bombers are showering on us in the shape of short bursts of machine gun bullets which streak through the dust alarmingly close by. My shirt and tunic are soaked with sweat from heat and fright. Nothing short of a miracle can now lift the armoured car out of the hole which its spinning wheels are digging ever deeper and deeper as the motor races in a desperate effort to wrench the heavy hulk out of its impending grave. Horsbrugh-Porter, who has worked twice as hard as any of us, finally straightens up and reluctantly calls the whole thing off. All equipment and weapons are removed and Horsbrugh-Porter himself ends the life of the armoured car with his own pistol, shooting the engine full of holes.[77]

On their arrival at Galmarden, their sudden appearance scared off 'two suspicious-looking civilians' who were 'very busy looting the brewery.' In their flight, they abandoned a large wheelbarrow filled with bottles of beer in the middle of the road. This was an opportunity too good to be missed so the bottles were distributed amongst the now-thirsty crews. The vehicles were finally parked outside the village under the tall shady trees that lined the Moerbeke road. On their arrival, they found that Shand's and Arkwright's troops had already arrived. Falaise noticed that one of the armoured cars had a large anti-tank bullet hole in it. Eventually, they all sat around in the tall grass along the bank of the road when they were finally joined by Roddick's troop. Falaise then shared out the remaining bottles of beer he had held back. When Horsbrugh-Porter joined the group, having been on the wireless receiving new orders, he was the subject of much amusement, which made all the troop leaders laugh. Although no one was clean, the state of Horsbrugh-Porter exceeded them all. His

---

76   Falaise mentions one sergeant killed on the same day. There is no CWGC registration for this claim.
77   Falaise, *Through Hell to Dunkirk*, p.90.

hair and eyebrows were so covered with white chalky dust, and his eyes so lined with black wrinkles that he looked 'as if he had been made up to play the part of an old man in a school Shakespearian play.'[78]

The new orders were that the Squadron was to 'spread out in a rough semi-circular six-mile line, stretching between Vane at the northern end, to a point south of the Bois de Lessines near the Edingen–Ath road. They were to get across the Edingen–Gerardsbergen [Geraardsbergen] road before it was reached by the Germans.' Falaise wrote that 'there was no time to lose as according to the latest information the Germans had already passed through Edingen and were not far behind.'[79]

As they crossed the road, the Squadron was being engaged from all angles, so Horsbrugh-Porter sent the staff car and fighting lorry off to find somewhere safer to the west of the Lessines Wood. From the air activity, it appeared that the next German objective was the Lessines bridge. This was then accompanied by the sounds of heavy firing coming from the south where the German tanks and motorcycle troops were located. This indicated that they were attempting to reach Lessines using the main road which joined the Edingen road at Ghislenghien. Later, Shand recalled that it was at Lessines when looking through his glasses over the river that he could see a 'solid mass of German troops' which at first, he thought 'was an illusion.'[80]

The road in the north was being watched by Arkwright and his troop, and a squadron of the East Riding Yorkshire Yeomanry (equipped with light tanks) straddled it a mile to the east of Ghislenghien. Arkwright hurried towards the village of Silly, south of the road where most of the shooting was taking place, and three anti-tank guns were sent up from Ath to assist. According to Falaise:

> Unfortunately, they set up their position back of us and fired at the British tanks, mistaking them for German. Three of the light tanks of the Yorkshire Yeomanry are blasted by them and their occupants are killed before they can be stopped. They are ordered back to Ath.[81]

Slowly the pressure on A Squadron increased and the Germans were now attacking from all sides. The Squadron was hard-pressed. The Germans succeeded in taking the crossroads at Ghislenghien and occupied it with motorcyclists. These were followed by tanks, which were moving on towards Ollignies and Lessines. If they succeeded, they would cut the Squadron off from the rear. Eventually, the Squadron lost contact with the Yeomanry as they were retreating towards Ath, although they were understood to be 'putting up stiff resistance.'[82]

78   Falaise, *Through Hell to Dunkirk*, p.90.
79   Falaise, *Through Hell to Dunkirk*, p.91.
80   Shand, *Previous Encounters*, p.51.
81   Falaise, *Through Hell to Dunkirk*, p.91.
82   Falaise, *Through Hell to Dunkirk*, p.92.

Horsbrugh-Porter was also concerned about being cut-off, so he sent Falaise to Les Deux Acren, two miles north of Lessines to make sure that the bridge was still intact. He then gave orders that the Squadron were to 'all stay on this side of the river until 2000 hrs, and then, if possible, to retreat over the bridge.' The Regiment had received orders 'to hold out for eight hours longer than had previously been ordered, until 2000 hrs, unless seriously pressed.'[83] Falaise had only been in position on the bridge for approximately an hour when a DR arrived and informed Falaise that the Squadron was crossing the Dendre now and he was to go ahead immediately to Buissenal (J1237).[84] Buissenal was approximately 10 miles to the west and it was hoped that when they arrived there, they would get food and some rest. Falaise wrote, 'our day's job is over.'[85] However, Bishop's troop were struggling to reach the crossing.

On their way there, Bishop ran into a column of refugees that was so dense that eventually they 'gradually and firmly pushed his stationary armoured car into a ditch on the side of the road. The crews quickly got everything off the car, smashed the engine and they all got onto one of the other armoured cars to quickly get across the bridge before it was blown.' Bishop overheard Horsbrugh-Porter say under his breath "this has just about cost us our lives."[86] The bridges which the Regiment withdrew over at Bassilly and Lessines (Les Deux Acren), which had been prepared by a Field Company, were successfully destroyed once the Regiment had crossed.[87]

When Falaise arrived at Buissenal he was greeted by Hall. Falaise had not seen him since they last met in Lennick St. Kwinten two days before. He informed Falaise that:

> The town is already filled to overflowing with hundreds of frantic refugees and he has had a difficult time finding billets for the Squadron, adding that the armoured cars and transport lorries will have to spend the night under the trees of a large orchard. The only thing that I am really interested in is the fact that I won't have to run around and do the billeting, because I am so tired that I can hardly stand. He leads me to a farmhouse where our cooks are busy preparing supper and advises me to rest a bit until Horsbrugh-Porter arrives with the troops. Standing in the courtyard as if in a dream, I see Shand and his troop come roaring up the village road through the dusk, and the bleary-eyed, grey-faced, worn-out crews stumble out of the armoured cars. I enter the noisy kitchen of the farmhouse and Tich, our Mess corporal, seeing the condition I am in, silently pushes a wooden stool under me. I flop down, close my eyes, and fall asleep immediately.[88]

83   Falaise, *Through Hell to Dunkirk*, p.92.
84   TNA WO 167/452: 18 May 1940.
85   Falaise, *Through Hell to Dunkirk*, p.92.
86   Bishop, One Young Soldier, p.53.
87   TNA WO 167/452: 18 May 1940 and TNA WO 167/778: 18 May 1940.
88   Falaise, *Through Hell to Dunkirk*, p.93.

Along with Hall and other members of the B Echelon, the last of the Engineers rejoined the Regiment. Smith finally made his way back, their task for the day having been to concentrate on forming a complete roadblock in the area of Enghien which they did by cratering between the houses. Once complete, Smith sent his party back to RHQ while he stayed to support C Squadron. While out on a reconnaissance Smith found another small bridge which had been overlooked. He prepared it for demolition and only managed to destroy it moments before the arrival of a lone German tank.[89]

As Horsbrugh-Porter gave orders to the Squadron, a small girl entered the kitchen. She had an infant in her arms, and she begged for a little milk for the baby, her brother. She had walked from Brussels, 40 miles, in a day and a night. She was 11 years old and her parents, German Jews, were sick, and she said that she had left them lying on some straw in a barn nearby. The kind-hearted woman who owned the farm overheard the conversation and brought in some hot water in a basin to bathe the child's feet. She also gave her a pair of rubber shoes to replace her worn-out shoes, and the cook made enough sandwiches for the girl and her family. Falaise captured the final moments by saying:

> The brave child leaves the kitchen, she thanks us with exquisite politeness and, with the dignity of a queen, solemnly steps out into the dark night holding her tiny baby brother in her tired, aching arms and enters the straw-filled barn.[90]

At 2200 hrs, Lumsden received orders placing him in command of a force which was to cover the withdrawal of the 2nd Division on the front to include Ath – Grammont. A strong squadron from the 13th/18th Hussars under Major Wilfred Davies was also placed under his orders. Lumsden was to report to HQ, 5th Infantry Brigade, at the Ghoy Church (J2344), as soon as possible, where he would be given further troops to enable him to carry out his role. This meant that the Regiment had to move again in the dark as soon as it had replenished and embark on its third night of continuous fighting.[91]

By 2300 hrs, the armoured cars had been refuelled and their ammunition supplies replenished; the men had been fed and the wounded attended. The evening meal that night was a 'supper of canned soup, canned sausage, and canned potatoes.' A Squadron's new orders were that they were to depart at 0300 hrs, as the troops of the 2nd Division occupying the line of the canal had been ordered to withdraw at 0315 hrs.[92]

The day had been a difficult one but the wireless was the saving grace. The War Diary recorded that 'through the excellence of the wireless which gave perfect

89 TNA WO 167/778, 18 May 1940.
90 Falaise, *Through Hell to Dunkirk*, p.94.
91 TNA WO 167/452: 18 May 1940.
92 TNA WO 167/452: 18 May 1940.

communication on the whole front of the Regiment, it was possible to bring fire to bear on all tanks seen and to keep all troops advised of the Germans' movements so that there was never any question of anyone wondering what was happening on his right or left.'[93] On a day when contact with the Germans had predominately been with tanks, the *Regimental History* recorded that the only weapons the Regiment had were their 'speed and accurate reporting on the wireless.'[94]

Sunday 19th May

(Day Ten)

By dawn... both regiments had collected a surprising assortment of heterogeneous details, who were only too pleased to be controlled and to know what was happening on their front and flanks.
Lumsden[95]

Lumsden arrived at Ghoy Church at 0100 hrs, where he met Brigadier Gartland, Commander 5th Infantry Brigade, Brigadier Davidson, Commander Royal Artillery (CRA) I Corps (and temporary Commander 2nd Division), and the officer commanding the Field Artillery Regiment of the 2nd Division. He was informed that the Argyll and Sutherland Highlanders (a Machine Gun Battalion) were in Gramont, but the location of their RHQ was unknown. There were also some carrier platoons which would be left on various parts of the Divisional front, although their commander had regretfully not arrived at this conference. The problem for the 2nd Division was that they were not in touch with their own forward troops and were unable to give Lumsden the positions of any of their HQs.[96]

Lumsden thought the obvious solution to the problem was to allot separate sectors to the Regiment and the 13th/18th Hussars squadron so that they could make contact with all the various bodies and troops remaining on the front of the Division, inform them of their orders and act as the controlling HQ. It was decided that the location for the Force HQ would be Ghoy Church as it provided direct communication by telephone and wireless to the Field Artillery Regiment and by wireless to the 12th Lancers and 13th/18th Hussars.[97] This would be commanded by Lumsden, while the Lancers would be commanded by Clifton-Brown to whom he gave the task of co-ordinating with Davies from the 13th/18th Hussars. Their task was to cover the line of the river and to organise any troops in the area to assist him in his task.[98] Lumsden observed:

93   TNA WO 167/452: 18 May 1940.
94   Stewart, *History of the XII Royal Lancers*, p.356.
95   Lumsden Diary in Stewart, *History of the XII Royal Lancers*, pp.357-358.
96   Clark-Kennedy, 'Record of Service', p.10.
97   TNA WO 167/452: 19 May 1940.
98   Stewart, *History of the XII Royal Lancers*, p.357.

They quickly established themselves on the front, which was patrolled throughout its entire length, barges and boats were sunk or drawn over the west bank, bridges were reconnoitred to ensure they were demolished, and a special watch was placed to cover the locks. By dawn… both regiments had collected a surprising assortment of heterogeneous details, who were only too pleased to be controlled and to know what was happening on their front and flanks.[99]

At 0330 hrs, Machin woke Falaise and the armoured car crews. Their black shadows could be seen moving in and out of the trees and every once in a while, they were illuminated with the flash of a torch. One after the other, the drivers started their engines, and within 30 minutes the Squadron was leaving Buissenal and moving down the ridge above the valley of the Dendre south west of Lessines. The journey was made without lights over dirt roads and bumpy tracks. They reached their destination of Ostiches just before dawn.[100]

When they arrived, the 4th/7th Dragoon Guards RHQ had already established themselves in the village and Horsbrugh-Porter reported to their Commanding Officer. Bishop also made contact with the 4th/7th Dragoon Guards at Ostiches where Philip Verdin had a cup of tea ready for him when he arrived.[101] The village was deserted, except for the owner of a café-general store on the main square near where the Lancers had halted. The shopkeeper was serving coffee and giving away all that she had in her shop to anyone who wanted it. She told Falaise to take anything he liked and gave him a hot bowl of café-au-lait. She said that she wanted all "her shelves and counters to be bare" for when the Germans arrived.[102]

By 0600 hrs, the Squadron had dispersed from Ostiches with the troops deploying to their positions between Lessines and Papignies. The 4th/7th Dragoon Guards' light tanks were positioned on the right flank from Papignies to Rebaix. SHQ troop, with the two armoured cars, the fighting lorry, the staff car, and four DRs moved out of Ostiches for Wannebeck. The route selected was 'bumpy and dusty' which made the journey slow and as they reached the small hamlet of Enfer (which means hell in French) the first reports of German tanks came in.[103]

It was reported that there were two German tanks and some motorcycle troops making a crossing at Lessines, approximately two miles away. As if to confirm the reports the sound of 'intense gunfire' suddenly started up from that direction. When SHQ reached Wannebeck, they halted, and Horsbrugh-Porter took one armoured car forward on reconnaissance to Lessines. It was 0730 hrs, by the time Horsbrugh-Porter had returned and the news was good. The two German tanks had been 'stopped cold' and for the present all was well on the left flank. Horsbrugh-Porter decided to relocate

99   Lumsden Diary in Stewart, *History of the XII Royal Lancers*, pp.357-358.
100 Falaise, *Through Hell to Dunkirk*, p.97.
101 Bishop, *Some Young Soldier*, p.54.
102 Falaise, *Through Hell to Dunkirk*, p.97.
103 Falaise, *Through Hell to Dunkirk*, p.98.

the SHQ to higher ground. The new location was an isolated farm on the crest of a hill approximately a mile to the north near Sart. This was at the junction of road No. 60 leading east to Lessines (2 miles), and the road going south to Papignies (3 miles). There was plenty of straw at the farm so the men camouflaged the armoured cars to make them look like haystacks, while the lorry and the staff car were hidden in the farm buildings.[104]

While SHQ was in its new location, news came in from the Dragoons that they were 'up against some heavier tanks near Rebaix.' This was confirmed by RHQ which informed them that several German tanks had crossed the river at Rebaix and that the Dragoons were slowly falling back. Again, there were concerns that if the Germans succeeded in getting tanks north towards Ostiches and Lahamade the Squadron would be cut-off. The problem was compounded by the fact that the last of the anti-tank guns that had been with the Squadron had just been seen moving west.[105]

At 1000 hrs, the news was a little better and the Dragoons informed the Squadron that they had put up a good fight and had knocked out some of the heavier tanks, although others were now reported 'swarming' up the road between Rebaix and Ath. On receiving this information Horsbrugh-Porter sent Falaise down the Lessines road a few hundred yards to establish an observation post. Falaise recorded:

> I find a good position and place an anti-tank gun in the right ditch and a Bren gun in the left one. My gunners have a clear view of the road for nearly half a mile, and if any Jerry ventures before our sights, he will get a hot reception. I have been sitting behind the Boyes rifle for over an hour now. The sky is filled with light Heinkel bombers. At first, they fly along the valley, wasting their high explosive bombs on the positions that the anti-tanks previously occupied, and each time they pass over Wannebeck they dive down and machine gun its empty streets. Later, although it can't possibly see anything stirring on the road we are on, one of the bombers sweeps down on it, firing short bursts from its machine guns while we hug the muddy bottom of the ditches. The sound of cannon-ading which has died down in the valley ahead reaches us now with increasing intensity, not only from the south, but also from the south west, and seems to get nearer every minute. I have an awful feeling that this time we are really surrounded.[106]

At approximately 1200 hrs, Falaise was ordered to return to SHQ where he found that the armoured cars were already moving out, 'shedding' their straw coats as they went. While he was away, orders had been received for the remaining Dragoon tanks and the Regiment to reconnoitre the roads leading south and south west from Frasnes.

---

104 Falaise, *Through Hell to Dunkirk*, p.98.
105 Falaise, *Through Hell to Dunkirk*, p.99.
106 Falaise, *Through Hell to Dunkirk*, p.99.

While A Squadron was waiting for Falaise, several batteries of field artillery, followed by the tanks of the Divisional cavalry, passed their location as they started to withdraw behind the Escaut. Eventually, the rest of the Regiment also passed the A Squadron location.[107]

As soon as Falaise and his OP party had returned, Horsbrugh-Porter told Falaise to jump into Erne's armoured car which was to follow at the rear of the column. The SHQ packet moved at speed towards Lahamade, ensuring that they kept wide intervals between the cars. Horsbrugh-Porter was heading for the safety of the thick woods between Lahamade and Buissenal. He was warned that there was 'only one bridge left over the Escaut' at Tournai and that the German bombers were trying to destroy it, so he sent Falaise and the non-armoured elements of the Squadron to the other side of the bridge to wait for them.[108]

As the SHQ approached Lahamade, it was attacked by two large bombers which flew straight down the road as they were moving. The bombers dropped their bombs as the packet drove through without stopping. As they entered the village the bombs hit the houses at the village entrance 'blasting them to bits.' Horsbrugh-Porter's armoured car, which was leading the convoy, 'thunders ahead' and disappeared into 'the smoke and dust raised by the explosions.' The rest of the packet which was 200 yards behind him followed at speed into the village.[109]

It was 1300 hrs by the time all the squadrons were collocated at Frasnes where they were joined by what was left of the Dragoons: Falaise observed that:

> The remains of the Dragoon regiment are drawn up under the tall trees on the left side of the road. They have been badly knocked about. Three of their Bren Gun Carriers are loaded with the wounded and dying. I can't help wondering when and where these men will be attended to, as I haven't yet seen a British doctor or ambulance since the campaign began. My friend, Bob, the French liaison officer with that squadron, is sitting, with his eyes closed, at the back of a small, battered lorry with his dead British captain lying across his lap. I walk over to speak to him, and he smiles wearily as he recognises me. His breeches are soaked and stiff with blood and, as he asks me to light a cigarette for him, I notice that more blood is trickling down his right hand. He has been hit hard in the shoulder but doesn't seem to know it. I believe he is still suffering from shock and does not realise that his captain is dead. His only idea is that he must get him to a hospital. Our Squadron has been luckier and less exposed than they. We have had no major casualties and all our cars have returned, though some are badly scarred and have jagged, gaping holes in their armour plate.[110]

107 TNA WO 167/452: 19 May 1940.
108 Falaise, *Through Hell to Dunkirk*, p.99.
109 Falaise, *Through Hell to Dunkirk*, p.100.
110 Falaise, *Through Hell to Dunkirk*, p.100.

As the convoy entered Tournai, they could see there was 'not a single house left standing.' Down by the river, the railway station was ablaze and all the streets leading to and from the bridge were blocked by 'crumpled' houses. As the last of the light tanks crossed the bridge the Royal Engineers started to clear some of the heaviest debris to enable them to pass. As the convoy waited to cross, the German bombers returned. Seeking cover from the attack, Falaise's driver cleverly parked the staff car 'inside a blasted shop window.' It was a somewhat 'unorthodox position' and Falaise thought that as it looked 'like a wrecked car,' the Germans had ignored them. Falaise shouted to the lorry driver to back up a few hundred yards and get under cover and wait for his signal before they moved again. He found it difficult to believe that Tournai was the same place that the Regiment had visited only nine days before:

> The quaint houses are scorched and empty shells; huge blocks of cement, stones, bricks, steel girders, and burning rafters, lie across our way. Only the cathedral, with its seven beautiful spires, seems untouched, but the ancient and world-famous library filled with priceless medieval manuscripts which adjoin it is roaring with flames. Live wires from trolley cars lie twisted on the ground and at first, it looks as though we would never be able to get across the square. Two women run through the debris screaming, desperately searching through the smoking wreckage while a little farther away an old man, his white hair caked with blood, stands before what was his home poking aimlessly with a stick at the remnants of a huge dining room table. Jumping out of the cars, pulling the wires, and pushing stones and slabs of cement out of the way, we succeed in getting out of this hell. We are all so shaken by the horror of what we are seeing, by the wanton cruelty of this destruction, which is beyond belief, that no one says a word. Our faces are pale and grim; our eyes alone speak.[111]

Once across the bridge, they waited just outside the town for two hours for the Squadron to arrive. In the distance there was a 'tremendous explosion,' which indicated that the bridge at Tournai had been blown, although the Squadron had still not arrived. Bishop wrote that as they came to the bridge 'some idiot' blew it up deafeningly in their faces, choking and blinding them with smoke and dust.[112] Realising there was no further reason to wait, Falaise set off and *en route* they met a DR who informed them that the Squadron had gone off in the direction of Orchies. The Regiment reached Orchies at 1500 hrs but it proved to be very unsuitable as a billeting area, so it moved on to Bersée (H7519) where it refuelled and had a much-needed night's rest.[113]

Not knowing the Regiment had moved, Falaise set off for Orchies. When he arrived, another DR who was waiting just outside the village at the crossroads directed the

---

111 Shand, *Previous Encounters,* p.51 and Falaise, *Through Hell to Dunkirk*, p.103.
112 Bishop, *Some Young Soldier,* p.54.
113 TNA WO 167/452: 19 May 1940.

packet to Thumeries, a small village south of the Phalempin woods. There they found the rest of the Squadron and the transport echelon which had already established their billets. The armoured cars had to make a considerable detour to find another bridge over the Escaut. Their billets were in a large villa, with a farm and extensive orchard, which Bishop thought was 'perfect,' but Hall thought was 'dirty.'[114] Hall recorded that the bridge they found was a pontoon bridge to the north of Tournai. It had been mined and the Royal Engineers officer was concerned that Hall's lorries might set them off.[115]

For those who had been out on patrol, this was only the second good night's sleep they had managed since the beginning of hostilities.[116] Shand wrote that this period of the campaign was for him the most 'confused in his memory, chiefly through the lack of sleep.'[117] To the rear of their leaguer was a French anti-aircraft gun battery and Bishop wrote that they enjoyed the very rare sight of seeing three German bombers being shot down. Falaise commented that each time they shot one down they 'whooped' and shared litres of red wine, and the more they drank 'it improved their aim, and it was a heartening sight.'[118] The first 10 days had now started to take its toll on the Regiment's armoured cars, and as they rested in the orchard, A Squadron had been reduced to three troops of two cars, indicating each troop had lost at least one car to date.[119]

In the evening there were fresh orders and news. The rest of the world had known for some days that the Germans had broken through on the Meuse at Sedan on 17th May. A mechanised army had poured through the gap and was heading for the Channel, having already bypassed Cambrai and Arras. There was also a danger from German parachutists, dressed as civilians, fifth-columnists, and communists who had attacked isolated officers and attempted sabotage in different places, so there were strict orders that no officer or trooper was to go about alone or unarmed.[120]

That evening, Lumsden visited the I Corps HQ where he was thanked by General Barker for the good work that the Regiment had done in covering the withdrawal of the 2nd Division. At 1930 hrs, the Regiment was again placed under the orders of GHQ, and Lumsden was summoned to GHQ where he obtained the latest information and received orders for the following day. The refugee traffic with the resultant blocking of the roads was appalling, and he did not get back to the Regiment from Wahagnies until 2300 hrs, although he had only travelled a distance of 12 miles.[121]

114 Bishop, *Some Young Soldier*, p.54 and Hall Diary,19 May 1940, p.6.
115 Hall Diary, 19 May 1940, p.6.
116 Shand, *Previous Encounters*, pp.51-52 and Bishop, *Some Young Soldier*, p.54.
117 Shand, 'May 1940: A Memory', p.153.
118 Bishop, *Some Young Soldier*, p.54 and Falaise, *Through Hell to Dunkirk*, p.104.
119 Shand, 'May 1940: A Memory', p.153.
120 See also, Shand, *Previous Encounters*, p.51.
121 TNA WO 167/452: 19 May 1940.

6

Reconnaissance for, and the Battle of Arras

(20th–24th May 1940)

Monday 20th May

(Day Eleven)

A quoi ça sert ? Les Boches ont coupé la ligne au sud d'Arras. Tout est entre nous ici.
French railway worker[1]

I also ordered 12th Lancers with a field battery to move to Arras and carry out necessary reconnaissances south and south westwards, and to gain touch with the outlying portions of
PETREFORCE.
Gort[2]

The situation at this time was that the BEF was holding the line of the Escaut and that the German penetration between the French and British Armies had forced the British right flank to fall back to the line of the River Scarpe toward Douai. Cambrai was in the hands of the Germans, and reports and rumours were so prevalent that it was uncertain whether the Germans had reached Bapaume, Peronne and Albert. It seemed certain that in any case only mechanised formations and those in small packets could have penetrated into the area. A determined drive southwards, especially if the French were to make their long-promised counter-attack northwards, would produce far-reaching results. However, one of the most pressing issues for the Regiment was still the lack of accurate maps.[3]

---

1   What the hell is the use? Les Boches have cut the line south of Arras. It is all up with us
    here.
2   Gort, *Second Despatch*, p.5916.
3   TNA WO 167/452: 20 May 1940.

Early that morning Lieutenant Morris, the Signals Officer, had been sent in a 15-cwt truck to try and collect some more maps from the depot at Doullens. The Regiment now covered so wide an area that the stock of relevant maps was practically nil. Had the Regiment not been so well acquainted with this area, through their previous training, even greater difficulties would have been experienced. Morris entered Doullens from the west as German motorcyclists entered from the east, but fortunately thanks to the mass of refugees in the centre, was able to make his escape, albeit without the maps.[4]

Early that morning, Second Lieutenant Bailey and M. Eduard Michel, (*Agent de Liaison*), were also sent to make contact with the French Cavalry Corps which was operating in the area Douai – Arras. This appeared to be a fairly safe mission but unfortunately that was the last occasion on which they were seen, although they were reported to have been seen entering Arras in search of the Commanding Officer at the old GHQ in the town.[5] It is of coincidence that Bailey's father Percy had also been captured by the Germans in August 1914, while he was serving with the Regiment.[6] Once the Regiment's task had been completed with FRANKFORCE it was directed to 'carry out recces on the right flank of the advance of Major General Martel's Force. The Regiment was told to pay particular attention to the roads: Arras – Doullens, Arras – Amiens, Arras, and recces were to extend southwards as far as Bapaume.'[7]

After a good night's rest, Falaise wrote that 'the Regiment started out on this task in good order and with light hearts, as they were once more being employed in their proper role.' The squadrons moved off soon after dawn, each by a different route, to try and avoid refugees who still blocked all the roads and delayed the advance in varying degrees. On the road to Lens, A Squadron 'sped' towards Arras, Falaise counted 60 German bombers in the sky above Douai and saw artillery and troop-carrying lorries trying to move north but stuck in a jam. He presumed that they were going to the front, but it looked as if the front was all around them now. When Falaise arrived at a level crossing he noticed a train on its side and a dejected French railway worker sitting on a bench. When he asked him why no one was trying to right the train he said, "what the hell is the use? Les Boches have cut the line south of Arras. It is all up with us here." Falaise repeated to himself 'les Boches have cut the line... cut the line!'[8]

The first reports came in from Browne-Clayton, commanding B Squadron, saying that they had been heavily bombed whilst passing through Arras and that a large column of German tanks was reported approaching Arras from Cambrai. Lumsden, who had by now been given command of 1 Welsh Guards and H and E Troops, RHA, went to Arras where he met Major General Petre who was in command of

4   TNA WO 167/452: 20 May 1940.
5   Stewart, *History of the XII Royal Lancers*, p.359.
6   Stewart, *History of the XII Royal Lancers*, p.248.
7   TNA WO 167/452: 20 May 1940 and TNA WO 167/29/4: FRANKFORCE Operation Order No.2, 21 May 1940.
8   Falaise, *Through Hell to Dunkirk*, p.105.

the defence of the city. Lumsden's original mission was 'to remain in observation and carry out reconnaissances' on five specific roads leading to Arras, 'with the object of clearing up that situation on that front.' He was also directed to make contact with PETREFORCE in Arras.[9]

When Lumsden arrived he discovered that the Welsh Guards, assisted by the Military Police, were fully occupied protecting Arras and that the Horse Artillery guns were already in action under General Petre's orders against German tanks, which had now reached the eastern outskirts, so that his force never, in fact, came into being.[10] The German tanks were next reported south of Arras and it was obvious that they were persistently trying to outflank the BEF. B Squadron failed to make their way due south and had to move north to extricate themselves, rejoining the Regiment which was now watching the area to the west of Arras.[11]

A Squadron was ordered to reconnoitre the area south and south west of the main Arras – St. Pol road. Shand's troop was ordered to push on to Doullens to make contact with the 36th Infantry Brigade, with whom there were no communications. Shand did not reach the main road until the afternoon due to the volume of refugees in and around the dense mining district of Lens and Vimy. When he finally arrived on the Arras – St. Pol road, he found that that it too was also packed with refugees. Shand wrote:

> People whose means of transport varied from expensive limousines to their feet and whose common force of propulsion was blind fear. The whole country south of the road we knew well as it was our former billeting area.[12]

When Bishop woke in Bersée, he was aware that the Germans were now in the area of their former billets of Fonquevillers, Hebuterne and Monchy, and he remembered that all his kit and some of his 'most expensive uniform' were still in an attic in Fonquevillers.[13]

Arkwright's troop, to Shand's immediate left, encountered a 'strong force' in Avesnes le Compte.[14] Just as Shand heard about this over the wireless, his second car had a fuel blockage. as they were trying to clear it, the threat of an approaching column of German armour 'compelled them' to abandon and set fire to the car, and 'beat a hasty and inglorious retreat with eight men all loaded onto one car.' During their retreat, they were chased by German AFVs, but were able to give them the slip as a result of their 'superior knowledge' of the district.[15] Bishop experienced the same

---

9   TNA WO 167/29/2, Appendix 3, 19 May 1940.
10   TNA WO 167/452: Cover letter.
11   TNA WO 167/29/2, 20 May 1940.
12   Shand, *Previous Encounters*, p.52.
13   Bishop, *One Young Soldier*, p.54.
14   Trooper Baker is cited as being wounded. See Bishop, *One Young Soldier*, p.53.
15   Shand, *Previous Encounters*, pp.52-53.

refugee problems as Shand but overcame it by travelling across the 'open plain' and was fortunate not to be attacked by German aircraft.[16]

During the day, Bishop was lucky not to have been killed by elements of the French infantry which he described as one of 'those examples of bovine stupidity that get men killed for no reason':

> When I noticed unusual movement immediately to my rear, it gradually sank in that my troop was being laboriously and painstakingly stalked by French infantry. It was difficult to comprehend. Our guns were all pointing in the opposite direction. They could see us watching them as easily as we could see them, we wore khaki, some of us wore British tin hats and we were making no effort to hide from them. As all our cars carried a Union Jack for recognition purposes and there came a moment when I decided it was time to show one. My gunner and I stood on the top of my car holding the flag spread out. "Anglais!" we yelled. "Nous sommes vos amis!" But neither my French nor my flag had any effect. They came stealthily along the ditch on their bellies, pushing their rifles before them. Had not Colonel Herbert [Lumsden] at that moment driven up to and through them, accompanied by Squadron's French liaison officer [Falaise], I cannot think how things would have turned out. The LO bravely ran down the road, waving his revolver, to meet them. He cursed the advance sections and screamed abuse at them. "Yes," he told me, "they would have shot you dead. Les imbéciles! They had no officer."[17]

It was approximately 1500 hrs when A Squadron reported tanks in the area of Avesnes. Horsburgh-Porter, Falaise, and Erne halted just beyond Hermanville where they took their rifles and climbed to the crest of the hill along the left side of the road to see what was going on beyond it. From the crest, they had a wonderful view of the main road leading from Avesnes to Arras. Horsburgh-Porter was concerned that German tanks may have 'slipped in between the carts' in and amongst the refugees in the distance, something they often did. He sent Arkwright's troop forward to investigate:

> The major sends Sergeant Knight's armoured car ahead to reconnoitre the entrance to Avesnes. We follow it. Suddenly the sound of shots down the road brings us to a halt. A few minutes later Knight's armoured car returns. There is a large hole in the armour plate. They ran smack into a German tank half a mile from here and it opened fire on them before they had a chance to know what was happening. Corporal [Howard] Chambers[18] was killed, and the sergeant wounded in the neck, but the driver, with the greatest skill and calm, managed

---

16   Bishop, *One Young Soldier*, p.54.
17   Bishop, *One Young Soldier*, p.55.
18   Described as cheerful young and efficient. See Bishop, *One Young Soldier*, p.55.

to back his car and turn it around in the narrow road while the sergeant, without wasting a second, swung his guns toward the German tank and let him have it with his Boyes gun. He thinks he stopped it dead. Anyway, it didn't fire again or move. The major is all for going after the tank right away, but just as he reports the incident to the Colonel, we get orders to move back north of the St. Pol road immediately, as the Squadron on our left has reported that they see German tanks coming up the main road back of us heading toward Aubigny.[19]

After A Squadron had withdrawn, they passed through Aubigny without meeting any opposition and when they arrived at the little village of Bethonsart they decided it would be a good opportunity to bury Corporal Chambers:

> Speedily the men dig a grave in a small field 200 yards south of the church under the spreading branches of a large oak tree. This quiet pasture, surrounded by thick green hedges, is reminiscent of an English landscape. It is a fitting resting place for a soldier of Britain. After standing in reverent silence for a few moments, we return to the cars and move off at once, reaching Frevillers at 1800 hrs.[20]

As the Squadron arrived and passed the church, a group of French cavalry motor-cyclists caught up with the Squadron, shouting that they had found one of the Regiment's rear DRs lying on the road badly wounded. A lorry was dispatched to pick him up, but before the lorry arrived a French ambulance arrived and determined that the patient needed to go to the hospital. Knight and the other wounded men also had their wounds dressed but refused to be evacuated. Falaise recorded that:

> With typical British distrust of any foreign diagnosis, they tore up the tags on which the medical officer has so painstakingly written a description of their wounds with a request that they should be x-rayed at once since they are certainly full of steel splinters.[21]

The Squadron transport to the rear heard on the wireless that there were Germans in the village of Beaumetz. Hall asked Lumsden if he should 'try and get through' as he thought that with the 50 men he had with him, four Boyes rifles and four Bren guns would be enough for the task. Hall did not hear the reply from Lumsden, which was taken by his operator Trooper Higgs. The answer was no, and Higgs told Hall, that they were to move to Aix, north of Arras, on the Béthune road. It was only later he heard that he had had a 'tremendous rocket from the Colonel for daring to think

19   Falaise, *Through Hell to Dunkirk*, pp.107-108.
20   Falaise, *Through Hell to Dunkirk*, p.108.
21   Falaise, *Through Hell to Dunkirk*, p.108.

of attacking with unarmoured vehicles, inadequately armed. Hall stated that this resulted from 'an exaggerated idea of the efficiency of the Boyes.'[22]

By 1800 hrs, the Regiment had gradually been driven back by German motorcyclists, infantry, anti-tank guns and tanks, to a line of observation on the road Arras – St. Pol. The refugee traffic continued to be a very serious handicap to all movement on all the roads in this area. One troop which visited St. Pol reported that the town was 'impassable and resembled Tattenham Corner on Derby Day.' It seemed certain that the Germans intended to move via St. Pol to Boulougne.[23]

At Shand's location, they came up with a joint plan to defend the village with two vehicles from SHQ while Shand's and Arkwright's troops took up a position on the high ground to the west of the village overlooking the main road. A Squadron's position had been reinforced with two Panhards from the Cuirassiers. The Squadron stayed in location for what was a quiet evening and at midnight they were ordered to move to Festubert, where they were to feed and refuel.[24] When they arrived at the Echelon, they confirmed to Hall that Chambers had been killed. Hall was already aware of this as he had heard it on the wireless and he wrote in his diary that he had always been 'fond' of Chambers.[25]

That night, Bishop commanded Horsbrugh-Porter's car (so he could sleep) and led the squadron to Festubert 'through the moonlight' with his torch illuminating his map:

> By now we were in a country so far back that we had not been expected to operate there. There were no one-inch maps. Mine was a 1918 quarter-inch, hopelessly out of date. I got there, occasionally having to dismount to shine my torch on a signpost, more by instinct than good map reading, by practice, training, and the feel of the thing.[26]

When they arrived at Festubert there was a hot meal waiting for them. They were all ready for bed. To their dismay, they were ordered back after only two hours' rest to where they had just come from and, by dawn, they were back where they started.[27]

The War Diary recorded that 'during the day, the Regiment had been engaged by the 'German break-through formations which were mostly elements of Panzer Divisions and though casualties now increased it was still due to the excellent handling by the Commanding Officer and Squadron Leaders, no less than to sound troop tactics, that they were not much greater.'[28] The Regiment's reports made it clear that the Germans were already well to the west of Arras and driving hard for Boulogne. As the original

22   Hall Diary, p.6.
23   TNA WO 167/452: 20 May 1940.
24   Falaise, *Through Hell to Dunkirk*, p.109.
25   Hall Diary, 21 May 1940.
26   Bishop, *One Young Soldier*, p.55.
27   A Squadron Frevillers. See Falaise, *Through Hell to Dunkirk*, p.111.
28   TNA WO 167/452: 20 May 1940.

task was now impossible, the Regiment was to be placed under command of Major General Franklyn, 5th Division.[29]

Gort recorded in his *Despatches* that 'later in the day German tanks were reported to be 10 miles west of Arras and all endeavours by 12th Lancers to reach Doullens had failed.' By 1800 hrs, they were back on the line Arras – St Pol.[30]

Tuesday 21st May

(Day Twelve)
A 'bloody and successful little action'.
Stewart[31]

We might as well ride forth… on horseback. At least then there would be a reckless glamour to our adventure.
Falaise[32]

The morning started with the return of A Squadron from its overnight positions to Festubert where they arrived at 0400 hrs. The Squadron had been delayed when Shand had an altercation with a French tank regiment. Its colonel thought Shand was a 'suspicious character' and detained him for two hours.[33] During the return journey, Shand noticed that all the German vehicles had bright orange strips on their radiators. Falaise thought this was so their own planes could recognise them. On the St. Pol road near Bailleul, Horsbrugh-Porter's armoured car was knocked out by a German tank, wounding two of the crew. Falaise recorded that Horsburgh-Porter 'blasted the German tank… killing the three crew.'[34] By the time the squadrons had returned, the Regiment was again placed under the orders of Franklyn who was nominated as the commander of the troops in the Arras area. In accordance with his instructions, the Regiment moved at first light to reconnoitre the area to the north west and west of Arras and, at 0940 hrs, B Squadron reported that there were still tanks and a considerable quantity of German motor transport in Avesnes. While the Squadron was deploying, Hall and his soldiers stood around in the village watching the refugees going past. Some of his men found what they thought was a deserted *estaminet* and started to serve drinks to the refugees as they filed by, only to find the proprietor appearing as they distributed his stock. The soldiers quickly moved away saying "look out! Someone is pinching your beer!"[35]

29   Clark-Kennedy, 'Record of Service', pp.10-11.
30   Gort, *Second Despatch*, p.5916.
31   Stewart, *History of the XII Royal Lancers*, p.360.
32   Falaise, *Through Hell to Dunkirk*, p.113.
33   Shand, *Previous Encounters*, p.54.
34   Falaise, *Through Hell to Dunkirk*, p.111.
35   Hall Diary, 21 May 1940.

At approximately 1012 hrs, C Squadron SHQ was halted on the Arras – St. Pol road about three miles outside Arras and the road was full of refugees on foot and in carts. Captain Willis, Captain Byass and M. Linn, *Agent de Liaison*, were all outside their cars studying the map, as from reports received from the three C Squadron troops in front, the Germans did not appear to have advanced further than Avesnes on the Squadron front. A reconnaissance patrol was sent out from C Squadron to identify these tanks and reported that they were French. The question of recognition of Germans, Allied, and British AFVs was a real problem and one in which the Germans held a distinct advantage, as the *DLM* was mixed up with C Squadron as well as stray units of the Belgian Army.

A column of German 5.9" Howitzers was seen approaching down the Duisans road, but nobody realised that they were German until M. Linn recognised their helmets from about 200 yds distance. The column appeared to be entirely lost and as they came straight onto C Squadron SHQ the armoured cars opened fire on them at nearly point-blank range.

The *Regimental History* describes what happened next as a 'bloody and successful little action,' which resulted in all the guns being destroyed and only a solitary staff car getting away. Shortly after the engagement, Hunn passed through the scene and was 'shocked by the carnage'... He later discovered that the attack was conducted by Willis and Byass in their armoured cars and he attributed the success of their action to 'the aggression they displayed.' The Germans had been engaged 'at nearly point-blank range and never had a chance and were entirely destroyed before they had time to return the fire to any great extent.'[36] It was thought that the Battery was making for Frevent (H1300) but made an error in map reading and moved too far north.[37]

During the afternoon, two troops of B Squadron took several prisoners and killed a number of the Germans as they tried to advance in the open. During the process of rounding up the prisoners, the two troops were engaged by an anti-tank gun which had been moved up unobserved. This resulted in two cars being engaged, one being knocked out, and the other becoming ditched. The War Diary recorded that despite the enemy pressure their 'losses were comparatively slight,' however, attributed them to the fact they had captured prisoners:

> These casualties were in part due to the difficulty of coping with some dozen German prisoners who had been captured in the area. It is undoubtedly very difficult for armoured cars to cope successfully with prisoners, who are a definite encumbrance.[38]

36   Hunn Diary, p.9; Stewart, *History of the XII Royal Lancers*, p.360 and TNA WO 167/452, 21 May 1940.
37   TNA WO 167/452: 21 May 1940.
38   TNA WO 167/452: 21 May 1940.

Two of the casualties were Clark-Kennedy, who had been shot in the stomach, and Lance Corporal Fred Humpherson who was severely wounded. Both were brought in at 1500 hrs but the driver died at the scene and the fourth crew member, Trooper Campion, made his own way back.[39] The detail of this action can be found in the gallantry citations of Clark-Kennedy and Sergeant Pearton.

For the action they had been involved in, Clark-Kennedy was awarded the Military Cross. It stated that 'between 10th and 21st May this officer always showed the greatest daring and skill in handling his troop and thereby obtained much very valuable and accurate information about the Germans strength and movements. On 21st May in the area of Avesnes, by the bold manoeuvring of his troop, he inflicted many casualties on the Germans and captured several prisoners. Later the same day, when his leading car was hit by German anti-tank guns, he silenced the German's fire, and ensured the rescue of the crew.'[40] That said, it was not Clark-Kennedy who silenced the German fire but his troop sergeant.

Clark-Kennedy had been engaged by an anti-tank gun which Pearton subsequently destroyed. Pearton was awarded the Distinguished Conduct Medal and the citation stated 'the armoured car in front of this NCO was stopped by fire and overturned into a ditch in front of his car (Duisans – H4003). He then advanced and although his gunner, [Trooper Henry Westrop] was killed beside him, he silenced the fire of the German machine gun post, killed several of them, rescued two men from the leading car, and brought them back safely to the dead ground behind. Although Sergeant Pearton's car was hit twice by anti-tank gun fire, his brilliant marksmanship when under fire, his determination, and the inspiration which he gave to the remainder of the crew carried this exploit through to a successful conclusion.'[41]

Shortly after Clark-Kennedy's engagement, Corporal Feeney picked up a stray Labrador puppy. After giving it some food and water, he placed it on the floor inside his armoured car behind the driver where it slept. This was to have near-tragic consequences, as no sooner had the dog fallen asleep, than Browne-Clayton heard that there were three enemy tanks down the road and ordered his crew into action. In the absence of Feeney, Hunn acted as the gunner, and as soon as the German tanks were sighted, Hunn engaged with the Boyes rifle, but the shots just bounced off. When the tanks returned fire, Browne-Clayton ordered the armoured car to turn round but as Trooper Stevens was conducting his three-point turn, the terrified dog jumped over his shoulder and hid amongst the foot pedals of the car, making it 'almost impossible to drive.' This incident resulted in Browne-Clayton forbidding pets in the armoured cars.[42]

On their way back, Browne-Clayton and Hunn passed Clark-Kennedy's ditched armoured car, and Hunn was tasked to try and recover the vehicle. When he climbed

39   TNA WO 167/452: 21 May 1940 and Clark-Kennedy 'Record of Service', p.11.
40   TNA WO 167/452: 21 May 1940.
41   TNA WO 167/452: 21 May 1940.
42   Hunn Diary, 21 May 1940, p.10.

inside the turret, Hunn found Humphrey's body still inside. He described the scene inside the armoured car as 'most unpleasant,' and it made him feel 'very, very sick.' However, before Hunn was able to attempt to recover the vehicle, the German tanks which had continued their pursuit of Browne-Clayton started to engage the armoured car. Stevens attracted Hunn's attention by the 'frantic' sounding of the horn and as the armoured car pulled away at speed, Hunn dived into the open door as they 'sped to safety.'[43]

By the evening, the Regiment was on the general line between St. Pol (excluding) – Tincques (H2709) – Scarpe – Arras. RHQ and A Squadron arrived at Mont St. Eloi at 1600 hrs and when Hall caught up with them, he found them on the highest point which was 'crowned with trees.'[44] Fifty tanks, presumably German, were seen from the high ground moving north west on the Arras – St. Pol road until they reached the Aubigny ammunition dump. This was set on fire, whereupon the tanks scattered and halted, about one mile north west of Haute Avesnes.

A Squadron was sheltered in an abandoned farm on a hill to the west of the village, under the 'towering memorial which rose above it.' Horsbrugh-Porter assembled the Squadron and briefed them on what the plan for the Squadron would be if the counter-attack by the Franco-British force was successful. The plan was that the Squadron was to:

> Push forward right through the German-held territory to try and make contact with the French armies 30 miles south, who will be attacking in their direc-tion… of course the Regiment will be in the lead. We shall push forward as far as we can and, though we may be knocked out before we reach the other side, others behind us will carry on the good work and carve their way through.[45]

Knowing the shortfalls of the vehicles, Falaise thought that they 'might as well ride forth… on horseback. At least then there would be a reckless glamour to our adventure.'[46] When Horsbrugh-Porter dismissed the Squadron, they returned to their vehicles and 'silently went about their work: refuelling, greasing, replenishing ammu-nition and cleaning the guns.' Shand thought the role was suspiciously vague and, in fact, 'amounted to a suicide squad.'[47] Bishop agreed with Shand and thought even if they managed to pass the Germans the 'Frogs would let us have it.'[48]

Falaise noticed that Horsbrugh-Porter seemed to have something on his mind. Before the start of the offensive Horsbrugh-Porter was waiting for news of the birth of his child, news he was yet to receive. Now he did not know if he would even live to see it. After a few minutes, he tells Falaise "by God, I will make you the Godfather if we come back." Horsbrugh-Porter concluded their conversation by saying that he did not

43   Hunn Diary, 21 May 1940, p.10.
44   Falaise, *Through Hell to Dunkirk*, p.110 and Hall Diary, 21 May 1940.
45   Falaise, *Through Hell to Dunkirk*, p.113.
46   Falaise, *Through Hell to Dunkirk*, p.113.
47   Shand, *Previous Encounters*, p.53.
48   Bishop, *One Young Soldier*, p.56.

think Falaise should go forward with the Squadron as there was not a place in any of the armoured cars, and the only vehicle available was the staff car 'which would be suicide.'[49]

At 2100 hrs, Horsbrugh-Porter assembled the Squadron and told them that a counter order that 'the 12th Lancers will not operate tonight' had been issued and that the planned operation for the evening had been cancelled due to the failure of the counter-attack in the afternoon.[50] The news came as an anti-climax to the day which left some of the men emotional and disappointed. As night fell the Squadron moved down the hill towards Vimy and Lens to Bully Grenay (H4517) for the night. The B Echelon transport had been heavily bombed in this area immediately before the Regiment's arrival, and there were a number of fifth-columnist activities in the area, which was not surprising given the well-known communist activities of the Polish population in the area.[51]

On arrival at Bully Grenay, A Squadron had to force their way through the locked gates and doors of the farms and houses to find shelter for the men and armoured cars. This was because the houses had been 'abandoned' by their owners who had fled.[52] Eventually, they were billeted in the local doctor's house by his sympathetic wife. The house was modern with a carpeted bathroom in which Bishop 'wallowed in hot water and bath salts and had a shave in luxury.'[53] Eventually, Hall caught up with the Squadron, having been subjected to air attack on two occasions. Each time, his Bren gun jammed. Cruden had also had a puncture which delayed his arrival by 15 minutes. Hall, like Bishop, also took advantage of the doctor's wife's hospitality and the use of her bath.[54]

Wednesday 22nd May

(Day Thirteen)

The 'little plush monkey mascot had fallen from the bonnet and was now a shapeless, torn mess hanging on the mudguard. Behind where it had once 'gayly' sat there was a huge, jagged hole. Falaise did not want to go near the car, nor did he wish to be told 'what caused the dark brown stains inside the turret.'

Falaise[55]

'All day long pressure increased round his right flank, and an observation post of 12th Lancers on Mont St. Eloi could see at one moment as many as 48 German tanks.[56]

Gort[57]

---

49 Falaise, *Through Hell to Dunkirk*, p.114.
50 Bishop, *One Young Soldier*, p.56.
51 TNA WO 167/453: 21 May 1940.
52 Falaise, *Through Hell to Dunkirk*, p.116.
53 Bishop, *One Young Soldier*, p.56.
54 Hall Diary, 21 May 1940.
55 Falaise, *Through Hell to Dunkirk*, p.124.
56 Gort, *Second Despatch*, p.5917.
57 Gort, *Second Despatch*, p.5917.

Falaise was up at dawn. Since there were no orders for the day, he had a shave and some tea. He found a wireless in the house and listened to the news from Paris. He heard that Amiens and Abbyville [sic] had fallen to the Germans, but the situation was in hand, that the Allied forces were taking a severe toll on the Luftwaffe and that important reinforcements were being sent to the front. Falaise wrote 'it would be funny if it were not tragic, and it was like getting news from another world.' The general situation was that the Scarpe river line to the east of Arras was being held by the French, and west of Arras to Mont St. Eloi by the British Infantry. The situation 'was certainly not improving' as there was a gap between the two. Falaise thought the next mission would be to find out how far the Boches were getting.[58]

The Regiment was tasked to reconnoitre the Scarpe from Berles to Arras (not including the town), where they made contact with the 17th Infantry Brigade who subsequently extended their front to (H4204). The squadrons were tasked with trying to keep the Germans south of the river valley whilst the bridges were being prepared for demolition by Smith and his detachment of Royal Engineers. The situation to the Regiment's right was obscure, but it seemed certain that the Germans would continue their outflanking movement. A Squadron was therefore ordered to extend the area of the Regiment's reconnaissance out as far as Houdain (H3219).[59]

At 0800 hrs, A Squadron left for Neuville, two miles south west of Vimy where they found B Squadron waiting for orders. A Squadron was sent off to reconnoitre the heights to the north west of Villers au Bois on the Houdain – Arras road. In the valley beneath, a strong German force was attempting to push northwards across the Scarpe between Acq, Capelle-Fermont and Villers-Chatel in an attempt to turn the positions at Vimy and Lorette from the west. When SHQ A Squadron reached Villers au Bois, they compared the British and French maps, and the small track that should have led to Camblain was not on Falaise's map. However, they proceeded down the track which worried Falaise. The order of march was Horsbrugh-Porter, the staff car with Falaise in it, Erne's armoured car, the fighting lorry, Knight's armoured car and three DRs.[60] Bishop wrote that 'there was not less than 50 yards between vehicles, in single file… with another troop being well-ahead.'[61] Eventually, the track petered out and they found themselves in open fields with no trees for shelter.[62]

Just as they tried to work out where they were, the SHQ was attacked by three Messerschmitt fighters 'hedge-hopping at about 100 feet.' These were immediately followed by three more. The staff car, and the lorry made for the cover of two large haystacks, while the armoured cars and the DRs made their way across the field south

58   Falaise, *Through Hell to Dunkirk*, p.117.
59   TNA WO 167/452: 22 May 1940.
60   Bishop states that this armoured car was in third in line behind Erne's. See Bishop, *One Young Soldier*, p.56.
61   Presumably Arkwright, Bishop, *One Young Soldier*, p.57.
62   Falaise, *Through Hell to Dunkirk*, p.118.

to the cover of a hazel wood approximately 300 yards away.[63] In the process two of the DRs were shot off their motorcycles, as the armoured cars reached the trees, they engaged the Messerschmitts with their Bren guns. During the attack, Bishop took cover in shell holes dating from 1914-18 where he grovelled and 'prayed like never before.'[64]

The SHQ was under air attack for 10 minutes until the aircraft wheeled left and disappeared. Falaise found the two DRs who fortunately had only been wounded and sent them back to the Regimental HQ near Mont St. Eloi.[65] After the attack, Falaise's 'knees felt like rubber' as he anxiously tried to find his map to navigate his way out of the *cul-de-sac*. Falaise was now alone with a staff car and a lorry which were not designed for cross-country driving. The slightest map-reading error would lead them into the German lines. Having considered his options, Falaise decided to try and follow the armoured car tracks and catch them up.[66]

Eventually, Falaise caught up with the two armoured cars to discover that one of them had been knocked out by the armour-piercing rounds from the aircraft. Sergeant 'Doc' Johnson had been killed and Horsbrugh-Porter had been slightly wounded in his left hand when firing the Bren gun.[67] Johnson had been Bishop's wireless operator for the day and he described him as 'intelligent, unflappable, and a pipe-smoking young Englishman.' When they found him, he was still in the armoured car 'leaning against the set as if asleep; a cannon-shell had blown a hole you could put your fist through directly above him.' Roddick's armoured car had been put out of action and Trooper Jarret was wounded in the leg.[68] Falaise was also informed by Erne that Arkwright's troop had also had a 'sharp encounter and he had been severely wounded.' This brought the Squadron's total of wounded that morning to eight. While Johnson's body was being removed from Bishop's car, Horsbrugh-Porter went off to reconnoitre Acq. When he returned, the equipment was transferred from the damaged armoured car which was subsequently blown up.[69]

After the attack, Shand and Bishop were sent to the west of Vimy to hold the high ground as the French infantry were starting to pull out.[70] The surviving two armoured cars from SHQ and the remaining vehicles made their way to a position where they could see the valley below. In the distance, they could see the flashes of anti-tank gun fire as the Germans tried to cross the Scarpe at Acq a mile away. They also observed German troops advancing up towards their position on two small roads. After a while,

63   Bishop, *One Young Soldier*, p.57.
64   Bishop, *One Young Soldier*, p.57.
65   It is presumed this was the Regimental Aid Post.
66   Falaise, *Through Hell to Dunkirk*, pp.119-120.
67   Hunn Diary, 21 May 1940, p.10.
68   Bishop, *One Young Soldier*, p.57. Shand notes that Johnson was killed alongside Horsbrugh-Porter. See Shand, *Previous Encounter*, p.53.
69   Falaise, *Through Hell to Dunkirk*, p.120.
70   Bishop, *One Young Soldier*, p.57.

they moved north west to a chateau at La Haie, (which had been selected off the map) which was halfway between Gouy and Villers au Bois. Bishop noted that fortunately for all that Colonel Herbert had a 'truly accurate picture' of the situation.[71]

Just as A Squadron SHQ was leaving the chateau to move to Villers au Bois, two soldiers, Troopers Burns and Nutting, were seen running across a field waving and shouting.[72] They were from Arkwright's troop. They told them that their car had been knocked out and the third member of the crew was killed.[73] This meant that A Squadron had lost another armoured car, but this time with all its equipment. The two men were put in the lorry and the convoy made its way to Carency via Villers au Bois. It was there that they heard the full story of Arkwright's troop engagement when they had met some concealed German tanks.

Arkwright was severely wounded when trying to extricate the crew of his leading car. It had been knocked out and he was anxious to prevent the crew from being captured. Lance Corporal Chorley, the driver of his car and the only unwounded member of the crew, passed a wireless message to say what had happened. He then drove alone to a Casualty Collecting Station at Béthune. Trooper Bishop, the wireless operator, although wounded in the face kept his set in action sufficiently long for Chorley to be able to pass the message. Chorley picked up a fresh crew upon his return to the Regiment and the car was back in action within three hours.[74]

Shand described the death of Arkwright as a 'tragic loss to everyone. He was only 20 and a most charming person.'[75] That evening, the two damaged armoured cars arrived showing the scars of the day. Falaise saw Arkwright's armoured car and the first thing he noticed was that the 'little plush monkey mascot had fallen from the bonnet and was now a shapeless, torn mess hanging on the mudguard. Behind where it had once gayly sat there was a huge, jagged hole.' Falaise did not want to go near the car, nor did he wish to be told 'what caused the dark brown stains inside the turret' which he could see from where he stood.[76] Hall had also heard about the wounding of Arkwright and the deaths of Johnson, Hudson, and Smith. Hall wrote that Sergeants Sewell and Thorpe were tasked to clean 'up the car, which wasn't too pleasant,' and 'was relieved' as he had said he 'would do it if there were no volunteers.'[77] For his actions Chorley was awarded the Military Medal. The citation read:

71   Bishop, *One Young Soldier*, p.57.
72   Bishop, *One Young Soldier*, p.57.
73   There is a distinct lack of clarity, regarding this event. Arkwright recorded the crew surnames as follows: Chorley, Nutting, Burns and Bishop. This amounts to more than a single crew.
74   Falaise, *Through Hell to Dunkirk*, pp.117-122.
75   Shand, *Previous Encounters*, p.53.
76   Falaise, *Through Hell to Dunkirk*, p.124.
77   Hall Diary, 22 May 1940.

In the area of Houdain on 22nd May, three other members of the car were wounded; he extricated his car with great coolness and fine judgement and drove to a dressing station which he found unaided. Through his skill and presence of mind, he saved his car and probably the lives of his car commander and wireless operator [Trooper Bishop], who were both very seriously wounded.[78]

Despite the efforts of the Regiment, the Germans pressed on with their attack with infantry supported by tanks before the demolitions could be completed. RHQ had a very good Observation Post on Mont St. Eloi from which point at one time 48 German tanks could be counted operating across the front of the Regiment, and infantry was seen debussing in three different places. Mann was bombed and shelled on the top of Mont St. Eloi, so moved down the reverse slope, leaving a telephone line to the OP on top which was manned by Butler (see Map 13). RSM Fox was sent forward to deal with the German lorries and infantry which were seen in the valley below. Butler passed directions by telephone to Lumsden who transmitted them by wireless to Fox. The latter was thus able to destroy the German lorries with his Boyes rifle and inflicted at least 30 casualties. Whilst he was inspecting a Humber staff car which the Germans had captured and were using, to see if he could find any papers or maps, he was compelled to shoot with his revolver one of the occupants who had returned. When it was seen that the Germans were stalking first from the right and then from the left, Fox was ordered to withdraw. He did so in good order, under the covering fire of Sergeant Booker, the Orderly Room Sergeant, who was his gunner. The key to Fox's success was subsequently recorded in his obituary:

> He became a proficient horseman and won the Young Soldiers' Cup for skill with the sword, lance, and revolver. But the rifle was his real weapon. For years he coached and shot with the rifle team. Which explains his dashing solo action in his armoured car near Mount St Eloi, where he was able to destroy German lorries by fire from his Boyes rifle and inflicted at least 30 casualties on the German infantry.[79]

Notwithstanding Fox's personal skill with the Boyes rifle, the key to the success of the day was the maintenance of communications and as such Sergeant John Thurston's action in maintaining communications between Lumsden and Fox was rewarded with a Military Medal. The citation included his previous 'devotion to duty and untiring work' but included the actions at Mont St. Eloi, stating that through 'his personal disregard of bombing and his quick and skilful passing of messages, it was possible to cause the destruction of seven German lorries carrying infantry into action against us.'[80]

78   TNA WO 167/452: 22 May 1940.
79   *The Delhi Spearman* (1982), p.78 and TNA WO 167/452: 22 May 1940.
80   TNA WO 167/452: 22 May 1940.

As the day progressed, the Germans gradually advanced. The tanks had driven the Regiment's armoured cars into the enclosed country of the river valley and the infantry and anti-tank guns gradually advanced, stalking the cars as they went. The Regiment was eventually forced to withdraw to the general line Bouvigny – Souchez, staying in touch with the *DLM* on their left.

During the evening, two columns of Germans were seen and reported moving north east from Fresnicourt (H3515) – Verdrel (H3615) and from Houdain towards Hallicourt. They halted on the high ground for the night. The Regiment remained in observation until dark. A report that one or two German tanks had reconnoitred Béthune was confirmed by A Squadron. A German plane was shot down by Bren gun fire by Brinton's Troop, C Squadron, and the crew of two taken prisoner. After dark, the Regiment withdrew to Festubert to feed and refill.[81]

When Falaise reached Festubert, it was already full of French troops and the Regiment's Echelon. Hall told him that he had a hard time trying to find anywhere for the Squadron and had to settle for four small, isolated houses approximately a quarter of a mile to the north outside the village. Falaise found eight medium French tanks in the village centre, by the church, also looking for billets. The last time they spoke, Falaise had told Hall 'that it would only be a matter of time before surrender, as they were cutting them off in the north.'[82] Therefore, Hall made the journey to Festubert 'at speed,' and he felt relieved when he crossed the canal bridge at La Bassée. Hall wrote that he thought Falaise appeared to be 'very defeatist.'[83] While Falaise was trying to resolve the billeting issue, more than 20 German Heinkels bombed the village and Falaise and Machin sought cover in a half-filled ditch of dirty water, where they spent 10 minutes wondering if they would ever let them 'relax a bit.' An hour later SHQ arrived and it was nearly dark before the rest of the Squadron finally joined them.

On their arrival, Erne told Falaise that they had had 'some exciting moments' since he left. Erne recounted Horsbrugh-Porter's earlier encounter with a German light tank. This was a result of him being his usual 'rash' self where he went on, alone, down a sunken country road to see what 'was going on beyond the next hill.' The tank that he nearly encountered could not be seen from his position but could be seen from Erne's. Erne tried to draw attention to Horsbrugh-Porter by firing at the out-of-range German tank. As both Horsbrugh-Porter and the German tank adjusted their positions around a farmhouse, Horsbrugh-Porter saw the tank and thought it was 'friendly,' so dismounted from his armoured car and waved his Union Jack. Erne continued to engage the German tank, eventually, Horsbrugh-Porter realised something was wrong, and the German tank 'turned tail' and drove away in a cloud of dust over the ridge to safety.[84] As Falaise tried to sleep, he reflected on the last 24 hours:

81   TNA WO 167/452: 22 May 1940.
82   Hall Diary, 22 May 1940.
83   Hall Diary, 22 May 1940.
84   Falaise, *Through Hell to Dunkirk*, pp.123-124.

After a hasty meal, we all lie down exhausted on the tiled floor in the main room of the café where we are billeted. Through the broken shutters, the glare which illuminates the sky to the west paints the ceiling above me ruddily and reminds me, as I lie sleepless and tossing, that six miles away Béthune is in flames and that somewhere among this mass of raging fire and crumbling ruins there is a hospital where my friend Peter lies dying. Last night he and I shared the same mattress, and this morning as we started off, he gave me his final tin of pipe tobacco, saying that he wouldn't need it any more. A tremendous explosion rocks the earth coming from the direction of La Bassée. The last bridge over the Aire Canal has been blown up.[85]

Hall waited for all the Squadron to arrive. He prided himself in always waiting to ensure everything was done, even if it meant that he had less sleep than most. On this occasion, he was so exhausted that he 'cracked up' and fell asleep while waiting for dinner. He later wrote that 'pride had come before the fall.'[86]

Thursday 23rd May

(Day Fourteen)
It was to be our most unlucky day of the war.
Shand[87]

On 23rd May, at last light, A Squadron had been recalled once more to Festubert. The Regiment was given the same role of watching the right flank of the troops engaged in the battle for Arras and was still under command of FRANKFORCE (GOC 5th Division). The original orders were that LUMSDENFORCE would 'carry out recces under separate instructions (given verbally) in the area west of the road Arras (inclusive) to Béthune and as far south as the Arras to St. Pol road. Tasks, in particular, were to report the presence and movement of German AFVs.'[88] The Germans had been kept under observation from first light, but this was the final phase of the confused and desperate fight for Arras.[89]

In addition to fulfilling his FRANKFORCE task, Lumsden had a 'hunch' that the advancing German forces were swinging in from the west and therefore decided to send the five remaining armoured cars of A Squadron off on a long-distance reconnaissance (40+ kms) patrol towards St. Omer and Hazebrouck (GHQ's location).[90]

---

85   Falaise, *Through Hell to Dunkirk*, pp.124-125.
86   Hall Diary, 22 May 1940.
87   Shand, *Previous Engagements*, p.54.
88   See TNA WO 167/452: FRANKFORCE Operation Order No.1, 21 May 1940.
89   Stewart, *History of the XII Royal Lancers*, p.362.
90   Note Shand states 'three troops of two cars' in Shand, *Previous Engagements*, p.54.

Given the extreme distance, Horsbrugh-Porter took the Squadron's 8-cwt wireless truck with him to act as his rear-link.[91]

At 0300 hrs, Falaise heard the noise of the idling motors of the armoured cars as they were driven out of the sheds in the darkness and Shand recalled that:[92]

> The Squadron… was detailed on this day to go to the west of St. Omer… There had been a report that German tanks were over the big canal there, but this was very vague indeed. However, we set off, and I can remember this very well because our journey took us to the rear of GHQ and some other sacrosanct areas where the war didn't seem to have arrived at all. For one thing, there was no German air activity there, you could see men washing their vehicles and polishing themselves up, all very impressive. In Hazebrouck, which is just east of St. Omer, I was stopped by Military Police and asked what was I doing, I suppose one did look a little dirty; it was a bit difficult to convince then that one was on a respectable military mission. It happened again only a mile or two out of Hazebrouck.[93]

When Falaise arrived at his location he described the countryside as 'probably the least suited in all France in which to fight':

> I can see how easy it must be for the Germans to advance through the densely inhabited, but undefendable villages and suburbs of this mining district. Huge slag heaps, over 300 feet high, provide the Germans and their parachutists with ready-made OPs from which they can command these flat lowlands and its net of highways.[94]

While the Squadron was deploying, Bishop had been given a separate task and was sent with his troop at 0345 hrs to Béthune. His task was 'to find out if reports that the Germans had occupied the place were true.'[95] When Bishop arrived, he:

> Found it bombed to smithereens. Rubble, corpses, dead horses still in the shafts of overturned carts, ankle-deep broken glass everywhere, but no Germans. Six streets converged onto a sort of island signpost in the town centre. I was told to stay there covering these streets. It was a vile place in which to start a day and I was not disappointed when orders, at last, came through that I was to rejoin the rest of the Squadron already on its way to St. Omer… On reaching Ellinghem [Ebblinghem], en route for St. Omer, other British troops assured us that "Jerry

91 Hall Diary, 23 May 1940, p.9.
92 Falaise, *Through Hell to Dunkirk*, p.127.
93 Shand, Exercise ACROSPIRE, p.74.
94 Falaise, *Through Hell to Dunkirk*, p.129.
95 Bishop, *One Young Soldier*, p.58.

was in the very next village." But he was not. Instead, we only found an isolated anti-aircraft battery that, not surprisingly, seemed extremely pleased to see us for a big ugly brute of a German tank was breezing confidently along a parallel road. I noticed that it had a Nazi Rag draped across it as aircraft recognition, scarlet, and white in contrast to the bits of foliage that decorated our own vehicles in a touching attempt to camouflage them.[96]

The rest of the Squadron had used the Hazebrouck – St. Omer road as their main axis, 'spreading out' after Hazebrouck towards St. Omer. By 1200 hrs, the Squadron was in a very exposed and dangerous position as the BEF was now not only being outflanked from the east and south but now the west as well. Falaise thought this situation had 'exhilarated' Horsbrugh-Porter who was 'patrolling fearlessly' in his armoured car and taking delight in personally reconnoitring the most 'hazardous spots.'[97] Shand wrote that when they reached Renescure they encountered various German forces that were stationary, but it was obvious they were on their way eastwards (see Map 14). However, they were completely unaware that the German infantry had filtered through the wooded country on either side of the road and would later engage the Squadron from the flanks with 'calamitous results.'[98]

During the afternoon, Horsbrugh-Porter reported that there were only a few Royal Engineers and artillery batteries in the area. He said that the Germans had been able to cross the river in the area of Renescure (H1950).[99] The guns were from 392nd Battery of the 98th Field Regiment Royal Artillery which had been sent up the night before and they had placed single guns covering the bridges at St. Momelin, St. Omer, Arques, Renescure, Wardrecques, Blaringhem and Wittes.[100]

On rejoining the Squadron, Bishop joined Shand on patrol when he noticed a 'big black tank' came 'swanning along with an enviable lack of caution,' to join another tank that had already stopped. Bishop observed:

> They were perhaps 400 yards away. I was willing them not to see us when Bruce started rat-tatting with his Bren, pouring tracer bullets into a wood occupied by German infantry on a bank the other side of the road from the tanks. The second tank traversed its gun, so I loosed off at it with the Boyes rifle and hit it on the side of the turret. For all the effect it had I might have been a little girl trying to hurt a heavyweight boxer. It can only be by the grace of God that it did not retaliate. Perhaps its crew had not even noticed. I hit it a second time, and then suddenly rain began to come down as if someone had pulled a chain. Andrew [Horsbrugh-Porter] told Bruce [Shand] to observe the tanks and, perhaps luckily

96   Bishop, *One Young Soldier*, pp.58-59.
97   Falaise, *Through Hell to Dunkirk*, pp.127-128.
98   Shand, *Previous Engagements*, pp.54-55.
99   TNA WO 167/452: 23 May 1940.
100 Ellis, *The War in France, and Flanders*, pp.129-130.

for him, also gave him a separate task. He then led the remainder of us up a side road, passing a British gun which had just been knocked out, its crew lying dead beside it.[101]

Horsburgh-Porter asked Lumsden if he could counter-attack the Germans on the high ground to the north and north west to enable the Royal Engineers to withdraw from Renescure and to enable the battery to be recovered. The reason for asking for Lumsden's permission was that the previous direction given was 'never to get involved.'[102] However, Bishop saw the action as being a little more spontaneous:

Our Squadron Leader acted swiftly and saved us from total destruction. He unhesitatingly swung off the track through a ploughed field yet to be sown. The track was not marked on the map and was as likely as not to be a dead end. The main lot of German infantry was lining the headland, in this case a shallow bank some 50 yards to our right. Bullets filled the air and I guessed most of them were ours for the Germans would scarcely have had time to collect themselves. A line of armoured cars coming round the corner must have been just as unpleasant for them as suddenly bumping into them had been for us. The ruts grew deeper and muddier and the 15-cwt truck, which had somehow got itself between Andrew and me, stuck in front of me. To stick was to stop. Trooper Pearce, a Reservist, was my driver that day and I shouted to him to "keep going." He could only do this by passing the bogged truck – and he did it. Unflustered by my yells and with admirable presence of mind, he swung the car out into the furrows and skidding and yawing, managed to regain the track successfully. It was a very good, cool piece of driving and the men off the truck scrambled aboard my slowly moving car as if they were catching a bus in the rush-hour. I then saw that the DRs, Owens, and Cotton, had also stuck, coming to grief in the ruts on their motorcycles. "Keep going!" I shouted, "to stop now was to stop forever." Then SSM Tree who was in my car, sank cursing to the floor, hit in the back of the neck. Somehow, he continued to hand me up fresh magazines of ammunition for the Bren, which I was holding like a hose over the turret, off its mounting, to be able to change direction more quickly. I was firing from the armpit, tracers making aim unnecessary. Andrew was also standing upright in his turret in the car ahead, probably doing the same. The Germans quickly recovered from their surprise, and we now came under a heavy crossfire from small arms. No car got through without casualties.[103]

---

101 Bishop, *One Young Soldier*, p.59. The Renescure gun was destroyed by mortar fire and the gun and crew at Wittes were captured. If Bishop's two tank accounts are linked, then Shand's MC action was in the area of Ebblinghem.
102 Shand, Exercise ACROSPIRE, p.75.
103 Bishop, *One Young Soldier*, pp.59-60.

As a result of the mud, the 15-cwt truck and two motorcycles had to be abandoned and Bishop's armoured car ended the course with 10 men in and on it. SSM Tree had been wounded with a nasty flesh wound which had scored a 'groove through the back of his neck.' The only other damage was a bullet hole in Bishop's spare petrol tank, otherwise the car and the occupants went unscathed.[104] This was not the case for Horsbrugh-Porter's armoured car. During the counter-attack, Erne, who was with Horsbrugh-Porter, was so severely wounded by anti-tank gun fire from the rear that he died of his wounds. The same afternoon, in a separate action, Roddick was also unfortunately killed when his troop ran into German tanks in the vicinity of Lynde.[105]

The separate task that Horsbrugh-Porter had given to Shand was to extract the Royal Engineers from their billets. By the time Shand had found them in an isolated chateau, the major in command was somewhat 'agitated.' Shand described the action in his typically understated way as 'a nerve-wracking operation under the eyes of German tanks':

> We extricated them all quickly, under the noses of four German tanks who failed to see us. I gave the Sappers a few minutes' grace in which to get away and then followed. As luck would have it, we were seen by the German infantry in the woods who opened up with everything they had, including anti-tank guns. We tore down the road out of Renescure, brilliantly covered by Sergeant Lewis, now commanding a troop, and reached safety without being badly hit.[106]

Subsequently, it was believed that the Germans had been able to move at least four tanks to the east of the canal and it was only through the intrepid actions and good fire of Shand's troop that these tanks were discouraged from advancing eastwards at a most inconvenient time. Falaise wrote that Shand 'by his clever and incessant manoeuvring' succeeded 'in drawing away the tanks.[107] Four tanks had also been reported by the Royal Engineers who thought that they were the same ones reported by the Regiment.[108] It would appear sequentially that Roddick's death took place before Shand's secondary task. Lewis as the troop sergeant had then taken command of the troop and joined Shand.

By the end of the afternoon, there was only one car in SHQ to act both as forward and rear-link. When Horsbrugh-Porter returned from his counter-attack, in which Falaise had not been involved, he noticed Erne's 'mangled crumpled body in the bottom of the turret' and a large hole right through his own armoured car.[109] The

---

104 Stewart, *History of the XII Royal Lancers*, p.362; Bishop, *One Young Soldier*, p.62.
105 Letter The Royal Lancers Museum Derby.
106 Shand 'May 1940: A Memory', p.154 and Shand, *Previous Engagements*, p.55. The latter described Lewis as 'a tower of strength.' See Shand, *Previous Engagements*, p.36.
107 Falaise, *Through Hell to Dunkirk*, p.128.
108 TNA WO 167/29/6: Report of Major Walkey RE, 23 May 1940.
109 Falaise, *Through Hell to Dunkirk*, p.128.

information that the Squadron had gained at such 'grievous expense' was of great use, as GHQ were unaware that the Germans were in the area of Renescure. The War Diary records that 'the Regiment received the very warm thanks of Major General Franklyn for the information which they had given him during the battle for Arras which he said had been invaluable as air reports had been singularly lacking.'[110] Their task complete, Bishop observed:

> Together we ran to Linde [Lynde] where the rest of the Squadron was now halted. Nearing Linde, the DRs and I were surprised to encounter a rocklike sergeant-major of Artillery, standing quite alone in the pouring rain, proud and smart in a khaki greatcoat, webbing equipment, gas mask, and tin hat. Being young, rather out of breath and more than fairly frightened, I enquired, probably as if he was very old and stone-deaf, if he realised that the Germans were in the next field. His admirable reply: "Thank you, sir, I heard the firing"... If the knocked-out gun we had passed early on was the right flank of this sergeant major's battery position, then his guns would indeed have been captured but for 'A' Squadron, 12th Lancers.

Whilst all the squadrons were engaged with the Germans, RHQ at Hulluch was engaged by one or two rifle shots fired by a fifth-columnist at the HQ. The gunman was captured by the RSM who handed him over to the local *Gendarme* who saw to his execution. The Regiment recorded that 'the French infantry who had been in the same area as the Regiment withdrew in the face of the German advance and were never seen to come to blows with him, or make any serious attempt to hold on to their successive positions.'[111] However, Clark-Kennedy was later keen to point out that this criticism did not apply to the *DLMs* who had fought with 'great gallantry throughout the campaign.'[112]

During the afternoon, the Regiment gradually withdrew eastwards to the line of canals from La Basse to La Heute Deult [Deule], with RHQ located at Meurchin (H5723). It was here that Smith rejoined the Regiment having been tasked at 1500 hrs by Lumsden to reconnoitre and prepare the remaining three bridges for demolition. He found that one had already been destroyed and the other two had been prepared. One of the remaining bridges to be used for the Allied withdrawal was guarded by British infantry, although it had been prepared by the French. The French corporal who was in charge of the demolition was found to be 'extremely drunk.' The French NCO told Smith he had tried to blow the bridge but nothing had happened. Smith and his team identified the problem and blew up the bridge, after assisting the infantry to lay anti-tank mines on the approach to the crossing which they were still

110 TNA WO 167/452: 23 May 1940.
111 TNA WO 167/452: 23 May 1940.
112 Clark-Kennedy, 'Record of Service', p.12.

going to stay and guard. Smith could not understand the mentality of a person who entrusted the destruction of an important river crossing to one individual who was not even a French Engineer. This and other incidents, in which the Allies withdrew in front of the Germans, and never seemed to get to grips with them, made Smith wonder if the 'Allies were really trying.'[113]

Later that evening RHQ, the Royal Engineer detachment and the B Echelon moved to the area of Carnin – Allenes while the Regiment moved to Fleurbaix.[114] Once Smith had completed his task, he returned to RHQ to find the new location had been thoughtfully located in a wine merchant's house, and it did not take long to discover 'he had a very good line in champagne and brandy.'[115]

For their actions both Horsbrugh-Porter and Shand were recognised for their gallantry. Horsbrugh-Porter was awarded the Distinguished Service Order. The citation stated that 'in spite of being wounded, he continued in command when his services were indispensable, clarified the situation, and in face of a superior force of German tanks and infantry with anti-tank guns, checked the Germans advance, and enabled our guns and troops to get clear, finally extricating the last of his Squadron with great skill. Had it not been for this bold and decisive action the Germans would have captured our guns and had a clear road to Hazebrouck.' Shand's MC citation included his action at Renescure and specifically his action with Bishop and the German tanks 'in the area of St. Omer on May 23, by the fearless manoeuvring of his troop, he was able to cover the withdrawal of a column of our lorries and guns in the face of fire from four German tanks which, without his intrepid intervention, would have been free to do great damage to our troops,' but all this had come at considerable cost.[116]

Falaise did not find out about Roddick's death until he returned to the Squadron that evening. He said he could tell there had been another tragedy by their faces. Horsbrugh-Porter 'gripped his arm tensely and moved him away from the other armoured cars in the courtyard':

> He tells me that brave young Andrew had been killed that afternoon… It is only later on that I find out through the others how gallantly he went to his death while attacking a greatly superior force of German tanks. Poor boy! This put the Squadron's score at three officers killed and four men wounded in less than 24 hours. We are all so depressed that we can't even speak to each other, and our supper is left untouched.[117]

---

113 TNA WO 167/778: 23 May 1940.
114 TNA WO 167/778: 23 May 1940; Clark-Kennedy, 'Record of Service', p.12.
115 TNA WO 167/778: 23 May 1940.
116 See TNA WO 167/452.
117 Falaise, *Through Hell to Dunkirk*, p.130.

That evening Hall, who shared Horsbrugh-Porter's room, wrote that 'Andrew was terribly upset that night.'[118] Later, his troop sergeant (Lewis) wrote to Roddick's parents saying, 'that he was held in great esteem by all of us, they had confidence in the decisions he made, that he led them well and was responsible for several successful actions against the Germans.'[119] Shand thought him like his uncle [Lumsden], 'a man of humour, humanity, and a permanent twinkle in his eye' recollected that:

> We were a sad and depleted Squadron when we rejoined the rest of the Regiment that night near Lille. Bishop and I were the only remaining troop leaders, each with two cars. Horsbrugh-Porter had received another flesh wound during his counter-attack, but was gallantly carrying on, and… Falaise was acting as Second-in-Command, talking on the rear-link back to RHQ, and generally trying to keep our spirits up. The only consolation was that our information had been of real use in establishing the truth of the encirclement of the BEF. We had one day of rest here and I think it was then that we first heard something of the intended evacuation.[120]

Bishop recorded in his diary that evening:

> I had never sat down to a grimmer little supper, with just a wounded Squadron Leader and Bruce, with John and Andrew being killed that day.[121] The last time Bishop had seen Roddick was earlier in the day when it was raining and he brought his car up beside mine onto the grass verge. The rain was running in rivulets off his helmet. It was bucketing down. "What the hell's happening, Tim?" he called. "God knows" was my unhelpful, but I suppose truthful reply.[122]

The armoured car situation for the Regiment was now becoming critical, and Butler (the Technical Adjutant) went to Arras to collect the only two spare Morris armoured cars in France. This, however, was not enough to bring the Regiment back to full strength. A Squadron had five cars, B and C Squadron had six remaining, giving the Regiment a total of 17 from the 36 the squadrons had deployed with.[123] Falaise observed:

> The Germans have also dropped leaflets in French and in English asking us to surrender and showing a map of northern France which outlines their front up

118 Hall Diary, 23 May 1940, p.9.
119 Letter The Royal Lancers Museum Derby.
120 Shand, *Previous Engagements*, p.36 and Shand, 'A Memory: May 1940', p.153.
121 Bishop, *One Young Soldier*, p.61. Erne is buried in Wormhoudt Communal Cemetery, Row F. Grave 13. Roddick, buried in Lynde Churchyard, France
122 Bishop, *One Young Soldier*, p.59.
123 Clark-Kennedy, 'Record of Service', p.12.

to the sea, attempting to prove to us that we are completely surrounded. Some of our men who have picked up these messages laugh at them. They don't understand and refuse to believe that we are cut-off from the rest of France. To them, it is propaganda which is just as well.[124]

Shand recorded it as their most 'unlucky day of the war.'[125]

Friday 24th May

(Day Fifteen)
Halt Order (Halt Befehl) from Hitler

This quiet interlude perplexes some of us and even causes rumours that there has been sort of an armistice. Personally, I wonder if it is not rather the lull before the storm.
Falaise[126]

A Squadron was woken at 0200 hrs and ordered 'to pack up and get ready to move forward to Lens and Vimy.' However, the order to move never came, as the situation had deteriorated so much. Falaise thought that there was probably nothing that they could do to help.[127]

At 0300 hrs, the Squadron was ordered northwards to the village of Bois Grenier, four miles south of Armentieres. The journey took two hours and, when they arrived, they found the village full of Belgian refugees. Previously, when the Squadron had its full complement of armoured cars, finding billets for a full Squadron would have been an issue. However, with the now much-reduced Squadron the task was quickly done. It only took two farmhouses to accommodate the troops and a small villa was found for the officers.[128] The rest of the Regiment was in the area of Fleurbaix (H5339).[129]

The day was remarkably quiet. There was no 'rumbling of guns' and the sky was filled with singing birds instead of German bombers. Some were perplexed by the quietness and there were even rumours that there had been sort of an armistice. Falaise thought it was 'the lull before the storm.'[130] The Regiment used the day as a maintenance day. It was the first full day it had had since the beginning of the hostilities. The armoured cars were serviced, the weapons cleaned and all the crews were able to take a well-deserved rest.

---

124 Falaise, *Through Hell to Dunkirk*, pp.129-130.
125 Shand, *Previous Engagements*, p.54.
126 Falaise, *Through Hell to Dunkirk*, p.133.
127 Falaise, *Through Hell to Dunkirk*, p.133.
128 Falaise, *Through Hell to Dunkirk*, p.133.
129 TNA WO 167/452: 24 May 1940. This is the shortest diary entry from that period.
130 Falaise, *Through Hell to Dunkirk*, p.133.

During the day, 19-year-old Trooper Laurence Gillam from the B Echelon was sent out in his lorry with a small party of men to bury one of their casualties in the cemetery at Armentieres. When they arrived, they had to break open the gates in the dark and dig the grave themselves. While they were digging an attractive French girl flung herself across the body, weeping and waving a photograph. Gillam could only assume that the dead man made her think of someone she knew. When they returned, the Regiment had been scattered and they pulled off the main road into a wood. As they did so, Gillam stumbled over a trip wire connected to a shotgun set for poachers and was hit by 70 or 80 pellets. They were 'up his nose, in his ears and all round his backside.' His friends picked them out in the kitchen of a French house, laughing far more than Gillam, who could not sit down for a long time. He considered himself wounded more times than any man in the army.[131]

Shortly before dinner, the Squadron gathered in a neighbouring manure-littered courtyard and listened to a small portable wireless (a gift from Lord Nuffield to the troops) which had been set up on the rear of a lorry so they could listen to the King deliver his Empire Day message:

> The men stand at attention while the weak batteries of the damaged set sputter forth "God Save the King," and they hear with grave attention and respect the voice of their ruler, which is barely audible. Then I notice their chests out thrust and their eyes gleam with pride as these last words of their sovereign's speech reach their ear… "Let us go forward to that task as one man, a smile on our lips, and our heads held high. And with God's help, we shall not fail." An inspiring sight, this small group of battle-worn men standing in a rural courtyard at the drawing in of the day, so far from their homeland, and yet suddenly taken there in spirit for a fleeting moment by the magic of a battered wireless haltingly transmitting to them the voice of their King.[132]

Falaise said that he felt as if he had 'intruded' on a family gathering and that it would be becoming to tiptoe away and leave the Englishmen together.[133]

Smith and his Royal Engineers rejoined the Regiment at Fleurbaix and requisitioned a carpenter's shop for garage and a billet:

> While the drivers were attending to vehicles Johnson went into the yard at the back and by alternate spasms of coaxing and cursing managed to get some of the carpenter's fowls into a shed. The encounter in the shed was short but very sharp and the final issue was never in doubt. Roach prepared the potatoes and Clout provided leeks for the second veg. Johnson was unanimously elected cook and

131 J. Harris, *Dunkirk: The Storms of War* (1980), pp.41-42. It is unclear who the fatality was.
132 Falaise, *Through Hell to Dunkirk*, p.134.
133 Falaise, *Through Hell to Dunkirk*, pp.133-134.

while the meal was cooking each member of the detachment had his hair cut by Hourigan who in turn had his cut by Roach. By the time the hair-cutting was finished Johnson announced the lunch, and everyone agreed that it was magnificent. It was greatly assisted by the wine merchant's champagne and topped off with his brandy. The war was then forgotten for 12 hours.[134]

For Hall and A Squadron, there was a new issue. They no longer had enough armoured cars for all the personnel in the Squadron. Furthermore, they lacked the transport to carry the crews, so Hall was lent a lorry by C Squadron to carry all the spare personnel from the abandoned armoured cars.[135] Hall also had personal and self-inflicted issues, as for most of the day he had slept, on and off, outside in the open and as a result got very sunburnt. Shand noted that the few remaining Squadron officers were all 'very depressed' and that he would never forget how Falaise would try to make them laugh with his stories of the 'domestic troubles' of the Hollywood stars.[136]

134 TNA WO 167/778: 24 May 1940.
135 Hall Diary, 24 May 1940, p.9.
136 Shand, *Previous Encounters*, p.55.

7

Defence of Ypres and the Yser Canal

(25th–28th May 1940)

Saturday 25th May

(Day Sixteen)

As an immediate step, 12th Lancers were sent off early on 25th to watch the left flank of II Corps on the Lys, and gain touch with the right flank of the Belgians.
Gort[1]

By now we had lost so many armoured cars the Regiment was down to half its strength.
Hunn[2]

At 0615 hrs, a staff officer arrived. Lumsden was roused from slumber and told that the Headquarters had been unable to contact the 13th/18th Hussars to reconnoitre in the area of Courtrai, where it was reported that the Germans had formed a bridge-head and that the Regiment must move forthwith to report on the situation in that area. The primary concern was the left flank of II Corps and the possibility that 'a gap' might be opened up between them and the Belgian Army.[3] A Squadron was the first to move off and all squadrons had packed up and moved in a little over an hour after the order was received.[4]

A Squadron was on its way to Belgium by 0700 hrs. The Squadron's understanding of the situation was that the Germans had broken through the Belgian lines south of Bruges and north of Courtrai and the Regiment's mission was 'to keep watch on the

1   Gort, *Second Despatch*, p.5922.
2   Hunn Diary, 25 May 1940, p.10.
3   Stewart, *History of the XII Royal Lancers*, p.363.
4   TNA WO 167/452, 25 May 1940.

left flank of the BEF II Corps on the Lys River and establish contact with the right flank of the Belgians.'[5]

At 0830 hrs, A Squadron crossed the Belgian border at Le Bizet, north of Armentieres, with orders to reconnoitre east of Roulers within the Belgian sector and confirm the German positions. This was still a journey of some 40 miles and the route would take them over the British battlefield of the First World War: Hogstreet [sic], Ypres, Passchendaele, finally arriving at Roulers at 1000 hrs. When they arrived, the town was animated and quite normal. The shops were still fully stocked and the people had not fled, nor did they intend to, and the square was almost entirely covered with sleeping Belgian soldiers sprawled across the cobbles.[6]

Shand and Bishop in their two cars were sent to reconnoitre Ingelmunster and try and find the Belgian GHQ.[7] At the same time, Horsbrugh-Porter and Falaise went off in the staff car to find the whereabouts of a Belgian infantry brigade which was believed to be holding a line between Ingelmunster and Winkel St. Eloi.[8] *En route*, despite being shelled by German 105-mm, they found the Belgian Infantry Division HQ at Roulers. On their way, they had heard that Shand's troop was under heavy artillery fire and had 'just had a car put out of action.'[9]

As Shand and Bishop arrived at Ingelmunster one of the 'ubiquitous' Storch aircraft was circling the place and dropping the occasional flare, and Bishop wrote that he had rarely entered a place with 'greater trepidation.' The place was full of 'scared Belgian infantry,' lying in the roadside ditches just outside the town. They had completely ignored a wounded and bleeding civilian in the middle of the road, so Bishop took him out on the bonnet of one of the cars. Halfway through Ingelmunster, Bishop and Shand suddenly came under point-blank small-arms fire. It was not easy to identify where it had come from, but afterwards, they all agreed that it could only have come from top-storey windows either side of the street:

> Luckily it did not last. Our gunners raked the windows while our cars reversed at speed. By now Trooper Wessel had become my driver. A flamboyant character, he gave a yodel as he went into reverse. Like Pearce of the ploughed field, he kept his head and showed coolness and skill, turning the car, and facing back to Roulers, while my guns never let up. We were now sitting ducks in the narrow street, but at least the firing from within Ingelmunster had ceased.[10]

5   Falaise, *Through Hell to Dunkirk,* p.135.
6   Falaise, *Through Hell to Dunkirk,* p.135 and Bishop, *One Young Soldier*, p.61.
7   Shand, *Previous Encounters,* p.56.
8   Falaise, *Through Hell to Dunkirk,* p.135 and Bishop, *One Young Soldier*, p.61.
9   Shand did not lose a car. It is possible this was Miller-Mundy.
10 Bishop, *One Young Soldier,* p.61.

During the attack in Ingelmunster, two 'ill-placed' civilians who were standing by the roadside were wounded.[11] However, the threat now came from the air as they were attacked by low level Messerschmitt 109s:

> This time it was rooftop rather than treetop height, again and again, guns blazing. The noise alone almost stuns a man. As in the hazel wood, I got everyone out of the car to huddle in a small cellar while I crouched on the floor of a tiny earth-closet. The planes howled along the line of the street, having it all their own way. Our cars were much holed and battered, but mobile, nor were there were any casualties so that when we were recalled to Wytschaete we were able to comply.[12]

Outside Ingelmunster, Shand, Bishop, Miller-Mundy and Henderson all met up. Henderson informed them that he had just had his 'DR killed, and a car wrecked.' The Regimental war diarist's entry for the Miller-Mundy incident reads that 'B Squadron had lost one car of 3 Troop in the area of Moorseele (H75), where they had encountered German infantry. A lucky shot had hit the steering of the lead car which as a result overturned in a ditch. Trooper 'Jock' Cowie, the DR, was unfortunately shot when turning round, and Henderson succeeded very skilfully and boldly in recovering the crew of his ditched car uninjured. Bishop concluded that like every place that May, he 'was not sorry to leave it.'[13]

As regards the rest of the Regiment, the War Diary recorded that first contact was made with the Germans at 0940 hrs in the area of Lendelede (H8464). Contact was also made with other Allied troops south of the Menin–Courtrai Canal and with the Belgians on the left in the area of Iseghem (H86). It was soon verified that although Courtrai was still holding out, the Germans had been able to cross the canal in the area of Harlbekie and were advancing westwards.[14] At 1010 hrs, the Regiment reported to GHQ that the line south of Roulers was 'all quiet.'[15]

By 1315 hrs, the Germans had pushed forward so many infantry and anti-tank guns supported by a few tanks that the Regiment was forced to withdraw down the Courtrai – Menin road. Mann lost an armoured car in the area of Lederghem where he had delayed over two hundred Germans and at least two anti-tank guns for the greater part of the day.

At 1600 hrs, the war finally came to Roulers when it had its first air raid, whereupon the civil population ran for shelter leaving the Grande Place deserted. Horsbrugh-Porter and Falaise again decided to go out in the staff car to try and make contact with the colonel commanding the infantry on the line west of Izegem. Eventually, they found the HQ in the small hamlet of Okene. The colonel told them that "the Germans

11   Shand, *Previous Encounters*, p.56.
12   Bishop, *One Young Soldier*, p.61.
13   Bishop, *One Young Soldier*, p.62 and Hunn Diary, 21 May 1940, p.10.
14   TNA WO 167/452: 25 May 1940.
15   TNA WO/167/29/8: 25 May 1940.

had succeeded in gaining a foothold in Izegem" which was approximately a mile away and it appeared that the Belgian infantry who were still holding out in Ingelmunster would have to retreat, or risk being cut-off. Immediately Horsbrugh-Porter heard this information he wanted to report this new development by wireless and to do this he needed to go back to Roulers.

At 1708 hrs, the Regiment reported that 'a gap was opening up in the Menin area where the enemy advance neared the outskirts of Menin and towards Moorseele.' At 1725 hrs, they reported that they had become involved in an infantry battle in the area of Menin – Roulers. The Regiment also reported that it appeared that the Belgians were doing 'little or nothing to restore the situation on their front.'[16]

Within an hour the Belgian troops started to withdraw along the canal towards Roulers and A Squadron was ordered to move five miles west. Immediately they moved the SHQ it came under air attack one mile north east of West Roozebeke [Westrozebeke]. The attack was conducted by Heinkels and Messerschmitts and it was clear they were the intended target:

> The major and I are crouching behind the wall of a smelly pigsty. I hear the bullets punching holes through its tiled roof. Our cars are hidden under sheds around the farmyard. The neighbouring fields and hangars of the adjoining granary are filled with troops belonging to a Belgian artillery supply echelon. Their terrified horses are milling around wildly, neighing with fear, and running into the barbed wire fences as they try to get away. Every time a bomb crashes, many of them are killed. The personnel, too, seem to be suffering heavy casualties. On the road directly ahead of us, three trucks have been stopped, their drivers killed by the strafing. There is nothing we can do about it, but wait and hope. At first, we try shooting at the planes with Bren guns, but give it up as a bad job. The more we shoot at them, the more they come back at us. If we keep quiet, they may forget us

At 2200 hrs, A Squadron was ordered back to Wytschaete approximately six miles south of Ypres. On the way, they found the road blocked with so many British and French vehicles all heading north that it was practically impossible to move. The night was very dark and no one used their headlights:

> I wonder how the drivers can make any headway at all against this unending stream of trucks, guns, and infantrymen which fills the highway, overflows on the neighbouring fields and leaves us no room to pass. It takes us more than two hours to cover 20 miles and when we reach Wytschaete, we have to remain in the cars to wait for further orders.[17]

16   TNA WO 167/29/8: 25 May 1940.
17   Falaise, *Through Hell to Dunkirk,* p.138.

After his day with the Belgians, Horsbrugh-Porter 'reported that III Corps HQ and First Army HQ that he had visited were obviously not in touch with the actual situation in the field on their front and that they had been busy making grandiose arrangements for a counter-attack in which the Regiment was expected to co-operate, whereas in fact no very strenuous resistance was being offered to the German advance on this front.' Browne-Clayton wrote that when he met the young Belgian staff officers, they were as 'pink and powdered as when they had last met them a fortnight ago.'[18] Shand, who had spent all day looking for the Belgian GHQ eventually found it, but on returning late that evening to SHQ, observed that no one was interested as Belgium had either 'capitulated' or was about to do so, and the long patrols just produced nothing but 'gloomy news' of the impending capitulation.[19]

B Echelon was again heavily bombed that day and one other rank was killed. Hall had been sent out during the day to try and pick up a wireless set from the Hopkinson Mission near Cassell, but notwithstanding his best efforts and assistance from the Commanding Officer of the 13th/18th Hussars, he could not find them so returned to the Regiment just as they were moving out.[20] During the evening, the Regiment gradually withdrew and crossed to the west of the Yser Canal moving to Neuve Eglise (H5350) for the night.[21] Hunn wrote that 'by now' they 'had lost so many armoured cars the Regiment was down to half its strength.'[22]

Sunday 26th May

(Day Seventeen)
Just before 1900 hrs, Winston Churchill ordered the start of Operation Dynamo.
One engaged in some strange interviews in quest of information. I was beginning to have less and less of an idea of what was happening, save that the Germans were doing rather well.
Shand[23]

It is a pity that GHQ never notified me that he [Lumsden] was on my left or instructed him to report to me the result of his observations. Considering that in the final stages GHQ were out of touch with the situation, I think that the best plan would have been to have placed the armoured car regiment directly under my orders.
GOC II Corps[24]

18   Stewart, *History of the XII Royal Lancers*, p.364.
19   Shand, *Previous Encounters*, p.56; Shand, 'May 1940: A Memory', p.154.
20   Hall Diary, 25 May 1940.
21   TNA WO 167/452: 25 May 1940.
22   Hunn Diary, 25 May 1940, p.10.
23   Shand, *Previous Encounters*, p.56.
24   Brooke, 26 May 1940, in A. Bryant, *The Turn of the Tide 1939-1943* (1957), p.101.

On 26th May, the Regiment was again ordered to reconnoitre the area Roulers–Werwicq – Ypres in front of 4th Battalion Gordon Highlanders which had occupied a position on the line of the Ypres–Comines Canal. Contact was made with the Germans and with the Belgians on the left, in the area of Zonnebeke (H66, see Map 15).[25]

A Squadron moved out at 0300 hrs towards Nieukirk [Nieuwkerke – Nueve Eglise]. Everyone was hungry and tired as no one had slept or eaten and everyone was close to exhaustion. The Squadron consisted of SHQ and only Bishop's and Shand's troops, which were down to just two armoured cars each, and therefore were kept very busy.[26] The journey was slow as they encountered the same traffic jams as before and it was nearly dawn before they reached their final destination, where they halted in front of the church in the square. The transport echelon had arrived there last night and was already billeted in a group of farmhouses a mile south west of the village.[27]

The church door was wide open. From the outside, Falaise could see 'the altar brightly lit with candles and the priest standing in his white and gold vestments giving communion':

> Seeking solace, I step into this unbelievable haven of peace, of 'peace on earth, good will toward men' and kneel down. The sight of the ancient walls surrounding these rituals which have gone on unchanged for centuries through the upheavals of war and shocks of revolution suddenly restores some faith in myself and in humanity, a faith of which at the moment I am in dire need. When I leave the church, I feel mentally more serene, on solider spiritual ground.[28]

Horsbrugh-Porter decided to leave Falaise and the staff car in Nieukirk and he sent the rest of the armoured cars to Ypres.[29] The intention was that Falaise was to get some rest, although this was not to be as at approximately 0800 hrs the town was subjected to an air attack which unfortunately caught a convoy of 20 ammunition trucks. The resulting devastation in the town was immense so Falaise moved out and joined the transport echelon on the outside of town. When he arrived there he was 'saddened' to hear about the death of Lance Corporal Chandler, one of Hall's men.[30] Hall recorded the incident in his diary:

> Well, after settling in, I decided to shave and had just finished when I noticed nine German bombers in the Bailleul direction. I was shaving at the back of a Mess lorry in a yard. Then I happened to glance over my shoulder and said, "My God, look!" to Eldridge and Park who were standing near. There were another

25   TNA WO 167/452: 26 May 1940.
26   Shand, *Previous Encounters*, p.56.
27   Falaise, *Through Hell to Dunkirk*, p.139.
28   Falaise, *Through Hell to Dunkirk*, p.139.
29   Falaise, *Through Hell to Dunkirk*, p.140.
30   Falaise, *Through Hell to Dunkirk*, p.140.

nine coming low over Neuve Eglise. The only obvious shelter was a somewhat dirty cowshed with stone walls into which we ran and flung ourselves flat on the floor. There were two lots of bombs; the first lot was right on top of us; we thought each would hit us. Their scream was one of the most unpleasant sounds I have ever heard. There were six that seemed right on us, the next further away.

We came out of the shed but for a few moments some more came and I took shelter in an air raid shelter dug by the farmer's wife and some troops who had been there before. This however was not so close. We sorted ourselves out and went to see whether there were any casualties in the other places in which our lorries parked. I found one bomb had fallen by the side of the road, close to where Allis, on look-out, was lying, and had hit a Belgian soldier who was lying next to him in the ankle.

Then Rowland came running up saying "Chandler's hit, sir!" I ran all the way to where he was and found he had been killed, struck in the head, the heart, and the wrist. He had been sheltering behind a bank and a bomb burst on the wrong side of it. We buried him just by where he had been hit, on the top of a mound from where we could see Mount Kemmel to the north and the plain of northern France to the south.

The curious reaction to this state of fear was that I found myself very hungry and went and ate bully, sardines and biscuits with butter and marmalade. The bomb had produced the largest crater and it burst just behind the little yard in which the cook's lorry was parked, not hurting anyone. The splinters must have passed over their heads. Two pieces did hit the lorry in which two were sheltering and lodged in haversacks.[31]

Horsbrugh-Porter heard that the Germans were through northwest of Ypres, so sent Bishop on a lone-car mission to Poperinghe to confirm or otherwise. Bishop had a 'jumpy sort of journey,' and he stated that he 'missed having a lead car,' but eventually came upon a Belgian HQ at Pilchem. Here he was shown a marked map by a very demoralised young Belgian ADC who spoke public school English. He was very angry that we should have offered help and then proved to have been 'of no help whatsoever.' Bishop told him that they were doing their best, but the ADC shouted back:

"No! No! Too late!" He said that there had been a tremendous lot of Belgian casualties at Poel Kappel (where our own RHQ had been the day before). He was an intelligent person and the utter futility of further resistance to this juggernaut of a German Army had got him right down. I was not thinking that way at all, but then my home was not in Belgium.[32]

31   Hall Diary, 26 May 1940, p.10.
32   Bishop, *Some Young Soldier*, p.62.

Bishop reported the situation over the air to Horsbrugh-Porter who then sent him off to Zonnebecke, as it had been reported that the Germans had broken through 'somewhere there':

> Again, I was very glad to find that they had done no such thing. I reported this to Horsbrugh-Porter who told me to go on to Dixmuide. Here I encountered a cheerful officer of the 8th Cuirassiers, who appeared to be in full command of the local situation and was as refreshing to meet as the poor Belge had been depressing. So, Horsbrugh-Porter told me to come back to Ypres, where he posted me, in my car, under the Menin Gate itself, to watch the eastern approaches to the town. The different attitude of our Allies from that of our foe was here apparent. A little Belgian walked up to my car where I had an extensive field of fire and cover from the air as well as being able to see a long way. He asked me if "I would mind moving further away if that is, you intend to fire your guns." There were, he explained, wounded men in the Cloth Hall and they needed quiet. Fortunately for all concerned, I did not have to fire my guns, but I stayed where I was.[33]

Bishop was eventually recalled back to SHQ at Westvleteren, as the German cavalry was reported to be swimming the canal to the north. Before leaving Ypres, Bishop helped himself to a case of champagne (quarter bottles) from the local wine merchants. All the shops had been left open, abandoned, and deserted. Across the road from the Cloth Hall, there was a high-class confectioner full of beautiful chocolates for the taking. 'It was a schoolboy's dream come true but, oddly enough, no one in his troop had a sweet tooth.'[34]

While Bishop had been in Ypres, Shand was sent on a long trip to Roulers and Thourout where he found all the Belgians very 'uncommunicative.' At Roulers he had a discussion with the Burgomaster:

> Who kept breaking into Flemish, which made conversation very difficult, and pointing at the statue of Nurse Cavell which adorns the centre of that town. Finally, he made me the symbolic gift of an apple and I was left in some doubt about the whole affair. This sounds highly irrelevant now, but one engaged in some strange interviews in quest of information. I was beginning to have less and less of an idea of what was happening, save that the Germans were doing rather well.[35]

Shand also wrote that he had been responsible for the destruction of an 'enormous iron swing bridge' at Schoorbacke. When Shand arrived at the bridge he found it

33   Bishop, *Some Young Soldier*, p.62.
34   Bishop, *Some Young Soldier*, p.63.
35   Shand, *Previous Encounters*, p.56.

Lieutenant Bishop's armoured car parked beneath the Menin Gate on 26th May 1940. (Warre)

under command of a French sapper sergeant who refused to blow the bridge or show Shand where the fuses were. Bridges to the left and right of Shand's location were being fired. The French sergeant still refused to fire the bridge even with the imminent arrival of the Germans being anticipated and even the production of Shand's revolver did not persuade him. It was only after being 'compelled to use third-degree methods on him' that he complied. Shand recorded that the bridge 'disintegrated with the most stupendous noise and bits of it continued falling for some time.' It was only a few minutes later that German armoured cars and tanks arrived and he withdrew 'under their spirited fire.'[36]

At 1100 hrs, Falaise noted that more planes came over, but this time two of them were shot down by anti-aircraft fire. During the whole morning, there had been a 'loud and incessant thundering of artillery fire toward the east in the direction of Warneton and Ypres.'[37] Falaise wrote that there was suddenly a 'heavy cloudburst, which gave them a respite from the raiders':

> I take shelter in a small shack where I find an old man sitting quietly smoking his clay pipe as if nothing disturbing were going on around him. We get to talking and I discover that he earns his living in rather an extraordinary way. Since the last war, in which he took part, he has been smuggling coarse tobacco over the French border two miles away and selling scrap iron which he dug out of the surrounding battlefields rusty remains of the millions of shells which ploughed up this sector. This in a modest manner, of course, just enough to keep him provided with food, shelter, tobacco, and an occasional nip of schnapps. He tells me that the only thing worrying him about this present war is that he thinks the indiscriminate way in which bombs are dropping all over the countryside will make it more difficult to collect later. He also fears that perhaps the German steel won't be quite up to quality! He then confides to me that his business, which was beginning to wane, underwent a boom when this war started, and the price of scrap metal doubled.[38]

At 1400 hrs, Horsbrugh-Porter told Falaise to go to Woesten (five miles northwest of Ypres) to look for new billets for the Squadron. The Squadron arrived two hours later, but Horsbrugh-Porter informed Falaise there had been a change in the plan and they were now going to Westvleteren, (five miles north west, near the Furnes road). Falaise 'scrambled' onto the back of Shand's armoured car and they left. Shand told Falaise the reason for the change was that the Germans had 'breached the line between Menin and Warneton' and were driving a wedge between the Belgian and British troops in the direction of Wytschaete.[39]

36   Shand, *Previous Encounters*, pp.56-57.
37   Falaise, *Through Hell to Dunkirk*, p.141.
38   Falaise, *Through Hell to Dunkirk*, p.141.
39   Falaise, *Through Hell to Dunkirk*, p.142.

The reports from A Squadron had shown that Ypres was only been held by approximately 20 Belgian sappers. This fact was immediately reported to GHQ by Lumsden in person, who informed the C-in-C of the situation, and within five minutes orders had been issued for a garrison to be sent to the town as soon as possible. At 1700 hrs, Lumsden ordered B Squadron to take over from A Squadron and take control of Ypres until a suitable garrison could be found. Davies's Squadron from the 13th/18th Hussars was in the area and co-opted to watch the southern exits. By these means, it was possible to ensure the defence of the town until the arrival of more troops. Smith and his sappers were sent with Browne-Clayton to take control of the crossings.

When Smith arrived in Ypres, three crossings had been partially prepared for demolition and were due to be completed and fired on orders. Smith went to the HQ of the Belgian sappers to see the officer in charge and then accompanied him on a visit to all the bridges to find out exactly how they were charged and what methods of firing they proposed to adopt. Smith observed:

> These Belgian sappers were quite clearly delighted at the chance of passing on the job to someone else and it was amusing to see the rapidity with which they vacated the town. It is also amusing to note that the bridges that were really prepared and fired by these Belgians were on the west of the town. The Germans, of course, were advancing from the east.[40]

On his return, Smith took Earl and Johnson and posted them each on a bridge and explained the Belgian method of firing and the location of the charge. He gave them instructions that the bridges were to be wired for electrical firing. Smith then took his own party to the forward bridge at the Menin Gate. Each detachment worked hard at the task and by dark the preparation of the charges was complete, with the wiring circuits in place. There was then nothing to do but to sit tight and wait for the order to fire the bridges.

In the evening, the promised garrison for the town started to arrive. The first arrivals were troops from the 50th Division. During the night, Smith was called to see the Commanding Officer of the East Yorks and was informed that his men were going to defend the crossings. Patrols from the East Yorks would be operating in front of Ypres and the bridges would be blown on his orders. In the absence of orders to this effect, the bridges were to be blown on the immediate approach of the Germans. Smith visited Earl and Johnson and conveyed these instructions to them and then returned to the Menin Gate. During the hours of darkness, Hourigan inspected his firing circuits to find that they had been cut by a tank which had mounted the footpath. The damage was repaired and the rest of the night was quiet.[41]

---

40   TNA WO 167/778: 26 May 1940.
41   TNA WO 167/778: 26 May 1940.

Menin Gate Bridge Blown by Smith. (<http://ww2talk.com/index.php?threads/2nd-lieutenant-d-a-smith-mc-101st-royal-monmouthshire-field-company-royal-engineers.33595/>)

At 2000 hrs, Falaise was still struggling to find billets for A Squadron as all potential accommodation was already filled with soldiers of all nationalities and refugees. He finally managed to get the transport echelon, the armoured cars and their crews some space in a farm just outside the village, near the crossroad to Poperinghe. The location was far from ideal as there was constant traffic going by. An hour later, having walked at least three miles and been turned down by every house owner, he lost his patience and 'dragged' the Burgomaster from his dinner to force the unwilling female owner of a small house (dress shop) to accept our Mess:

"You must sleep on the brick floor and be careful to leave the place clean," says the vinegary spinster, but Machin and Tich have already occupied a corner of her stove and they tell me that if I can keep this witch out of the kitchen, they may be able to give us a hot meal. Shand and Bishop have fallen asleep the minute they sat down on the floor; their heads flopped on their chests. Horsbrugh-Porter says that it looks as if we might get a few hours' sleep and not leave until daylight tomorrow.[42]

42   Falaise, *Through Hell to Dunkirk*, p.142.

Hall's interpretation of the situation was that the dress shop owner 'obviously had German sympathies.'[43]

While A Squadron had been at Ypres, the Germans had continued their advance and the Regiment was finally withdrawn over the canal so that the bridges could be destroyed. C Squadron had been ordered to reconnoitre in the area of Passchendaele. During this operation, Second Lieutenant Holford's troop was heavily shelled with the result that he lost a car and a DR. On the completion of their task, the Squadron left a troop at Boesinghe.[44] B Squadron remained in Ypres and was ordered to hold it 'at all costs.' When Hunn arrived at Ypres, he noted a few tanks of the 13th/18th Hussars and some two-pounder anti-tank guns were also there to help them:

> My armoured car was positioned beside the arch of the Menin Gate That night as I went through the town, everywhere was deserted. There was no sign of life; shop doors were open; it was a ghost town; so quiet and eerie that one felt very uncomfortable.[45]

The remainder of the Regiment withdrew to the vicinity of Woesten where they were in position to cover the BEF's left flank.[46]

Monday 27th May

(Day Eighteen)
At the request of the Mayor of Woesten, the horses which survived were given to him to feed the civilian population which he said had been very short of meat, owing to the influx of refugees.
Regimental War Diary[47]

On 27th May, the 50th Division under Major General Martel took over command of Ypres. The Regiment was placed under his orders, which were that the Regiment should reconnoitre to the east and north east of Ypres to observe the German movements.[48]

The Regiment reconnoitred in the area Dixmuide – Roulers – Ypres and information was soon given to 50th Division that a gap had formed in the Belgian line and that their right was swinging back in a north easterly direction. The Regiment remained in touch with the Belgian Army in the area of Roulers and covered the gap

43   Hall Diary, 26 May 1940, p.10.
44   TNA WO 167/452: 26 May 1940.
45   Hunn Diary, 26 May 1940.
46   TNA WO 167/452: 26 May 1940.
47   TNA WO 167/452: 27 May 1940.
48   TNA WO 167/452: 27 May 1940.

between them and the left of the 50th Division which was gradually extended during the course of the day northwards to Boesinghe.[49]

A Squadron were all packed up and ready to move by 0500 hrs and waited for orders. At 0600 hrs, they were informed that it was possibly going to be a rest day and they were to stay where they were. This was welcome news as the armoured cars needed servicing. During the morning, the men got on with sleeping, washing, and cleaning weapons. Falaise thought the morning had 'dragged' and noted that they were 'hardly being disturbed by the German aircraft.'[50] Hall recorded the morning slightly differently saying 'that the German bombers bombed around the farm where the transport and Officers' Mess was, and some men spent the day in air-raid shelters in the farm… but never very near to us.'[51] Bishop wrote that he and Shand spent the morning asleep in the back of Horsbrugh-Porter's Mercury staff car, in which Bishop managed five 'undisturbed beautiful hours.'[52]

B Squadron was sent to the line of the River Yser at Nieuport, Schoorbrakke and Dixmuide. It was attacked en route by a formation of Stuka dive bombers as they passed through a town:

> We took cover in a wood until the attack ended. A small detachment of French cavalry was also seeking the protection of the leafy trees. One of the cavalrymen was in tears as they were due to abandon their horses and he had no wish to allow his mount to fall into Germans hands. He asked if one of us British would shoot the animal. A volunteer drew his pistol and asked the tearful Frenchman to hold the horse's head steady. He then pressed the trigger and both the horse, and its owner fell to the ground, the bullet having passed through one into the other. Fortunately, the French officer who had witnessed the incident took care of the casualty.[53]

On reaching Nieuport, B Squadron was 'greeted' by heavy shellfire and the Germans were trying to capture the bridge which was prepared for demolition:

> Strong German forces quickly arrived to support the leading elements. 4 Troop fought bravely to stem the tide. The Troop Leader, Peter Miller-Mundy, was slightly wounded, Paddy Thornton the gunner also and Trooper Chappell, the wireless operator, was killed. However, with the aid of 3 Troop, the Germans were delayed until a stronger force of infantry and tanks arrived to relieve them. All ranks were by now completely exhausted; only three nights' sleep had been possible in two and a half weeks of fighting. Although we suffered a number of

49   TNA WO 167/452: 27 May 1940.
50   Falaise, *Through Hell to Dunkirk*, p.143.
51   Hall Diary, 27 May 1940, p.11.
52   Bishop, *One Young Soldier*, p.63.
53   Hunn Diary, 27 May 1940, p.10.

casualties, on considering the actions in which the whole Regiment had been involved, it was fortunate there had not been more.[54]

Meantime, in Ypres, Smith, on doing the rounds of his position, was surprised to find the covering party of the East Yorks had been withdrawn and Hourigan had been left to hold the bridge alone with Roach. After an hour, Smith had managed to get the East Yorks to return to the bridge. No sooner had Smith resolved the problem than Earl's bridge was coming under fire from machine guns on the east side of the canal and by the afternoon it was clear that the Germans were definitely within striking distance and there seemed no reason for further delaying the orders to fire the charges:

> Anti-tank guns were brought up and put in position at the Menin Gate and at 1600 hrs, orders were given that the bridge at the Menin Gate should be fired. This was done with complete success and without causing any structural damage to the Gate but causing irreparable damage to the car of the colonel of the East Yorks, the machine being completely wrecked by falling masonry.[55]

On returning to RHQ at Woesten, Smith was tasked to go to Noordschote to destroy barges on the canal. When he returned, he found that Earl and Johnson had returned safely from Ypres having successfully completed the destruction of the bridges.[56] The War Diary records that 'it was only thanks to the hard work and devotion to duty of this officer and his handful of hard-working sappers that the destruction of the bridges round Ypres was completed in time.'[57]

At midday, Lumsden visited A Squadron and informed them as to 'the seriousness of the situation.' He informed them that there was 'no further question of trying to make a break for it through the ever-thickening German lines to join up with the French armies in the south and that the British High Command had decided that the only way out of the trap was to head for the coast around Dunkirk, and get off as many men as possible while other troops try to hold the Germans... The first to embark would be the wounded, the non-combatants and the numerous troops of the Army Supply Corps.'[58] Falaise had heard that a tank brigade which made the raid around Arras on 21st May was already safely back in England and wondered what would happen to the Lancers who had 'been acting as rearguard ever since 12th May.'[59]

There was also bad news from the Belgian side and talk of surrender. Falaise contemplated the impact of the left flank of the BEF being exposed:

54   Hunn Diary, 27 May 1940, p.10.
55   TNA WO 167/778: 27 May 1940.
56   TNA WO 167/778: 27 May 1940.
57   TNA WO 167/452: 27 May 1940.
58   Falaise, *Through Hell to Dunkirk*, p.143.
59   Falaise, *Through Hell to Dunkirk*, p.144.

If that happens, our left flank will be completely unprotected and we must shorten our line by withdrawing behind the Canals running from Nieuport to the region south of Dunkirk. Ypres is still in British hands, but for how long? Roulers has fallen and there seems to be little cohesion in the Belgian lines. German patrols have been encountered many miles this side of them, and wiped out, one in particular as it was trying to get across the Yser-Ypres Canal six miles east of here. The French troops, under Generals Blanchard and Prioux, are still holding out around Douai and the Lys River, keeping the Germans at bay along the Franco-Belgian border.[60]

At approximately 1600 hrs, three British Hurricanes flew over the A Squadron location. They were a welcome sight and the troops cheered them as the pilots dipped the wings of the planes and showed their markings.[61] The Hurricane that flew over was the only Allied aircraft Bishop had seen to date and he toasted the pilot with champagne. Bishop was also aware that the Germans had started to drop leaflets telling the British to lay down their arms, with a map showing that they were surrounded. Bishop thought this would have the opposite effect and it was more likely to 'spur British soldiers to fight to the death.'[62]

During the evening a German mounted patrol crossed the canal to the north of Ypres, swimming it in the face of the Regiment 'but was annihilated.' At the request of the Mayor of Woesten, the horses which survived were given to him to feed the civilian population which he said had been very short of meat, owing to the influx of refugees.' The War Diary records that 'it was on this day that the news of the intended withdrawal of the BEF from Belgium first became generally known.'[63] The Regiment withdrew to the area Woesten – Elverdinghe for the night, where they were ordered to watch the left flank and rear of the 50th Division in case the Germans attempted to cross the canal north of Ypres.[64]

As the Regiment was coming to terms with the capitulation of Belgium, they were unaware that one of their brother officers, Lieutenant Piers Edgecumbe, had been killed while on attachment to Phantom Force (Hopkinson Mission). Upon his death, Captain Tony Warre, who was also 12L and Edgecumbe's Squadron Leader, wrote to the Lieutenant's parents on 31st May, remarking that:

> On the evening of 27th May, our unit was in the village of Wormhout... The Brigadier wanted to know as far as possible the position of the enemy before

60   Falaise, *Through Hell to Dunkirk*, p.144.
61   Falaise, *Through Hell to Dunkirk*, p.144.
62   Bishop, *One Young Soldier*, p.63.
63   TNA WO 167/452: 27 May 1940.
64   TNA WO 167/452: 27 May 1940.

falling at night. Piers' section received the order to reconnoitre a part of the sector, and this is when his armoured car was hit by a missile.[65]

In a letter addressed on 28th July 1989 to the Regimental Secretary of the 9th/12th Lancers, Warre remembered that Edgcumbe had disappeared with his teammate while carrying out reconnaissance in the Cassel sector and that they had probably been burnt in their armoured car. He wrote that he did not think that his body was ever found. However, the following statement subsequently came to light:

> When I returned to my tavern [Hunter's Rest], a burned armoured vehicle was in front of my house. I went into the house and in the kitchen there was a big mess, traces of struggle, and blood everywhere. Cast parts of my fire [place] had obviously been used as projectiles. Continuing the inspection of the house, I arrived in the adjoining barn with a pigsty where two bodies were lying. The two bodies (of the British soldiers) were buried in the pasture of the tavern with what remained of their effects.[66]

Photographs later acquired from German sources showed that the side-door of Edgecumbe's armoured car outside Hunters Rest was open, possibly indicating that the crew had escaped, and drew doubts on Warre's statement that they had probably burned to death in their armoured car. This led to the re-examination of a previously unidentified body and a meticulous study of the dental records assisted by the statement made previously by the CWGC that the body had 'hair on the blond side, leather jacket with four pockets (army issue) and a photo of a young girl on skis.' The CWGC were not to know that Edgcumbe had skied with his girlfriend shortly before. This information was sufficient to formally identify Edgcumbe's body. As a result of Guy Rommelaere's research, Edgcumbe was reinterred at Esquelbecq Military Cemetery with full military honours on 27th May 2022.[67]

Tuesday 28th May

(Day Nineteen –Belgium Surrenders)
Early on the 28th the leading German mobile troops and tanks had reached Nieuport, and they would have arrived there unopposed had it not been for the work of a troop of 12th Lancers.
Gort[68]

---

65   Research carried out by Guy Rommelaere at the Commonwealth War Graves Commission's Esquelbecq Military Cemetery near Dunkirk.
66   Rommelaere.
67   Rommelaere.
68   Gort, *Second Despatch*, p.5928.

This meagre but stout-hearted little force then proceeded to dominate the situation.
Stewart[69]

At approximately 0730 hrs, the Regiment came under the orders of the 3rd Division. General Montgomery arrived at RHQ at Woesten (H5267) and said that the "3rd Division was moving into position north of 50th Division, and that the leading elements were already in position on the canal running west north west from Ypres, that his left would extend as far north as Noordschote, and that at his request the Regiment had been placed under his orders." He then said that he wanted "the Regiment to cover his left flank and would be quite satisfied if they extended the front to include the bridge at Forthen (H4980). He wanted them to ensure the defence of the crossing at Noordschote until his troops were firmly in position."[70]

During the course of 27th May, reconnaissance by the Regiment, in particular by A Squadron, had established the fact that the Belgian Army was retreating in a north and north easterly direction rather than to the west. This withdrawal would expose the left flank of 50th Division and the BEF, therefore, 'the arrival of 3rd Division was most welcome.'[71] However, from the information that the Regiment had gathered, Lumsden had a 'hunch' that the Belgian Army would not long be continuing the struggle and that their withdrawal from the fighting would be known to the Germans and would leave a gap between the left of the BEF and the sea.[72] It therefore, seemed imperative that the Regiment should extend their front to the Channel coast and this decision was made on the initiative of Lumsden.[73]

The Regiment's dispositions were C Squadron on the right in the general area of Dixmuide with orders to link up with the left of the 3rd Division. A Squadron was in the centre, in the area of Schoorbakke, and B Squadron was on the left in the area of Nieuport.

Lumsden's decision to move further east to the line of the Yser River and canal resulted in there being fewer bridges to destroy between Noordschote and the sea at Nieuport than on the Furnes Canal. That said, in reinterpreting Montgomery's orders, the requirements of 3rd Division would still be fulfilled.[74] The Regiment's fears regarding the Belgian Army proved correct and there would be more ground over which to fight a delaying rearguard action whilst the bridges over the Furnes canal, about which nothing was known, were prepared for demolition.[75]

Smith had been ordered the previous day to make a reconnaissance of the bridges over the canals in the area of the canal junction at H5575 to Noordschote. Therefore,

69   Stewart, *History of the XII Royal Lancers*, p.367.
70   TNA WO 167/452: 28 May 1940.
71   TNA WO 167/452: 28 May 1940.
72   Shand 'May 1940: A Memory', p.154.
73   Clark-Kennedy, 'Record of Service', p.13.
74   Corps Recce Study Day, 'Salvation of the BEF 10-31 May 1940', p.25.
75   TNA WO 167/452: 28 May 1940.

Smith was immediately despatched to destroy them, his order being 'to deny to the Germans and demolish the bridges over the Yser Canal.' Smith began his task on the left flank of the 3rd Division, moving progressively northwards via Dixmuide to Nieuport. No Belgian or French troops were seen attempting to take up a position in this area, except for a few Belgian bridge guards.[76]

That morning, Willis gave C Squadron the order that they 'were to fight to the last man and the last round.' This message in some way counteracted the German messages which had been dropped by leaflets the previous day. The leaflets read 'British Soldiers! Lay down your arms! Why go on Fighting?'[77] 'The combination of Willis's words and the leaflets had exactly the opposite effect on his Squadron

German surrender leaflet. (Author's collection)

and Hunn (like Bishop previously) thought it 'was more likely to spur British soldiers to fight to the death.'[78]

The first contact with the Germans was made by C Squadron at Dixmuide where Mann reported that a black Mercedes Benz open touring car, carrying a white flag and four fully armed German Officers, had passed him travelling west at high speed through Dixmuide. He said that he had been so busy trying to arrange for the blowing up of the bridge that this car had evaded him in the first instance, but that he was in pursuit. He soon gave up the fruitless chase and returned to Dixmuide to ensure the destruction of the bridge.

76   TNA WO 167/452: 28 May 1940.
77   MC awarded for services with the Trans-Jordan Frontier Force in 1939.
78   Hunn Diary, p.12; Bishop, *One Young Soldier*, p.63.

Dixmuide Bridge. (Author's collection)

It was now known that a German staff car was in the area and it was very desirable that it should be stopped. Owing to the great dispersion of the Regiment, which had suffered numerous vehicle casualties and was on approximately a 16-mile front and already fully engaged in trying to get all the bridges blown, this was no easy task. It was a case of "calling all cars, black car containing German Staff Officers last seen moving west from Dixmuide expected to move north, stop it or shoot." The car was next reported moving north in the area of Pervyse and then seen in Nieuport by Browne-Clayton when it had been joined by two other similar cars. The occupants were conversing with what appeared to be both Belgian and French Officers. The Germans were fully armed and, as Browne-Clayton was only in an unarmoured Morris truck, he did not feel competent to tackle them single-handed and quite rightly merely kept them under observation (see Map 16).[79]

No attempt was made by the Belgians to interfere with these German officers whom they appeared to be expecting, nor did the few French or Belgian troops in the area make any efforts to stop them or intervene. From the Regiment's perspective, this was a 'completely unauthorised parley.' After a short conversation, the three cars moved south, but the only one that was seen again managed by a stroke of ill-luck to re-cross at Dixmuide but at a price, as the three officers in the back were 'hard hit.' It seems certain that these Germans reported that there were no troops in the area

79   TNA WO 167/452: 28 May 1940.

Nieuport to Dixmuide which they had traversed; that the bridges were still intact and that their columns must hasten their advance. As subsequent events proved, this was already well underway.[80]

At the point of a revolver, Mann persuaded the Belgian officer in charge of the demolition chambers that the bridge had to be blown. He finally pressed the switch, but there was no result; Mann then inspected the charges on the bridge. They had obviously been tampered with. On his return he found a French major who told him that he would now take command, that his troops were fast approaching, and that Mann need bother no more about blowing the bridge. Mann asked: "Where are your troops for the defence of this bridge, I cannot see any?" and was told: "They are just the other side of the canal and will be here immediately." Mann went to look for himself, found there were none, and returned hot-foot in search of the French major who he was by then convinced was a German masquerading as a Frenchman, but he had vanished into thin air. Mann again persuaded the Belgian officer to show Smith exactly where and how all the charges were laid, and with the assistance of some new fuses and an exploder, the bridge was blown 'handsomely' at the second attempt. The *War Diary* noted that the Belgian Engineers never 'stinted' in the amount of explosives in their demolition charges.[81]

Smith's own account adds perspective to the responsibility placed on himself and Mann. 'Try to imagine two Second Lieutenants holding a discussion what to do next when two German staff cars drove past… The bridge was full of refugees streaming west [over the bridge] and we had to clear these. Ned Mann fired over their heads and the flow miraculously stopped. We had no idea what was happening on the other side of the bridge.'[82]

No sooner had Mann placed his troop of armoured cars in a position to watch the approaches to the bridge than they had to withdraw slightly to avoid the explosion. In fact, within 10 minutes of the bridge being blown, the first party of German motorcyclists arrived 'full tilt' at the bridge, closely followed by infantry in lorries. It was quite obvious from the way they arrived at the lip of the crater, and the look of surprise on their faces when they found the bridge blown, that they had been told to seize the bridge at all costs as there was no adequate defence on the Regiment's side and the bridge had been intact. However, well-directed machine gun fire soon accounted for the motorcyclists and many of the men in the leading lorries. Nothing stirred for half an hour until German ambulances arrived to remove their wounded.[83]

Mann was now reinforced with a second troop under Brinton so that there were four cars available to cover the road and railway bridgehead to keep Dixmuide under machine gun fire. Brinton joined 21-year-old Lance Corporal Cyril Glarvey in a

80   TNA WO 167/452: 28 May 1940.
81   TNA WO 167/452: 28 May 1940.
82   Smith to Charrington correspondence dated 12 April 1997 and TNA WO 167/452: 28 May 1940.
83   TNA WO 167/452: 28 May 1940.

house where they could better see what was happening both on the other side of the canal and in the town. It was soon noticed that some Germans were trying to make a reconnaissance of the bridge but with well-directed fire, Glarvey was able to kill five Germans in eight shots. This helped discourage any close reconnaissance of the canal. The cars kept up a continuous fire on any signs of movement. They saw numerous vehicles approaching Dixmuide from Roulers, which must have been a substantial force as they counted some 250 vehicles entering the town. They reported that the road to Dixmuide from Roulers as far back as they could see was a solid mass of German motor transport. This was reported back for the RAF to bomb.[84]

2nd Lieutenant Mann's action at Dixmuide on 28th May 1940, by John Oldfield Stewart.
(*History of the XII Royal Lancers*)

For their actions at Dixmuide, both Mann and Glarvey were rewarded for their gallantry. Mann with a Distinguished Service Order and Glarvey with a Military Medal. Mann's award of the DSO was a rare distinction for a Second Lieutenant:

> The bridges were blown, with the assistance of Lieutenant Smith… By his (Mann's) skilful dispositions and bold leadership, he inflicted so many casualties

84   TNA WO 167/452: 28 May 1940.

on the head of this German column that he was able, when reinforced by another troop, to contain the Germans east of the Yser Canal for over seven hours, by which time more than 250 vehicles had been counted entering Dixmuide and the road... was a solid mass of transport. Had he failed, by less bold action or less skilful dispositions, to deceive the Germans as to his true strength and thus to contain this overwhelmingly superior force, the Germans would, during the first few hours, have had a clear road to two of the beaches from which the BEF finally embarked.[85]

The 'many casualties' referred to in Mann's DSO citation were mainly inflicted by Glarvey. There is a degree of conflict in the reports on Glarvey's action as to whether he sniped or had a Bren gun, however his citation read:

> With orders to snipe any Germans who tried to reconnoitre the bridge which had been blown, or who tried to advance down the street. By his very accurate fire, he inflicted a number of casualties on the Germans and cleared them completely from the street, thereby helping very materially to check the German's advance at a most critical time. His coolness, judgement, and devotion to duty set a very fine example.[86]

By this time, A Squadron was reduced to one car in SHQ and two troops each of two cars. Shand took over the bridge at Schoorbaake [Schoorbakke] about 1000 hrs and Bishop the bridge 1½ miles to the south east. Contact was made with C Squadron on the right and with B Squadron on the left. A French colonel in this area reported that his troops were withdrawing over the Schoorbaake bridge and would hold the canal bank in that area, but this promise was not implemented (see Map 17).

As soon as Smith had completed the destruction of the bridge at Dixmuide he continued northwards along the canal to Schoorbaake and Stuyvenskerke [Stuivekenskerke] where Shand and Bishop required his help with the bridges, and to help in the destruction of barges and boats which had been towed across to the western bank of the canal. Bishop wrote that he 'parked the two cars allocated to him under some Dutch barns, everything, men, cars, arms, was by now composite.'[87] 'The small boats were sunk with a small burst of machine gun fire but the large barges were better and more quickly dealt with by a slab of gun cotton and a long fuse, which ensured their sinking rapidly.'[88] At one point Sergeant Lewis, Shand's troop sergeant, 'was exchanging shots across the canal with no less than four German armoured cars

---

85 TNA WO 167/452: 28 May 1940.
86 Clark-Kennedy, 'Record of Service', p.13, states, 'Bren gun mounted in a house' and the TNA WO 167/452 says 5 kills in 8 shots. See TNA WO 167/452, 28 May 1940 and Stewart, *History of the XII Royal Lancers*, p.366.
87 *Bishop, One Young Soldier*, p.62.
88 TNA WO 167/452, 28 May 1940.

and six tanks.'[89] It was after this engagement that a Belgian Commanding Officer informed Bishop:

> That the war was over, the Allies were laying down their arms, we are going home… Scheme over, return to barracks, and thank the Lord for that.'[90]

These were the infantry that Shand and Bishop had been supporting. They suddenly stood up and marched off in fours towards the Germans, with the same Commanding Officer holding a white flag. Bishop wrote that this act was something that 'affected him personally.' Bishop thought that this would have an adverse effect on his soldiers 'but quite the reverse. As usual in adversity, extra witticisms broke out.'[91]

Shortly after the bridge at Schoorbaake had been blown, the Germans attacked Dixmuide and Nieuport. A Squadron was subsequently withdrawn towards Furnes and held in support of B Squadron who were hard pressed at Nieuport. Henderson's troop had already blown one bridge and helped to arrange for the opening of the flood gates. The second and larger bridge at Nieuport was still intact and had not been prepared for demolition so Smith's expert advice and help were urgently needed.[92]

The first troop to enter Nieuport was 4th Troop, B Squadron, under Miller-Mundy, who arrived in the area at approximately 0930 hrs. The town had already been heavily bombed, several bombs falling only a few yards from the bridge. Soon after his arrival, it was subjected to a second wave of incendiary and HE bombs and machine gun fire. One of the German bombers was shot down by two British fighters (see Map 18).[93]

By 1100 hrs, Miller-Mundy had completed his reconnaissance of the area and taken up a position about a quarter of a mile north east of the bridges where he observed a number of refugees and many Belgian military vehicles on the roads. Most of the Belgian officers were concerned with discussing whether their King had, or had not, capitulated. Many of the better ones, particularly those belonging to the cavalry and Air Force, seemed to think that he had and expressed their very clear disgust. A number made enquiries as to how they could join the British Army as they obviously wished to continue their struggle against the Germans.[94]

At approximately 1100 hrs, the first patrol of German motorcycles with sidecars arrived from the direction of the coast. They passed amongst some lorries sandwiched in between refugees and it was very difficult to recognise them. It was not until they were almost level that they were identified and immediately engaged. The leading one was killed instantly and whilst the remainder were being shot one of them ran right up to the car and tried to shoot the crew through the revolver slots. The whole

89   Stewart, *History of the XII Royal Lancers*, p.368.
90   Bishop, *One Young Soldier*, p.64.
91   Bishop, *One Young Soldier*, p.64.
92   TNA WO 167/452: 28 May 1940.
93   TNA WO 167/452: 28 May 1940.
94   TNA WO 167/452: 28 May 1940.

of the patrol, including the one next to the car, was accounted for, with the exception of one at the rear of the patrol who was able to turn and escape by mingling with the refugees.[95]

During this short but intense firefight, Miller-Mundy, his gunner and the wireless operator were all wounded. The driver was killed. Lance Corporal Thornton, the gunner, continued to fire despite his wounds and the balance of the casualties of approximately ten to one in favour of the Regiment was largely due to his bravery. Two bullets passed through the wireless set and another snapped off the aerial but fortunately did not put the set out of action. A wounded Czechoslovakian was taken prisoner and said there were some 30 German lorries with infantry following close behind them. Miller-Mundy made the necessary dispositions to meet this second party, as the reinforcements were only just starting to arrive in the area to take up a defensive position on the canal bank. He was subsequently reinforced by another troop, under Henderson, as it had proved impossible to blow up the second bridge in Nieuport.[96]

This reinforcement freed Miller-Mundy, under the direction of his Squadron Leader, to go and try to find the French Officer who was said to be in charge of the engineers responsible for the destruction of the bridges. The Regiment's supplies of engineering material had run very low and it was imperative that the French engineers be found so that the bridge could be blown. Unfortunately, the search proved fruitless.[97]

As British reinforcements arrived in the area, the remaining cars of B Squadron were collected for the defence of Nieuport. Miller-Mundy and Henderson eventually withdrew, handing their position over to two light tanks from the 15th/19th Hussars and 100 soldiers from the 75th Field Regiment, Royal Artillery (without their guns) from the 2nd Armoured Brigade.[98] For his action Miller-Mundy was awarded the Military Cross, his citation specifically mentioning his action at Nieuport 'by his bold tactics in moving east of the River Yser to meet the Germans who were approaching fast and in greatly superior numbers, he was thus able to check their advance for several hours, thus giving time and space for the bridges to be prepared for demolition and blown up.'[99]

As Hall was withdrawing with his transport, he arrived at Oeren on the Yser Canal where he was told to guard the bridge. Hall sat on it 'with the toughest men he could find... Corporals Melville, Rowland, Adams and Cook, accompanied by Lance Corporals Chorley, Syms, Godden and Noble with two Bren guns and two Boyes rifles.' A Belgian officer showed Hall the firing circuits. Eventually, the order came to blow the bridge just as the Royal Engineers arrived. He lit the fuse and ran, and

95   TNA WO 167/452: 28 May 1940.
96   TNA WO 167/452: 28 May 1940.
97   TNA WO 167/452: 28 May 1940.
98   Clark-Kennedy, 'Record of Service', p.13; Stewart, *History of the XII Royal Lancers*, pp.368-369 and J. Thompson, *Dunkirk: Retreat to Victory* (2009), p.129.
99   TNA WO 167/452.

the bridge went up in a most 'satisfactory manner.' Later in the distance, Hall heard 'the nicest sound' he had ever heard, 'a loud bang in the distance and Tim [Bishop] reporting on the wireless "Bridge blown."'[100]

It was now approximately 1900 hrs and orders were issued for B Squadron to remain and cover the bridges at Nieuport until after dark when the new garrison was in position. As it became dark, shouting could be heard from the far side of the canal. The German reinforcements had by this time driven the Regiment's cars to the west of the bridge and were located in the warehouses on the east bank. In the failing light, they could not be seen or located. Motorcyclists could be heard coming and going and it was not long before heavy mortar fire was put down in three definite areas on the Regiment's side of the canal. By constantly making small moves, this fire could be avoided. During these engagements, Trooper Nunn with great coolness managed to shift a lorry full of ammunition which had been abandoned in the area and which looked as if it might be set on fire at any moment.[101]

A detachment of artillery had also arrived in the area and an officer and two sergeants very gallantly tried to destroy the bridge with hand grenades. It was now dark and, under cover of machine gun fire from the Regiment, they crawled up to the bridge but as they came within throwing distance a green Verey light was sent up by the Germans and heavy machine gun and mortar fire opened up all along the bank of the canal. Their infantry could be observed by its light on the far bank. Two or three grenades were thrown, unfortunately without damaging the bridge. The two survivors of this gallant party returned, the third having been killed outright by a mortar shell.

Nieuport was now burning in several places. With heavy artillery and mortar fire falling on the town, it served no purpose leaving armoured cars there in the dark and they were withdrawn clear of the town. A Squadron continued to watch the bridge at Furnes. The bridge on the Schoorbaake–Furnes road had not been destroyed and it was probable that the Germans would arrive within a few hours. Lieutenant Colonel Kimmins, RA, GHQ Staff, who was co-ordinating the defence of this sector, obtained permission for the bridge to be blown. This was done and A Squadron remained in Furnes throughout the night covering the crossings.

The decision Lumsden made to extend his line to the coast and fill the gap left by the Belgians has been seen by historians as crucial 'in the salvation of the BEF' as it prevented Montgomery's 3rd Division from being encircled. Lumsden's sacking by Montgomery in the desert four years later was linked to Lumsden outshining Montgomery at Dunkirk. 'Perversely,' Montgomery 'never forgave' him.[102]

Lumsden's own opinion of his relationship was recounted in the Cavalry and Guards Club in approximately 1941 to a potential officer, John Robson, who asked Lumsden 'why he had left the Eighth Army' to which he replied:

100 Hall Diary, p.11.
101 TNA WO 167/452: 28 May 1940.
102 Corps Recce Study Day, 'Salvation of the BEF, 10-31 May 1940', p.25.

You may think the desert is a huge place but there wasn't enough room for two shits in it and, as I was junior, I had to go.[103]

This came as no surprise to General Richard McCreery who remarked shortly after his appointment

> He saw Herbert Lumsden shortly afterwards and there is no doubt he was worried. He gave me the clear impression that he felt he would not get on with General Montgomery. Certainly, the two never hit it off. I have never known what was the origin of the trouble between them, but I suspect that there had been some misunderstanding during the critical withdrawal back through Belgium.[104]

Montgomery stated later that Lumsden had 'not pursued the Africa Korps hard enough.' However, Churchill thought highly enough of Lumsden to appoint him 'as his Military Representative to General MacArthur in the Far East where he was tragically killed in a Japanese suicide attack on the USS New Mexico.[105] MacArthur said of Lumsden 'it is superfluous for me to speak of the complete courage that this officer so frequently displayed in this theatre over the last year.'[106]

Montgomery himself wrote he was in a 'pretty pickle! Instead of having a Belgian Army on my left I now had nothing and had to do some rapid thinking.' He does not credit Lumsden with the initiative or mention the 12th Lancers in his memoir at all.[107] Montgomery stated that when he appointed Lumsden as GOC X Corps he 'hardly knew him and so could not agree with complete confidence; but accepted him on the advice of others.'[108]

It would appear that historians have redressed the point of initiative and Blaxland observed in *Destination Dunkirk* that Lumsden's decision 'was to prove one of the most fragile but crucial threads in the delicate, complex, and chancily woven pattern of the BEF's survival.'[109] The Regimental Record of Service written by Clark-Kennedy is somewhat more self-effacing, simply stating that Lumsden's decision 'contributed greatly to the safe withdrawal of the BEF to the Dunkirk perimeter.'[110]

103 *The Delhi Spearman* (2006), p.119.
104 *12L Regimental Journal* (1959), p.40.
105 Charrington, *Spearmen*, p.137.
106 *The Delhi Spearman* (2006), p.119.
107 B.L. Montgomery, *The Memoirs of Field Marshal The Viscount Montgomery of Alamein* (1958), p.57.
108 Montgomery, p.103.
109 Blaxland, *Destination Dunkirk*, p.272.
110 Clark-Kennedy, 'Record of Service', p.13.

8

Organisation of the Beaches and the Final Embarkation

(29th–30th May 1940)

Wednesday 29th May

(Day Twenty)

We drained the sumps and ran the engines until they seized up and then fired Boyes anti-tank bullets into the engines before pushing them into one of the Canals.
Shand[1]

By the morning of 29th May, the withdrawal of the BEF to the Dunkirk bridgehead was now in full swing. The actions of the Regiment were now much circumscribed. This was the last day the Regiment would be employed in their armoured cars as there was sufficient infantry to take over their role. The Regiment, as its last task (with much-depleted numbers), had held a front of some 16 miles.[2]

During the course of the morning, the Regiment ceased to be under the orders of the 3rd Division. It had no further need of their services and they came under command of II Corps. In the afternoon, the Regiment was ordered to withdraw to Ghyvelde and get in touch with the OIC II Corps Troops Embarkation Beach at La Panne.[3]

While the Regiment was handing over to the infantry, the B Echelon transport was now assembled at Vincquim, cut-off by the mass of French and other transport which had moved towards the coast and was now blocking every road. The B Echelon vehicles of B Squadron, to the north of the canal in the Nieuport area, were eventually deliberately immobilised. The squadron was finally ordered to scuttle their vehicles

---

1   Shand, *Previous Engagements*, p.57.
2   Clark-Kennedy, 'Record of Service', p.13.
3   TNA WO 167/452: 29 May 1940.

and prepare to embark. This order came from some unknown source and it seems doubtful whether the general order given for people to embark in this haphazard fashion was wise.[4] During the move to Dunkirk, Browne-Clayton directed SQMS Harvey to take Trooper Skinner who had been seriously wounded in the leg and was in severe pain direct to one of the piers. Harvey was successful in getting both himself and Skinner on board HMS Icarus.[5]

Falaise wrote that at 0100 hrs he was sitting with the Colonel, Shand and Bishop were also sitting up, but were both fast asleep. Horsbrugh-Porter, however, was wide awake and raring to go and was planning a heroic last stand at a certain bridge. To make up for the Squadron's deficiency in armoured cars, his plan was a forlorn-hope party of men on foot. The cooks, Machin and Tich, volunteered along with everyone else for the job. Falaise inwardly questioned the soundness of the move as a good military strategy but half-heartedly offered his services on the condition that he was allowed to have a sleep beforehand. He wrote that if that were not the case, he certainly would not be able 'in his present state, to draw a bead on an elephant at 100 paces as that would require keeping his eyes open and that is the one thing of which he felt totally incapable.'[6]

At 0400 hrs, A Squadron's remaining five armoured cars and the fighting lorry 'rumbled slowly out of the farm through the gluey mud in the cold drizzly night.' They were heading north towards Furnes and Nieuport. It was planned that the transport echelon would follow at 0500 hrs, heading for Ghyvelde, a village six miles north east of Dunkirk.[7]

The journey for the Echelon vehicles on roads which had previously been blocked by refugees and were now blocked by the retreating armies was most difficult. Trooper George Delaney, driving Lumsden's staff car, found himself 'dodging between haystacks' while under attack from Stukas and, when seven miles short of La Panne, Delaney was stopped by the Military Police and told, "Sorry mate, drain your oil and smash your beloved car up as much as you can in that field over there." In Delaney's obituary it said that 'George was not a happy soldier' as his staff car meant everything to him. Eventually, with a water bottle full of cherry brandy for his wife Eileen, he made his way to the coast.[8] The Military Police told Hall it would not be possible to get through to Ghyvelde as it was a one-way street. As he moved closer the numbers of ditched vehicles increased and he only got through by 'dint of pushing every other lorry out of the way.' His final obstacle was 20 horses left tethered in a narrow lane. At the end of the journey, which took two hours, Hall was most 'proud' of his efforts and they arrived just in time for breakfast.[9]

4   TNA WO 167/452: 29 May 1940.
5   *The Delhi Spearman* (1992), p.91.
6   Falaise, *Through Hell to Dunkirk*, p.149.
7   Falaise, *Through Hell to Dunkirk*, p.149.
8   *The Delhi Spearman* (2001), p.95.
9   Hall Diary, 29 May 1940.

Falaise noticed that the farther they went, the roads and adjacent fields had 'taken on the aspect of dumps filled with what once was the fine materiel of the BEF. Overturned trucks, equipment, broken cases with thousands of unopened cans spilt out and heaps of cigarette packages and clothing were strewn everywhere in the mire.' As dawn broke, he saw the many 'freshly-dug graves and bloated horses putrefying in the fields. There were long lines of worn-out troops trudging wearily on amidst the wreckage.' The troops were 'from all the Allied countries, French, British, Belgian, all in disorder, all retreating.'[10]

At 0500 hrs, A Squadron's armoured cars took up positions on the bridges at Nieuport along with the French Dragoons who were already in position and in control of the situation. Despite the fact they had not seen the Germans since yesterday, the German field guns started to find the range of the bridges and several 105-mm shells burst above them. Soon, a Henschel observation plane hovered overhead, an 'ominous token of unpleasant things to come.' During the morning, sometime before midday, Shand was detailed to control the traffic and try and separate the French and British into separate streams, which he described as 'most exasperating' work which had to be conducted under 'considerable aerial bombardment.'[11]

At 1400 hrs, the Germans launched a dive bomber attack on their position which lasted for over half an hour, and the French Dragoons suffered many casualties as the Stukas took turns diving down. As the bridges started to come under pressure, they began to be blown in turn. The unfortunate consequence was that the Belgians who had not already crossed had 'to remain on our side' and were now trapped between the Germans and the coast.[12]

An hour later, the forward troops received orders to withdraw and join the Regimental rendezvous at Ghyvelde. The French troops flooded the whole district south of Furnes as a defence against German tanks, and the narrow roads which were barely above the level of water-covered fields, were 'jammed with retreating troops.' The Squadron proceeded with the greatest difficulty, finally reaching the French border, and halted south of Ghyvelde. The moment the Squadron 'dreaded,' finally arrived. The battle-scarred armoured cars were lined up alongside the canal. Horsbrugh-Porter gave the order to dismount and that they be stripped of ammunition and weapons and anything else which could have been of any use.[13] Shand wrote, that they 'drained the sumps of the latter and ran the engines until they seized up and then fired Boyes anti-tank bullets into the engines before pushing them into one of the canals.'[14]

At Vincquim, B Squadron was given the same task and Hunn wrote that they undertook it with 'heavy hearts.' All the vehicles were drained of oil and water and

10   Falaise, *Through Hell to Dunkirk*, p.150.
11   Shand, *Previous Engagements*, p.57.
12   Falaise, *Through Hell to Dunkirk*, p.150.
13   Falaise, *Through Hell to Dunkirk*, p.151.
14   Shand, *Previous Engagements*, p.57.

the engines were run until they seized. The wireless sets were removed, dismantled and smashed with sledgehammers and the tyres and wheels on the cars were made 'unserviceable.' When the task was complete, they dowsed the camouflage nets in oil and petrol, placed them inside the cars and set light to them. Finally, like the other squadrons, they pushed their armoured cars into the canal.[15]

Once A Squadron had destroyed their armoured cars, 'heavily-laden,' they made their way to Ghyvelde. Falaise looked back and bid 'farewell' to the armoured cars which had been their 'faithful companions which, though inadequate in many ways,' had rendered unfailing service in most difficult conditions. The armoured cars were 'now merely hulks of steel' which were 'sluggishly sinking into their muddy graves.'[16]

Eventually, they reached a large field on the outskirts of Ghyvelde where all the officers and men were destroying and burning their personal kit and everything they would not be able to carry along with them. 'A huge bonfire had been started' and suitcases full of linen, boots, records, etc., everything they had carried for so long and cherished, was reluctantly thrown into the blaze.'[17]

By 2000 hrs, the retreating Squadron was under 'strong and savage air attack from squadrons of Heinkels and Messerschmitts which were machine gunning and bombing the villages.' Falaise noticed 'dozens of abandoned French artillery horses. Some were dead, while others were whinnying and galloping around, trying to escape.' The 'din' was terrific, and 'every available weapon was turned against the planes and thousands of bullets were whizzing In every direction.' Falaise took refuge in a shallow ditch 'to quiet' his nerves. He took up a rifle along with everyone else and crouched low, the threat was now as equal from both the air and the ground. After an hour, the noise subsided and the Squadron stood around not knowing what to do and waiting for orders.

In an attempt to find out what was going on, Falaise wrote that Horsbrugh-Porter captured one of the French artillery horses and rode bareback to the village to find out what he could.[18] Before he left, Horsbrugh-Porter tasked Bishop to 'go and find the transport,' so like Horsbrugh-Porter, Bishop 'caught hold' of one of the many horses which had been turned loose and set about his 'impossible task'. He recorded that the horse he found had a 'French officer's saddle, grey with quite a bit of quality.' Eventually, after a mile and purely by luck Bishop found the transport.[19] On his return, Bishop led the dismounted Squadron to the transport so they could gather and go for a hot meal. Bishop noted that one of the soldiers had found a 'terrified terrier

15   Hunn Diary, 29 May 1940.
16   Falaise, *Through Hell to Dunkirk,* p.151.
17   Falaise, *Through Hell to Dunkirk,* p.151.
18   Falaise, *Through Hell to Dunkirk,* p.152. Bishop states that he gave Horsbrugh-Porter his horse after he found the transport.
19   Bishop, *One Young Soldier,* p.65.

pup inside one of the ditched trucks,' and was now sharing his food with it. The soldier said that the "right bastard" that had left it there must already be on their way home.'[20]

Lumsden eventually returned and briefed the Regiment that they needed to be ready to leave for the coast at 0300 hrs. He told them that many ships had been sunk by the Luftwaffe during the afternoon and evening and so the evacuation was not proceeding very fast. However, it appeared that the evacuation had been promised air protection for tomorrow. Shand wrote that when they left for La Panne, before dawn, they left their 'lorries and spare baggage' burning behind them. Bishop noted the same, although said that when they left, 'the Regiment was still together and fully armed.'[21]

As it became clear that the Regiment would be leaving at some point. According to Falaise:

> I feel very miserable as I think of the thousands of French soldiers of the Cavalry Corps trapped and cut-off from us 60 miles away, fighting to the last around Douai and Lille. It is their sacrifice which may perhaps enable us to get away. Machin brings me a cup of hot tea to cheer me up. I roll up in a blanket, lie down on the wet grass near an abandoned truck and try to sleep, and do not think of tomorrow.[22]

It was understandable that Falaise should view the situation through the eyes of his fellow countrymen. However, for the soldiers of the Regiment the perspective was different. They had been beaten but not defeated and now they were going home. Hall wrote, 'it was a curious reflection on the way the men's spirits were affected. At first, knowing that they were to leave some time in the future, they were depressed and quiet, but when they heard that they were to embark for England the next morning they were so cheered that when a Bosche aeroplane appeared they let off every rifle and Bren gun there was.' That evening they destroyed their 'lorries and slept a little having first drunk everything they could manage.'[23]

Thursday 30th May

(Day Twenty One)
The Commanding Officer had been 'personally and directly ordered by the C-in-C to re-organise the embarkation beaches at La Panne owing to certain difficulties which had been experienced on that beach.
War Diary[24]

---

20 Bishop, *One Young Soldier*, p.65.
21 Shand, *Previous Engagements*, p.57; Bishop, *One Young Soldier*, p.66.
22 Falaise, *Through Hell to Dunkirk*, p.151.
23 Hall Diary, 29 May 1940.
24 TNA WO 167/452: 30 May 1940.

On the way, I met Herbert Lumsden who, with his excellent 12th Lancers, was controlling the beach and organising embarkation parties.
GOC II Corps[25]

It was just after 0300 hrs when A Squadron assembled in the dark to move off towards Adinkerke. The Squadron set off carrying on their shoulders their Bren guns, Boyes anti-tank rifles and cases of ammunition. The first part of the journey followed 'a smuggler's path' that was covered in ammunition along a ridge of sand dunes which lay approximately a mile south of the main Dunkirk – Furnes road. The march across the dunes was 'heavy going' and they often had to stop to allow the more tired ones to catch up. After approximately two miles, they crossed the French border and turned north once more into Belgium reaching the road which ran alongside the Dunkirk-Furnes Canal. The next two miles towards Adinkerke felt like 10. When they arrived they halted at the back of a farm near a narrow bridge over the canal.[26]

Falaise was 'worn out and soaked with sweat, and needed to stop as he felt he could not walk a step further.' In the farm there was an old well in the courtyard with plenty of clear water so, while the cooks made tea, Falaise soaked his head and was relieved by its coolness. Lumsden arrived at the farm and briefed the officers 'that from the look of things the Regiment might get off but warned them that if they were to get aboard a ship, they would most probably have to swim for it.' So, he advised the officers to get rid of everything, except weapons, ammunition, and respirators. Fortunately, some of the men found a dozen abandoned bicycles probably left there by the Belgian troops. They used them as carriers for the heavier guns and the ammunition cases for the next move.[27]

At 1100 hrs, A Squadron was assembled on the side of the road waiting for the order to march across the bridge leading to La Panne. After waiting for 30 minutes, the signal to march was given and they stepped-off towards the canal in troop column formation with wide intervals between each troop. The bridge was guarded by a platoon of British infantry, with instructions to stop the French soldiers from moving towards the coast, as only British soldiers were allowed to cross. It was only by the intervention of Horsbrugh-Porter and Shand who linked their arms through Falaise's, insisting that he was part of the Regiment and that he was allowed to stay with the Squadron (see map 19).[28]

On the bridge, Falaise was surprised to find Captain Ciriez, another *Agent de Liaison* with the British army corps. His job was to divert the French troops towards the south to Bray-Dunes and Malo les Bains as these were the only points where the French were to be taken off. He explained that this was 'to avoid confusion as strict

25   Bryant, *The Turn of the Tide*, p.118.
26   Falaise, *Through Hell to Dunkirk*, p.153.
27   Falaise, *Through Hell to Dunkirk*, pp.153-154.
28   Falaise, *Through Hell to Dunkirk*, p.154.

discipline and control' was 'needed in an operation of this kind.' As they marched through the dunes, Falaise found 'hundreds of stragglers in French uniform, camping in gipsy-fashion around fires, some of them were drunk.' The lack of discipline in his countrymen 'infuriated' him. However, when he tried to shame them, he became embarrassingly uncomfortable when they explained that they were all men belonging to the older reserves and they knew that they were going to be left behind. They informed him that they had 'been told that the authorities had decided to give the first chance for escape to the younger fighting men who will be able to get right back into the scrap.' So they, the older men of the Services of Supply, had to stay behind and 'take what comes.' Falaise found it 'difficult to argue with these men, who were now sitting looking at him defiantly, and consoling themselves by eating and drinking everything those who were leaving them' had abandoned. These men only had a few more hours of freedom remaining. Apologetically, Falaise took his leave, daring not to look back and 'face their envious and anxious eyes as they watched the Squadron 'march down the road towards what they regarded as safety.'[29]

Finally, just outside La Panne, the Regiment halted under some pine trees. By the time A Squadron arrived, the two other squadrons were already there. For Falaise, it was the first time in a month that he had seen his friend Guy, the *Agent de Liaison* with B Squadron. They had much to catch up on and they talked about Pierre (Vaast), their colleague who was with C Squadron, and whom they had not seen since Neuville-St. Eventually, he joined them and as they chatted, 'they endeavoured to forget the bombardment and tried to forecast their immediate future.'[30]

At 1400 hrs, the Regiment marched off through the town. At the end of a narrow street, they could 'smell the tang of a salty breeze.' A few minutes later, beyond a narrow stretch of yellow sand, Falaise saw 'the glorious sight of the splashing surf, and stretching to the end of the horizon, the dark green waves' which might take them to England. The Regiment established themselves in two deserted villas on the seafront. It was here that they heard there was no immediate prospect of embarkation. The Regiment was assigned to police duties on the beach and to see that the embarkations were accomplished in good order.[31]

Lumsden had been 'personally and directly ordered by the C-in-C to re-organise the embarkation beaches at La Panne owing to certain difficulties which had been experienced on that beach.'[32] On the beach in front of A Squadron SHQ were four Bofors anti-aircraft guns and the Regiment took over and re-organised three embarkation points. They then assisted in the collection and forming up of motor transport vehicles as a jetty on the sand and into the sea from which it would be easier to embark troops. Parties were sent off to collect folding boats and rope from abandoned Royal

29   Falaise, *Through Hell to Dunkirk*, p.155.
30   Falaise, *Through Hell to Dunkirk*, p.155.
31   Falaise, *Through Hell to Dunkirk*, p.155.
32   TNA WO 167/452: 30 May 1940.

Engineer vehicles. Troops entering the bridgehead were met by boats on endless ropes which could be used to overcome any lack of watermanship in the troops embarking. Each squadron worked and looked after a single jetty.[33] Syms found a motorboat which they thought they would be able to use to tow out the rowing boats. With the help of some gunners, they managed to get it into the water.[34] However, despite the calm sea, there were no boats ready to take personnel on board until the evening.[35] On the seafront, thousands of British soldiers waited patiently for a boat; but none seemed to be coming near the shore. The men had been there all day, but no one had yet embarked.[36]

In the afternoon, Falaise went into town to search for food for the Squadron. When he returned to the waterfront with Machin and Lance Corporal Aldrich, laden with supplies, he saw that two destroyers had moved close to the shore and were now taking on men. After a while, as the German fire increased in intensity, all embarkation stopped and the destroyers steamed off slowly towards Dunkirk. Immense black clouds of smoke now stretched for miles. Falaise thought the 'oil reserves must be on fire.' The smoke over Dunkirk was now getting 'thicker and rising ever higher in the sky.'[37]

Suddenly, there was a 'roar of engines' as four German bombers flew directly at the Regiment at a height of less than 1000 feet. The crews of the Bofors battery got their gun into action and tracer shells streaked through the air which was rapidly filled with black smoke and the dark smudges of shell bursts. The Regiment took up its Bren guns and added 'their sharp crackle to the ear-rending racket.' Unperturbed and in perfect formation, the bombers flew over, dropping their bombs as they passed. Falaise stood 'flat against the wall of a villa where he found two British soldiers from another Regiment who crouched by his side. One looked near to breaking point and had his handkerchief stuffed in his mouth so as not to scream. His face was the colour of clay,' Falaise 'offered him some brandy, but he shook his head in refusal.'[38]

At 1900 hrs, the two destroyers (possibly the same two which had left earlier) moved back in towards the shore and the embarkation resumed. The process continued in 'perfect order and with unabated zeal' throughout the night. Soldiers of the Regiment rowed the waiting soldiers out to the two destroyers waiting in deeper water. The process was made all the easier by the 'dead calm sea.' Bishop himself made two trips and assisted with the rowing which he found hard work and said that 'it was two trips too many.'[39] However, towards the morning, the supply of boats started to fail and embarkation slowed off. The onshore wind freshened so that a higher degree of

33   Bishop, *One Young Soldier*, p.64.
34   Hall Diary, 1 June 1940, p.12.
35   TNA WO 167/452: 30 May 1940.
36   Falaise, *Through Hell to Dunkirk*, p.156.
37   Falaise, *Through Hell to Dunkirk*, p.157.
38   Falaise, *Through Hell to Dunkirk*, p.157.
39   Bishop, *One Young Soldier*, p.66.

watermanship was now required to keep the boats head on to the wind, whilst being rowed out. During the loading, Falaise saw Horsbrugh-Porter ankle-deep in the water helping soldiers into longboats. Shand wrote that 'the officers were appointed Embarkation Staff Officers (ESO) and were assisted by four subalterns from the Coldstream Guards who had been sent over from England the previous day to assist':

> The operation went pretty well, especially during the night when we were able to evacuate a great many walking wounded. We had fairly plenary powers over our jetties, and I think that junior officers probably got a certain sardonic satisfaction in asking those of senior rank to wait their turn before embarking![40]

However, not everyone took their direction well. A drunken and insolent Scotsman 'covered' Hall with his rifle. Fortunately, before Hall could draw his revolver, the man was restrained by his friends. When Hall called for the beach guard, he was surprised to find that they had already been withdrawn. Hall described it as 'not a very creditable incident.'[41]

When Horsbrugh-Porter finally came up from the waterline, he drank a cup of tea and as he ate a sandwich, he discussed with Falaise their chances of getting to England. Horsbrugh-Porter thought their chances were 'slim' but Falaise was far more optimistic and had confidence in the High Command. He thought they would do 'everything it could to save a man of such military calibre as Lumsden as they would need him later.' He also knew that 'he would not leave the beach until the last man of his Regiment was safely on board.'[42]

One of the most distinguished passengers the Regiment rowed out was Rear Admiral Frederic Wake-Walker who was given responsibility for everything afloat at Dunkirk, including the armada of small craft then being assembled.[43] Wake-Walker had been ashore and visited Gort. When Wake-Walker left Gort about 2200 hrs he asked "if a boat had been told to wait for him" but the reply was that boats were too precious to be kept hanging around, even for an Admiral at this stage of the evacuation. Wake-Walker wrote that he came across some 'men of the 12th Lancers attempting to float pontoons, and he 'persuaded' eight of them to paddle him out to the destroyer Worcester, his flagship of the moment, lying offshore:

> I placed four on each side and told them to wade out with it and get in when I told them. They got in two by two until only my Flag Lieutenant and I were still wading at the stern with the water well over our knees. Finally, we got in together and I started the soldiers paddling by numbers, rather like a racing

40   Shand, *Previous Encounters,* p.58 and Shand, 'A Memory, May 1940', p.155.
41   Hall Diary, 1 June 1940, p.12.
42   Falaise, *Through Hell to Dunkirk*, p.158.
43   Bishop, *One Young Soldier,* p.64; R. Atkin, *Pillar of Fire: Dunkirk 1940* (1990), p.186.

boat's crew. They soon picked it up, but I noticed there was already a good deal of water in the boat. The freeboard was about three inches, and the wavelets were washing up to my stern as I sat on the gunwale. So, we all got out and returned to the beach with our boat and emptied it… Reluctantly I had to reduce my crew by two and off we went again. This time things went all right and the soldiers, settling down in fine style, soon brought us to the Worcester.[44]

Hall wrote in his diary that 'late at night I went to see the Admiral in charge, who was closeted in GHQ with Gort.'[45] It is possible that Hall was sent to escort Wake-Walker to the beach. However, the absence of any other Royal Naval personnel on the beach was recorded in The *War Diary*. 'No attempt was made by the Navy to form an endless or towing rope between the beach and the ships, although the Regiment had by this time collected some nine miles of rope of varying thicknesses. A properly organised rope line by which passengers in each boat could pull themselves out leaving the crew to pull back the empty boat would have been invaluable and would have greatly speeded up the rate of embarkation.'[46] That said, Bishop wrote that he received invaluable help from a contemporary of his, a naval officer called Godman, who 'was everywhere at once, capless and bare footed, clad in only grey flannel slacks and a monkey jacket.' He read later he had been awarded the Distinguished Service Cross and he thought that if it were for Dunkirk 'he deserved it several times over.'[47]

A little difficulty was experienced with some Belgian officers who were all collected in one place and then marched down to embark. They were taught how to row, to keep the boat head-on into the wind, to embark equally from both sides of the boat, which had been pushed out waist-deep into the water, and then shown to which ship they had to row. Unfortunately, at the last moment, they forgot some of their instructions and poured into the boat from one side which then capsized and filled with water. The boats were baled-out, the rowlocks collected from the sea bed, the oars recovered, and the whole performance started again, but unfortunately with the same result. As boats were all too precious, the Belgians were regretfully marched from the beach and told to embark from the Mole at Dunkirk.[48]

44   Atkin, *Pillar of Fire*, p.188.
45   Hall Diary, 30 May 1940, p.12.
46   TNA WO 167/452: 30 May 1940.
47   Bishop, *One Young Soldier*, p.66. The Royal Navy put ashore a Beach Party of 12 Officers and 160 bluejackets.
48   TNA WO 167/452: 30 May 1940.

Friday 31st May

(Day Twenty Two)
The officers were told to get back in the sea, there were trailing ropes to clutch – we clutched.
Bishop[49]

The Regiment woke to 105-mm shells crashing in the streets in and around its locations. Falaise found Horsbrugh-Porter in the front room of their villa, 'worn out from his all-night vigil over the embarkation and from standing so long in the cold water and his expression was grim and smileless.' Since it appeared there was little prospect of getting off, Horsbrugh-Porter asked Falaise to go out again into the town and see what he could 'find in the way of food.' Between them, they emptied their pockets of what money they had left and Falaise 'went out on a buying spree.'[50]

Falaise took Machin with him into the town 'running from house to house,' eventually finding an open bakery where he bought 'several loaves of bread.' They then climbed 'over a back wall into a grocery store where they succeeded in buying some sardines and cheese, however, 'paying for them with almost their weight in gold.' Falaise decided that with what was left of the money, he would 'invest it in wine and beer.' Despite the ongoing shelling, they made their way back to the squadron with their precious cargo unharmed, where they were 'welcomed like long-lost brothers.'[51]

Initially, the Regiment was informed that it was to be relieved of their embarkation supervision duties at 0900 hrs, but it was now midday and they still had not been replaced. However, the destroyers that had been lying offshore and taking on men all morning pulled out again because of the intense shelling from the German batteries. 'Each time the destroyers put to sea; gloom settled in along the beach.'[52]

At approximately 1300 hrs, Horsbrugh-Porter arrived with the news that the Squadron was to assemble on the beach below the dunes at the western end of the town, having finally been relieved by the soldiers from 1st Division.[53] The Squadron marched off in single file along the heavy sand towards the rendezvous. When they arrived, they found the other squadrons and the 'Regiment were together for the first time since 10th May, all the Lancers reunited.' The men were lying around in the hot sun waiting for the return of Lumsden who had gone off towards Dunkirk. Horsbrugh-Porter and Shand found some deck chairs in which they lay sunbathing as if it were just an ordinary Summer day. Falaise was about to join them on the warm sand when the noise of aircraft engines made him sit up and take notice. Down the beach, he saw a flight of German light bombers flying straight towards their location.[54]

49   Bishop, *One Young Soldier*, p.67.
50   Falaise, *Through Hell to Dunkirk*, p.159.
51   Falaise, *Through Hell to Dunkirk*, p.159.
52   Falaise, *Through Hell to Dunkirk*, p.160.
53   Shand, *Previous Encounters*, p.58.
54   Falaise, *Through Hell to Dunkirk*, p.160.

Fifteen seconds later, bombs came thundering down on the dunes, the shore, and the hotel that stood at the western tip of the town a few hundred yards away. It was the same hotel that General Gort had been in only a few hours earlier and was 'repeatedly' hit. Falaise and Guy found a small plank and started to dig themselves in. While they were doing so, the planes flew out to sea and attacked one of the destroyers which managed to shoot one of them down. The planes then returned to the beach on a low pass to machine gun the soldiers on the beach before dropping five more bombs. Finally, the aircraft disappeared towards the smoke cloud which was now covering 'the whole of the Dunkirk area.'[55]

At approximately 1500 hrs, Lumsden arrived in a 'shooting brake staff car' which the driver had found on the beach.[56] Lumsden ordered that all the heavy weapons were to be placed in it and the Regiment was ordered to march towards Dunkirk, approximately 10 miles away. On hearing of a soldier who had arrived at the beach without his Bren gun, Lumsden sent him back to fetch it and told him not to return without it, whereupon the soldier returned four hours later.[57] Not only had the Regiment taken its own weapons but an additional 30 Lewis Guns that it collected on its march. The *Regimental History* stated that the Regiment saw it as a 'point of honour' to reach the beach with all its hand-held weapons.[58]

Horsbrugh-Porter placed the Squadron in arrow formation (Artillery), in order to minimise any casualties from artillery and air attack and made their way down the beach. This reminded Shand of his days in the Officer Training Corps (OTC).[59] Half way down the beach, Bishop looked back to see their previous area at La Panne 'being blotted out by heavy shellfire.'[60] After an hour of marching under 'the blazing sun, the formation became drawn out' as a result of being 'machine gunned and bombed three times. During this process, several men were wounded and had to be left at the Casualty Clearing Station.'[61] Horsbrugh-Porter walked ahead unflinchingly, shouldering parts of the kit of many of his exhausted men. Falaise wrote that he did not once slacken his pace or duck to dodge bombs and bullets. His 'magnificent bravery gave us the courage to keep on going.' Thurston thought the march was 'orderly' and was a 'magnificent sight and must have shown by example how a well-trained and disciplined Regiment could behave in such circumstances.'[62] Hall's personal experience was far less pleasurable. He wrote 'it was the most horrible walk' he had 'ever known,' and that they were completely out of condition and carrying far too much kit… It was only by keeping in step that he 'found the journey much easier' notwithstanding his

55   Falaise, *Through Hell to Dunkirk*, p.161.
56   Bishop, *One Young Soldier*, p.67.
57   Bishop, *One Young Soldier*, p.66.
58   Stewart, *History of the XII Royal Lancers*, p.372 and Falaise, *Through Hell to Dunkirk*, p.161.
59   Shand, *Previous Encounters*, p.58.
60   Bishop, *One Young Soldier*, p.67.
61   Trooper Bloom, Bishop, *One Young Soldier*, p.67 and Hall Diary, 1 June 1940, p.12.
62   Thurston, *Account*, p.2.

blisters.[63] Bishop wrote that 'hope made the march,' even for 'weak infantry,' a 'mere nothing.'[64]

At 1900 hrs, the Regiment was still stumbling along, dodging bombs. Eventually they were in France again having marched over seven miles since leaving La Panne. The march was tough going every inch of the way. Not far ahead, Falaise could see the large hotel of Malo Terminus two miles east of Dunkirk. Lumsden's car passed the column and halted about half a mile ahead of the Regiment. When the Regiment reached him, he told them that we had "come to the end of the road and must take to the water. We are going to embark!"[65]

At approximately 2000 hrs, from about a mile out to sea, two boats moved slowly towards the beach where the Regiment waited. The first was a small excursion steamer, the other 'was a queer-looking craft, a sand dredger that belonged to the Tilbury Construction and Bridging Company.'[66] Long boats and launches also started to make their way to the beach, 'and the sailors signalled to the Regiment to come out as far as they could into the water.' The conditions had changed from the previous day, and now the wind was rising and there was a swell as they waded out into the cold sea. Soon, they were shoulder-deep. Shand wrote that 'each of the squadrons waded into the sea until it was up to their chins, pulling themselves along ropes which had been tied to the boats.'[67] Bishop wrote that when the boats were full 'the officers were told to get back in the sea, there were trailing ropes to clutch – we clutched.'[68] In the meantime, the RAF fighters engaged the Heinkels and dispersed them, this resulted in two enemy bombers being shot down and a Hurricane diving 'straight into the sea a few hundred yards away.'[69]

The whole loading process took about 30 minutes. All the men had eventually clambered into the launches and one by one they boarded the steamer which pulled out rapidly as soon as it was full. The only people left neck-deep in the icy water were Lumsden, the three squadron leaders, two French liaison officers and Falaise, plus a handful of men. Once the steamer had left, the dredger came in slowly to pick them up. The heavy swell washed over Falaise's head and he lost the haversack he was holding above the water. In it, he had put a dry shirt, a sweater, some valued personal belongings (including his divorce papers) and a gas mask. 'He tried in vain to recover it but it sank to the bottom like a stone, waterlogged.'[70]

A launch then came in to pick up the soldiers and take them to the dredger, but its sides were too high, and Falaise did not have the strength to pull himself up. This was

63   Hall Diary, p.12.
64   Bishop, *One Young Soldier*, p.67.
65   Falaise, *Through Hell to Dunkirk*, p.161.
66   TNA WO 167/452: 31 May 1940.
67   Hunn Diary, p.16. Shand states 1900 hrs, *Previous Engagements*, p.59.
68   Bishop, *One Young Soldier*, p.67.
69   Falaise, *Through Hell to Dunkirk*, p.162.
70   Bishop, *One Young Soldier*, p.67.

a result of him being weighed down by his soaked uniform, steel helmet, and heavy riding boots. After several attempts, he was about to give up and loosen his grip as his fingers were numb with the cold. He wrote that he was sure he could not hold on for another minute and 'then four strong arms hoisted' him 'over the side' where he fell 'like a clod into the bottom of the launch.'[71]

Falaise was not the only individual who struggled to get into the small boats which came to collect them. Willis and one or two soldiers almost drowned whilst climbing onto the launch, as the latter was suddenly towed out into deep water and they were thrown back into the sea out of their depth, but with the aid of many lifebelts and some 'Herculean efforts' they were safely pulled on board. Thurston, who had already climbed into his boat, was pulled back into the sea by a panicking soldier of the Regiment. The soldier tried to use Thurston's waist belt to pull himself into the boat, which resulted in him being dragged back into the sea. Thurston was top-heavy with equipment and could not get his footing in the deep water and was only saved from drowning by an officer who had seen what had happened.[72] Hunn said that it took 'superhuman effort' to clamber aboard the small boats.[73]

The *War Diary* recorded that 'it proved yet again how important it was for all soldiers to be able to swim' and for some to know 'how to resuscitate the apparently drowned.' Had there not been many strong swimmers in the Regiment and others such as Trooper Doyle who knew how to 'life save,' the casualties amongst those embarking would have been 'appreciably higher.'[74]

By 2100 hrs the whole Regiment had embarked, with all the Boyes rifles and Bren guns, most of them finding places on the dredgers. The Regiment departed 'amidst some light shelling and an appreciable amount of bombing.' The Regiment's 'very charming hosts' had some 50 years' experience at sea, although some had never lost sight of the shores of Great Britain. Byass noted that the ship 'was commanded by a midshipman who looked about 12, assisted by a boatswain aged about 80 who had never previously been outside the River Thames.'[75] Once on board, Falaise wrote:

> My aching body feels dead. All I can hear is the roaring of the German motors sweeping over us, the screaming of the bombs and the loud explosions which jar my ears and practically blow the breath out of me. I hear Pierre, who is sitting next to me, say that a drink of brandy would be in order. I point to my left pocket, and he pulls out my flask. We pour brandy down our throats as if it were water... I am sitting stark naked on a heap of coal in the engine room of the dredger. My clothes are hanging near the furnace to dry, and I am trying to get warm.

71   Falaise, *Through Hell to Dunkirk*, p.162.
72   Thurston, *Account*, p.3.
73   Hunn Diary, p.16.
74   TNA WO 167/452, 31 May 1940.
75   Shand, *Previous Engagements*, p.59 and Hunn, Frederick (Oral history)/Imperial War Museums <iwm.org.uk> (accessed 11/7/22).

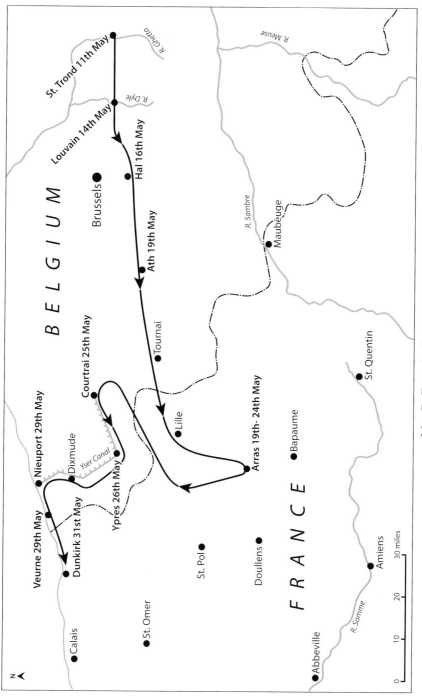

Map D From the Dyle to Dunkirk.

My whole body is shaking. I don't want to move, but just sit here where it is hot and stare at the flames of the boiler with my mind a complete blank. The craft is crawling along slowly because a near-hit bomb loosened some bow plates. The stoker says we are averaging only about two knots.[76]

Shand, however, wrote that he had 'absolutely no recollection of the journey back at all, as I think I slept the whole way.' This was possibly assisted by some rum that he was given, and he went to sleep 'in some sort of wheelhouse.'[77] Before he slept, Hunn took one last look 'at the glow lighting the smoke clouds over Dunkirk.'[78]

Saturday 1st June

(Day Twenty Three)
'Oh no," he said, "we march!" Everybody else went on the buses but the 12th Lancers, who had acquitted themselves so splendidly in the fighting, marched in threes with their arms swinging.
Gillam[79]

Falaise was woken when the 'chug-chugging of the engine' stopped. The stoker informed him that that they were off-course, lost in a minefield and that their best hope was to wait until daylight. Once Falaise's clothes were dry, he joined the others who were still fast asleep in a heap inside the wheelhouse.[80]

At 0600 hrs, when Falaise went on deck, he found that their boat had a mixture of French and British soldiers who were 'huddled together, lying on the filthy boards, dead to the world, down and out. The skipper hailed a passing minesweeper shouting,' "Which is the main road to Ramsgate?"[81] As Falaise lent on the rail feeling low and very weary, he had lost all his personal equipment and his revolver. All he had in his possession were 'some papers' and his diary which he had kept in his pocket.[82] Hunn was woken at approximately 0700 when someone shouted "Blighty!" Up to that point, he had been on deck having immediately fallen asleep.[83]

The Regiment landed at Margate at approximately 1000 hrs. Hunn recorded that the welcome from the inhabitants was 'fantastic. Tea, sandwiches, cake, and biscuits were distributed, and there was cheering, crying and laughter as these people showed

---

76   Falaise, *Through Hell to Dunkirk*, pp.162-163.
77   Shand, *Previous Engagements*, p.59.
78   Hunn Diary, p.17.
79   Gillam in Harris, *Dunkirk: The Storms of War*, p.132.
80   Falaise, *Through Hell to Dunkirk*, p.165.
81   Hall Diary, 1 June 1940, p.13.
82   Falaise, *Through Hell to Dunkirk*, p.165.
83   Hunn Diary, p.17.

their joy at our safe arrival home.' However, in their 'crumpled clothing, unshaven and weary faces' they 'look far from being victorious.'[84]

When Gillam arrived at Margate, he noted that there were temporary canteens set up. Double-decker buses were waiting to carry them to the station but Gillam wrote that the RSM was having none of that:

> "Oh no," he said, "we march!" Everybody else went on the buses but the 12th Lancers, who had acquitted themselves so splendidly in the fighting, marched in threes with their arms swinging. It was a small example of Regimental pride at work, that small thing which Gillam insisted made Dunkirk a success. They complained but they also put on 'bags of swank' and when an old lady offered Gillam a packet of 50 cigarettes, the RSM gently pushed her away. "Leave him alone, Mum," he said. "This is Army business."[85]

Shand described what they saw after disembarking:

> Margate on a beautiful, but perhaps not glorious, First of June was a miracle of organised chaos: some administrative genius had done his work most thoroughly. I note from a telegram which I still possess, sent to my mother, that we must have landed soon after ten o'clock. There was little Regimental cohesion as we had all embarked at Dunkirk on various ships, some of which docked at different ports. At least we knew that all our own troops had got away on some sort of vessel, though where they were at the moment, Heaven alone knew. I was worried about the faithful Smallridge, last seen in watery circumstances, but I assumed he would eventually turn up. Seemingly innumerable trains awaited the stricken Army which, primed once more with 'proper' English tea, provided by the Salvation Army and local organisations, was soon being dispersed all over the kingdom. Rupert Byass, Tim, and I had a compartment to ourselves and promptly dropped into heavy slumber. We were conscious that the train had stopped at the London Olympia station, but it had started again while we were thinking of getting out and we were carried on to Bletchley through a comfortable, sunlit afternoon. At Bletchley, there were charming ladies awaiting us with reinforcements of tea and cigarettes. I set off to find the RTO in charge to enquire about our destination, but was rebuffed brusquely for breaching security: "Don't you realise there's a war on?" I returned to my companions only to discover that Tim, with more enterprise, had consulted the engine driver who divulged that the train was bound for Warrington in Lancashire. We felt it somewhat unnecessary to travel there before being sent south again and with the help of the Station Master, a most courteous individual, were inducted into

84   Hunn Diary, p.17.
85   Gillam in Harris, *Dunkirk: The Storms of War*, p.132.

a London bound express [and] White's Club, whose portals had probably never seen three dirtier guests.[86]

Hall followed Shand and his party to White's, so Byass could cash a cheque for him, as he had spent all his money on fares and drinks. He described the scene when he arrived:

> So, the beautiful sight of Rupert with four days' beard, myself in a three days' one, with awful cuts where I had tried to shave on the train, and Bruce hatless in a blue jersey was seen entering White's.[87]

Shand subsequently reflected that:

> It was gratifying to receive congratulations and to know that we had done as well as we could, but after the initial euphoria the more recent memories came flooding back: the speed of modern warfare, the plight of the refugees, the horror of the continual air attacks, the crucifying lack of sleep and, particularly in our Squadron, the thought of those who had been killed, and also the moments of sheer unadulterated fear, especially in those periods of silent watching when you were waiting for something to happen.[88] One was left with some curious problems to deal with. I am sure there is an answer to them all now, the map problem, running off the maps, I am sure this is a thing that happens in every war. There was an immense problem having to deal with French and Belgian troops, and I think we should have known perhaps more about demolitions and things like that... somebody said that officers should have at least two languages... a degree in civil engineering and some training with the Diplomatic Corps before assuming command of a troop. I am sure we made the most terrible mistakes and got into fearful messes, I know we did, I know I did personally... but I can say this: we did communicate.[89]

On the Regiment's return to England on 18th June, Field Marshal Birdwood, the Colonel-of-the-Regiment wrote to the Regiment about their conduct and placed it as 'a glorious page in their history':

> This the first possible opportunity of telling you one and all of the real great pride I feel in being so closely associated as I am as your Colonel with every one of you who have taken such a great part in writing the most glorious page in the history

86   Shand, *Previous Encounters*, pp.59-61.
87   Hall Diary, 1 June 1940, p.13.
88   Shand, *Previous Encounters*, pp.62-63.
89   Shand, Exercise ACROSPIRE, p.75.

of our Regiment since Waterloo. I well realise what all of you have been through and I know how magnificently every one of you behaved through everything – we have to remember too that much is yet before us before we attain the complete victory over the Germans which I have not the slightest doubt will be ours in due course – I'd give all I have to be young enough to be with you.[90]

One of Lumsden's final acts before leaving the Regiment on promotion was to submit select names from his Regiment for greater recognition:

It is with the greatest personal regret that I finally finish my term of Command of the Regiment. To nobody has the privilege been given to Command a finer Regiment and it is on that account that I hand over my Command with complete confidence that the Regiment will ever add to its recent glorious successes. I should like to congratulate those whose services have been so deservedly rewarded and my only regret is that it has not been possible to forward the names of so many more, whom we all know were similarly deserving and whose excellent work contributed in no less degree to enhance the fame of the 12th Royal Lancers.[91]

The word used by both Birdwood and Lumsden to describe their conduct was 'glorious.' In recognition of their services, the Regiment was awarded the following Battle Honours:

- Dyle
- Defence of Arras
- Arras Counter-Attack
- Dunkirk 1940
- Northwest Europe 1940[92]

---

90   TNA WO 167/452: 18 June 1940.
91   TNA WO 167/452: 16 June 1940.
92   *12L Regimental Journal* (1957), p.51.

9

Concluding Thoughts

[Armoured cars are] 'invaluable for recce, and 12th Lancers have done marvels, but the Morris is not tactically or technically good enough.
Major General Pope, BEF AFV Advisor[1]

I can say this, we did communicate.
Shand[2]

The single purpose of this publication is to bring together all the known fragments of the 12th Lancer story of 1940 into what will hopefully be seen as the definitive story. Unlike the postwar Regimental history, the collective accounts have produced a complete narrative. Stewart did not serve with the Regiment that fateful year and therefore it cannot be seen as a primary source. While it benefits from Lumsden's and Browne-Clayton's diaries, it does not include that of Falaise, which was available at the time. Stewart's history is eulogistic, free from criticism, and lacks any of the errors and mistakes to which Clark-Kennedy, Shand, Hall and Hunn freely admit. For the most part, the individual diaries are not contemporaneous, despite being produced in a diary format and nearly all of them contain a degree of post-event rationalisation, possibly with the exception of Hall's. It should also be noted that the War Diary was written on the return to Britain, as like so many of the other unit's war diaries, it was probably water-damaged at Dunkirk.

Hall's narrative is important since it gives the only account of the delivery of logistics. At times he is critical and he is the only narrator who questions what his RHQ are doing, although this needs to be balanced against his rank, appointment and length of service. Hunn's diary is also important since it is the only account of B Squadron's

---

1   War Office AFV Department correspondence in D. Taylor, *Armoured Warfare in the British Army 1939-1945* (2022), p.20.
2   Shand, *5th Division Exercise ACROSPIRE; Battlefield Tour; NW France, and Belgium 1940* (1970), p.75.

war, which gives balance to the rest which is all from A Squadron. Despite this, for the most part, the story is an A Squadron commissioned officer-centric account. From their accounts, it is quite clear that they represent a period of history when officers still had servants and batmen and when the opportunity presented itself, they preferred to Mess together. This was built on a culture of knightly and chivalric values which abhorred the civilian casualties and saw their men board the boats at Dunkirk first.

The timing of the German invasion caught the BEF and the Regiment unawares. No one would choose to go to war without the Commanding Officer or Quartermaster. The fact that Lumsden would have appeared to have been posted away and subsequently recalled is not explained. The Regimental personnel were not prepared for the ferocity of the German bombers and indiscriminate bombing of the towns and the civilian population and what they saw affected them all personally.

Lumsden was universally revered and he was at the heart of his RHQ where he and his staff were able to process the information much quicker than GHQ. Indeed, it would appear that Lumsden had the best understanding of the overall German intent.

From a tactical armoured car perspective, the key to their success was their ability to communicate by wireless, not only to each other but rearwards to GHQ. This was the Regiment's unique capability, and without it, GHQ would not have been able to make the timely decisions that it did. It is unclear why the Regiment was repeatedly used as a divisional cavalry regiment. One can only presume that there was a deficiency which the Lancers were able to satisfy.

When the Regiment was reporting and scouting, Lumsden's direction had always been not to get involved, but when it was either necessary or the opportunity presented itself, the Squadron Leaders and Troop Leaders were always aggressive and fearless, even against tanks. Their offensive cavalry spirit prevailed. The post-war criticism of the Morris armoured car has the benefit of hindsight and the knowledge of the vehicles that were to follow. There can be little doubt that the vehicle was highly suitable for its role in 1939, but there was no armoured car which could destroy a tank or survive a direct hit from anything the Germans possessed. Their routine was relentless. There is a prevailing narrative of lack of sleep and fatigue which they tried to manage as best they could by creating extra sections from the SHQ armoured cars and rotating commanders.

C Squadron after Dunkirk. (RLMT)

Appendix I

Gallantry and Distinguished Conduct Awards

The Regimental Journal of 2005 made the following statement: 'Lord Gort made 31 awards of which 12 went to members of the Regiment.[1] The following awards have been compiled from the Regimental War Diary and *A Short History of the XII Royal Lancers 1945-1960*, which would indicate that the number was in fact at least 18.[2] However, the first two awards account for the post-nominal letters of Lumsden and Willis before embarkation in 1939 and are not included in the total.

MILITARY CROSS (First World War)

LUMSDEN, H., Lieutenant, RHA (1918)

> For conspicuous gallantry and devotion to duty during 13 days of continuous fighting in charge of a forward section. He invariably showed the greatest cool-ness and courage in the face of danger, keeping his section in action, and always volunteering for any officer's patrol work. As Forward Observation Officer he was consistently shelled whenever he moved his OP, and, although finally wounded, he continued to work and observe for his battery.

MILITARY CROSS (1938)

WILLIS, J.H., Captain (1938 Attached to Trans-Jordanian Frontier Force)

> For gallant conduct and courageous, cool, and skilful leadership while in charge of three troops during an action near Beisan on 2nd December 1938.

---

1   *Delhi Spearman* (2005), pp.73-74.
2   R. Brockbank & R.M. Collins, *A Short History of the XII Royal Lancers 1945-1960* (1994), p.57.

DISTINGUISHED SERVICE ORDER

MANN, Second Lieutenant E.C.

On May 28th, 1940, this officer was sent to Dixmuide with his troops to ensure the bridges over the Yser Canal were demolished in time and to hinder the advance of any enemy forces which might appear in the area. In spite of the work of enemy agents dressed as French and Belgian officers, the bridges were blown, with the assistance of Lieutenant D.A. Smith, R.E., at the point of the revolver, after a second attempt, 10 minutes before the arrival of a detachment of enemy motor-cyclists, who were immediately followed by a column of infantry in lorries. By his skilful dispositions and bold leadership, he inflicted so many casualties on the head of this enemy column that he was able, when reinforced by another troop, to contain the enemy east of the Yser Canal for over seven hours, by which time more than 250 vehicles had been counted entering Dixmuide and the road Dixmuide – Roulers was a solid mass of transport. Had he failed, by less bold action or less skilful dispositions, to deceive the enemy as to his true strength and thus to contain this overwhelmingly superior force, the enemy would, during the first few hours, have had a clear road to two of the beaches from which the BEF finally embarked.

2nd Lieutenant Mann's medal group. (Author's collection)

HORSBRUGH-PORTER (Captain, T/Major) A.M.

This officer commanded his squadron between May 10 to 29 with the greatest dash and energy so that he obtained much valuable information. In the area of St. Omer on May 23, in spite of being wounded, he continued in command when his services were indispensable, clarified the situation, and in face of a superior force of enemy tanks and infantry with anti-tank guns, checked the enemy's advance, and enabled our guns and troops to get clear, finally extricating the last of his squadron with great skill. Had it not been for this bold and decisive action the enemy would have captured our guns and had a clear road to Hazebrouck. On May 27 in the area Dixmuide – Roulers – Ypres, by his keen perception and continuous close co-operation with the troops in that area, he was able to gain information which was of vital interest to our Army.

Horsburgh-Porter's DSO medal group. (RLMT)

LUMSDEN, Lieutenant Colonel H., M.C.

During the whole period of operations from May 10 until embarkation, Lieutenant Colonel Lumsden commanded the 12th Lancers with vigour, initiative, coolness, and boldness. His regiment operated continuously and untiringly on the front and on the flanks and was an example to all of what can be achieved by a highly trained and disciplined unit, fearlessly led. For the great achievements of the 12th Lancers, Lieutenant Colonel Lumsden is responsible.

MEMBER OF THE BRITISH EMPIRE

KENNARD, Captain, R.M.

Will shortly be completing his tour of duty as Adjutant, during which time he has been most successful and by his skill and constant hard work has achieved much in the common good.[3] A great sportsman who by his physical fitness and self-control is able to work hard and for long periods, and this, coupled with knowledge, enables him to be the most efficient key man in his Regiment.[4]

MILITARY CROSS

SHAND Lieutenant B.M.H.

During the period May 10-28 this officer, by his skill and great daring, repeatedly acquired the most valuable and accurate information about the enemy while on patrol, and inflicted numerous casualties. In the area of St. Omer on May 23, by the fearless manoeuvring of his troop, he was able to cover the withdrawal of a column of our lorries and guns in the face of fire from four enemy tanks which, without his intrepid intervention, would have been free to do great damage to our troops.

MILLER-MUNDY, Second Lieutenant E.P.G.

During the period May 10-28 this officer, by his clever and fearless leading, inflicted many casualties on the enemy. On May 19, in area Ath, when helping to cover the withdrawal of the 2nd Division, one of his cars was damaged and while a tow rope was being attached a large party of enemy infantry arrived within 100 yards of the cars. By the accuracy of his fire, he inflicted so many casualties on the enemy he was able to tow the car to safety. On May 28, at Nieuport, by his bold tactics in moving east of the River Yser, to meet the enemy who were approaching fast and in greatly superior numbers, he was thus able to check their advance for several hours, thus giving time and space for the bridges, prepared for demolition, to be blown up.

---

3   Nominated by Lumsden on 11 July 1940, this is not specifically for Dunkirk.
4   TNA WO 373/75/583.

CLARK-KENNEDY, Second Lieutenant A.J.C.

Between May 10 and 21 this officer always showed the greatest daring and skill in handling his troop and thereby obtained much very valuable and accurate information about the enemy's strength and movements. On May 21 in the area of Avesnes, by the bold manoeuvring of his troop, he inflicted many casualties on the enemy and captured several prisoners. Later the same day, when his leading car was hit by enemy anti-tank guns, he silenced the enemy's fire and ensured the rescue of the crew.

SMITH, Second Lieutenant, D.A., Royal Monmouthshire Royal Engineers att. 12th Lancers.

This officer was attached to my Regiment throughout the period of 10-29 May. He was in charge of three detachments of Royal Monmouthshire Royal Engineers who throughout this period carried out invaluable work to delay the enemy's advance. They never failed to accomplish any task they were set. On May 11 and 12 he ensured the demolition of bridges over the R. GHETTE, which had been prepared by the Belgian Army. On 14 May despite enemy bombing, he completed the demolition over the R. DENDRE north of Louvain. At Ypres on May 26 in spite of continuous shelling and bombing, working day and night with a handful of men he prepared and fired the demolitions in front of the Menin Gate. On the R. YSER on May 28, yet again he made the demolitions a certainty. Without his immediate aid, many bridges would have remained intact.

DISTINGUISHED CONDUCT MEDAL

PEARTON, Sergeant A.M.

On May 21, in the area of Avesnes, the armoured car in front of this SNCO was stopped by fire and overturned into a ditch in front of his car. He then advanced, and although his gunner was killed beside him, silenced the fire of the enemy machine gun post, killed several of them, rescued two men from the leading car, and brought them back safely to the dead ground behind. Although Sergeant Pearton's car was hit twice by anti-tank gun fire, his brilliant marksmanship when under fire, his determination, and the inspiration which he gave to the remainder of the crew carried this exploit through to a successful conclusion. This SNCO was frequently in the leading car of his troop and never lost his dash. He finally lost his car when inflicting very heavy casualties on the enemy and, through his very fine leadership, was able to withdraw his crew to safety in spite of enemy fire.

WATSON, Sergeant J.E.

This SNCO showed the finest leadership and courage during all the actions in which his troop took part between May 10 and 25. He was always in the leading car of his troop which inflicted severe casualties on the enemy and obtained much valuable and accurate information. On May 25, when his car was finally destroyed by enemy fire, although wounded, he got back with another wounded man of his crew, whom he assisted, reported to his troop leader that his car was lost, and pointed out the positions of the two anti-tank guns which had fired at his car, thereby through his grit and forethought, ensuring the prevention of further casualties.

JAMES, RQMS, W.S.

This WO acted as Quartermaster to the Regiment throughout the period May 10-31, and it is due to his excellent common-sense, personal disregard for bombing, and exceptional continuous efforts that the Regiment never lacked for supplies, ammunition, or petrol, although constantly on the move during this period.

They Held the Road to Dunkirk Beach for their Comrades of the BEF, 14th June 1940. (*Daily Sketch*)

MILITARY MEDAL

THURSTON, Sergeant J.

> Throughout the period of continuous fighting from May 10 to 28, this NCO, through his complete devotion to duty and untiring work, both by day and night, maintained the wireless communication to his Commanding Officer's car in perfect condition. Thereby this vital link in the chain of communication from forward troops to GHQ. was maintained. At Mont St. Eloi on May 21, through his personal disregard of bombing and his quick and skilful passing of messages, it was possible to cause the destruction of seven enemy lorries carrying infantry into action against us.

CHORLEY, Lance Corporal L.

> This NCO drove his car with the greatest skill and daring at all times between May 10 and 28, and when his car was engaged by enemy anti-tank guns in the area of Houdain on May 22 and three other members of the car were wounded he extricated his car with great coolness and fine judgement and drove to a Medical Dressing Station. which he found unaided. Through his skill and presence of mind, he saved his car and probably the lives of his car commander and wireless operator, who were both very seriously wounded.

GLARVEY, Lance Corporal C.H.

> At Dixmuide on May 28, this NCO was placed in a house with orders to snipe any enemy who tried to reconnoitre the bridge which had been blown, or who tried to advance down the street. By his very accurate fire, he inflicted a number of casualties on the enemy and cleared them completely from the street, thereby helping very materially to check the enemy's advance at a most critical time. His coolness, judgement, and devotion to duty set a very fine example.

MENTIONED IN DESPATCHES

The following were Mentioned in Despatches – no citations available:

- Captain Kennard
- Captain Mabbott
- RSM Fox
- Sgt Cutler
- Sgt Syms

Appendix II

101st Royal Monmouth Royal Engineers and A Squadron Echelon ORBATS

101st Royal Monmouth Royal Engineers[1]

Second Lieutenant D.A. Smith
Lance Corporal G. Hourigan
Driver C.E. Roach

Lance Sergeant W.G. Earl
Sapper F. Jones
Driver A.V. Clout

Lance Sergeant J. Johnson
Sapper A.J. Batt
Driver G.E. Waller

A Squadron Echelon[2]

8 cwt Wireless truck (Morris)
Lance Corporals Syms, Higgs, Bloom.
Fighting lorry (3 ton Commer)
Corporal Clinton, Nash, Lance Corporal Burns,
Cook's Lorry (30 cwt Morris)
SQMS Butler, Troopers Duffy, Alayden, Maitland, McCabe.
Petrol Lorry (30 cwt Commer)
Corporal Turner, Lance Corporal Scott,

---

1   TNA WO 167/778.
2   Hall Diary, p.13.

Officers Mess (30 cwt Commer)
Sergeant Sewell, Lance Corporals Park, Eldridge Clay
Personnel (30 cwt Morris)
Troopers Cruden, and Wills
Personnel (3 Ton Commer)

Chandler, Allis (Allis drove the 30 cwt Crossley that C Squadron gave us and Cruden the 3 ton Bedford.; Syms driving his old Morris, Burns drove Chandler's lorry, when he was killed, Nash driving the fighting lorry. My [Hall] DR was usually Cotton of 3 Troop).[3]

---

3   Hall Diary, p.13.

Appendix III

Fatalities in Chronological Order

Service Number	Rank	Surname	Christian Names	Age	Date of Death	Comments
551908	Lance Corporal	Averill	Francis Joseph		11/05/1940	
316706	Corporal	Chambers	Howard	29	20/05/1940	A Squadron
549956	Lance Corporal	Humphrey	Fred	30	21/05/1940	B Squadron
3653496	Trooper	Westrop	Henry James	20	21/05/1940	B Squadron
321513	Trooper	Hudson	Bernard Frank	20	22/05/1940	A Squadron
319328	Sergeant	Johnson	Ronald Edward	25	22/05/1940	A Squadron
761153	Lance Corporal	Smith	Harold Albert	31	22/05/1940	A Squadron
89529	2nd Lieutenant	Roddick	Andrew Thomas George	21	23/05/1940	A Squadron
315432	Trooper	Cowie	John	32	25/05/1940	B Squadron
551890	Trooper	Head	Leslie George	26	25/05/1940	
321365	Trooper	Brown	David	20	25/05/1940	
550882	Sergeant	Chandler	William John	28	26/05/1940	A Squadron
87192	2nd Lieutenant	Edgcumbe	Piers Richard	25	27/05/1940	Phantom Force
321469	Trooper	Rudkin	Geoffrey Hugh	20	28/05/1940	Phantom Force[1]

Service Number	Rank	Surname	Christian Names	Age	Date of Death	Comments
2043653	Trooper	Chappell	William Anthony	20	28/05/1940	Phantom Force[1]
310772	Trooper	Edgeworth	Thomas William	44	17/06/1940	*Lancastria*[2]
318806	Trooper	Dudman	Eric Arthur Clifford	27	17/06/1940	*Lancastria*[2]
310811	Corporal	Sturgess	Thomas Ralph	31	17/06/1940	*Lancastria*[2]
551922	Trooper	Wort	Albert Edward	29	17/06/1940	*Lancastria*[2]

1   *GHQ Liaison Regiment RAC (Phantom) Roll Of Honour* <http://ww2talk.com/index.php?threads/ghq-liaison-regiment-rac-phantom-roll-of-honour.22568/> (accessed 21/11/22).
2   Died on board HMT *Lancastria*. See T*he Forgotten Tragedy: The Story of the Sinking of HMT Lancastria* <briancrabbmaritimebooks.co.uk> (accessed 21/11/2022).

Appendix IV

Regimental Historiography of the 12th Lancers at Dunkirk

Without the Twelfth Lancers only a small part of the Army would have reached Dunkirk.[1]

The Regimental Narrative

The Regimental narrative can be traced through the articles, obituaries in the Regimental journals, and in the autobiographies and diaries of the veterans. The overall story has an officer and A Squadron bias as a result of the available primary sources. The death of Lumsden in 1945 and the subsequent loss of his own War Diary has prevented his personal narrative from being part of the historiography, especially when it came to his own relationship with Montgomery. Clearly errors were introduced to the narrative as memories faded and stories 'were improved beyond repair.'[2] The narrative has been interrupted by two amalgamations, but the thread has been continuous as it ebbed and flowed through the Regimental journals.

The word Dunkirk was often used as a point of reference, as in other situations 'bore a remarkable resemblance to Dunkirk,'[3] or in obituaries there may or may not have been mention of the fact that an individual was present at Dunkirk or not.[4] Likewise,

---

1   Broadcast quote was made over the British Forces Network in Germany in January 1959. See *12L Regimental Journal* (1959), p.50.
2   Phrase taken from M. Forsyth, *The Etymologicon* (2013), p.9.
3   *The Delhi Spearman* (1993), p.91.
4   Major W. Fenton, *12L Regimental Journal* (April 1949), p.115; William Chalk, DR with A Squadron, (1976), p.61; Colonel E.O. Burne, as attached to the British Liaison Mission and evacuated from Dunkirk in 1940, *The Delhi Spearman* (1978), p.81, Bill Saunders 'Bill served with the Regiment until after Dunkirk, attaining the rank of SQMS, John Cruden, served with the 12L in France, where he was transport Sergeant at RHQ. After Dunkirk he went with the Regiment to Egypt, *The Delhi Spearman* (1981), p.44; Horsbrugh-Porter, served with Distinction, *The Delhi Spearman* (1981), p.75, Bishop, two armoured cars to continue the 21 days of "hell." Prior to evacuation near Dunkirk. When the vehicles

individuals who became members of the Dunkirk Veteran's Association, such as key figures like Reg Finch who was mentioned as having 'attended for many years the annual pilgrimage to Dunkirk.'[5] It was also used as a time reference, such as 'just 18 months after Dunkirk, the Regiment was once again in contact with the enemy,' or the Regiment moved on 31st May, seven years ago from Dunkirk.'[6] Occasionally there were mentions of the award of the Ned Mann Memorial Prize, but they did not feature every year.[7] Post-amalgamation with the 9th Lancers, there are very occasional references in *The Delhi Spearman* to 9th Lancer service in 1940 under the description of Dunkirk, which in itself was incorrect as the 9th Lancers left France from Saint-Nazaire, so this remained a 12th Lancer narrative and the exploits of the 9th Lancers have not been absorbed into the Regimental consciousness at all.[8]

As with all Regimental war actions, the story begins with the narrative in the War Diary. The War Diary was written by the Adjutant, Captain Ronald Kennard, and unlike many War Diaries it is type-written in flowing prose, instead of succinct bullet points or notes. The copy in the National Archives is a retrospective account written in response to a request to Lumsden for an account 'dealing with the operations in the area of Arras 19-23 May.' Lumsden's response was to send on 28th June 1940 a complete account for the period 10-31 May for which he apologised.[9] The fact that there was no original War Diary available would suggest that the original was lost during the evacuation.[10] As a result of it being written retrospectively, it contains elements of post-event rationalisation such as 'this set proved invaluable throughout the fighting which followed, and no less powerful set would have been of any use.'[11] It should be noted that there are no War Diaries for the 13th/18th Hussars and 4th/7th Dragoon Guards and the GHQ War Diary is also incomplete. The GHQ Command Post War Diary only covers the period 19th-5th May 1940, and there are no radio logs or surviving messages that would have been sent between RHQ to GHQ, and there are only fleeting textual references.[12]

had been destroyed, *The Delhi Spearman* (1987), p.80; George 'Nobby' Simmonds 'in the withdrawal to Dunkirk, *The Delhi Spearman* (1995), p.80, Lieutenant Colonel Neil Speke, He missed the Dunkirk campaign and did not get to the desert battlefield until early in 1942, *The Delhi Spearman* (1996), p.87.

5   *The Delhi Spearman* (1986), p.69 and *The Delhi Spearman* (1997), p.91.
6   *The Delhi Spearman* (2006), p.105; *12L Regimental Journal* (June 1947), p.1 and *The Delhi Spearman* (1981), p.3.
7   *The Delhi Spearman* (2006), p.8 and *The Delhi Spearman* (2010), p.8. Won by Captain N.M.T. Stafford in 2006.
8   *The Delhi Spearman* (1973), p.179; *The Delhi Spearman* (1974), p.124; Obituary Vere-Laurie, *The Delhi Spearman* (1982), p.50 and Obituary, Lord Mostyn, *The Delhi Spearman* (2000), p.83.
9   Covering letter TNA WO 167/452.
10 CAB 106/220: Bartholomew Committee Final Report (1940), p.27. The author only has access to a transcript and not the original manuscript.
11 TNA WO 167/452, 10 May 1940.
12 TNA WO 167/29/2-8.

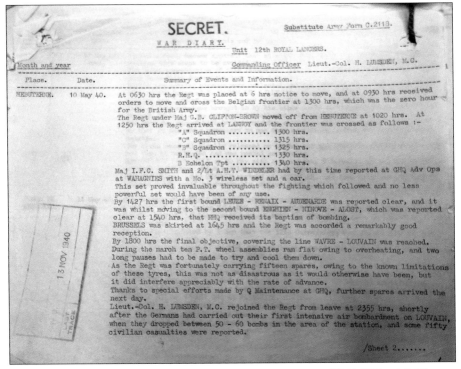

12th Lancers retrospective War Diary for the 10th May 1940. (TNA WO 167/452)

In 1940, Lumsden gave evidence to the Bartholomew Committee which looked into the conduct of the BEF before the evacuation, from the perspective of a possible invasion of mainland Britain by Germany. It noted the absence of war diaries:

> May I make it clear first of all we have practically no war diaries at the moment from which we can annotate the information. I think that situation possibly may improve, but at the present time as far as we can make out the majority were either lost at Dunkirk or destroued [sic] in the sea coming back.[13]

In the report, there was a section on armoured cars. It was the unanimous opinion of the committee that the ability of 'armoured car regiments with wheeled vehicles… to cover long distances with little maintenance was invaluable.' It thought the present organisation 'as a whole was considered suitable' but the number of troops in a Squadron should be increased from three to five. On the subject of communications, all wireless sets 'should have the [same] power of a No. 9 set.' The support by

13   CAB 106/220, *Bartholomew Committee Final Report* (1940), p.1.

Lieutenant David Smith was brought to the attention of the committee who noted that 'the attachment of one truck load of Royal Engineers to each Squadron proved most valuable' and while 'some engineers should always train with armoured car regiments, they should not be an integral part of the Regiment.'[14] For the Divisional reconnaissance regiments, it recommended that it was essential that each should have its own rear-link wireless and anchor set. In general, 'the BEF did not make the best use of wireless.' This was attributed to the 'lack of training practice in view of restrictions during the static period, the ingrained habit of wireless silence during this period and the fear of Direction Finding (DF).' It was 'recommended that a greater use of wireless should be made at all times, that restriction should be reduced to a minimum, and that once operations are joined, the maximum use of wireless should be made.'[15] It is clear that the committee listened to, and heeded, Lumsden's advice but the only tangible effect the Regiment would have noticed was the increase to five troops per Squadron as this report would not have been available to the general public until 1972.[16] One might also presume this vindicated the decision to retain wheeled reconnaissance and not to convert from armoured cars to tanks.

The first account of the Regiment's actions in May 1940 was written by Henry de la Falaise, A Squadron's *Agent de Liaison,* in his book entitled *Through Hell to Dunkirk* written in 1943. The book was published in America although parts of the diary had previously appeared in *The Field Artillery Journal* in Washington DC. Falaise dedicated the book to Herbert Lumsden and the officers and soldiers of A Squadron. The format of the book is 23 individual days, presented in a diary format, containing great detail of his own role supporting A Squadron. It is apparent not only he had a great affection and professional respect for Lumsden and the Squadron, but that he himself was a man of great courage. The language of the book at times is written in American-English using words such as 'highway' having been aimed at an American audience. From the numbers of copies currently available it would appear to have been published in relatively low numbers, which might explain the fact it is rarely referenced in other authors' works including Stewart's *Regimental History.* This is unfortunate as it is the most detailed autobiographical account of those published.

The first account was written in the first post-war Regimental Journal in June 1946. The first article was the obituary of Lumsden 'who was remembered with deep affection and pride by all those who were privileged to know him.' His period of command at Dunkirk was described as winning 'him an almost legendary reputation... equable, unruffled, and indefatigable, his command of the Regiment being authoritatively considered as a classic example of how an armoured car unit should be handled.' However, when it came to the first full article 'Record of Service of the

14   Bartholomew Committee Final Report, p.19.
15   Bartholomew Committee Final Report, p.16.
16   *History of the Public Records Act* <https://www.nationalarchives.gov.uk/information-management/legislation/public-records-act/history-of-pra/#:~:text=The%20Public%20Records%20Act%201967,be%20available%20for%20public%20inspection> (accessed 11/8/22).

Regiment During the War,' it was preceded by the statement that 'we regret that pressure on space has meant that the story of our service in France in 1939 and 1940 has been omitted. It will be published in our next issue of the Journal.'[17] The sequence of the Regiment's war service commenced with the Middle East written by Lieutenant Colonel Kate Savill, who commanded the Regiment during the period. The period from disembarkation to evacuation was subsequently published in the December of the same year. The article on Dunkirk was written by Lieutenant Colonel John Clark-Kennedy. It is unclear why the statement was made unless the article was simply not ready. However, as a consequence of the sequencing issue between the two editions, the Roll of Honour for 1939-40 was also inadvertently omitted. Dunkirk was not referred to again in the Regimental journals within a Regimental context until 1949 when it was mentioned in Colonel C.M. Truman's obituary.[18]

The next significant piece of work was written in 1950 by Captain Patrick Stewart MC when he published *The History of the XII Royal Lancers*. The book covered the period 1715 to 1945, so the Dunkirk 1940 action was written 10 years after the event. Stewart was an 11th Hussar and as such was a member of the Lancer's sister armoured car regiment. He did not serve with the Regiment in May 1940 and therefore the 1940 chapter cannot be considered as a primary source of information. The link between Stewart and the *Regimental History* was General Richard McCreery. Stewart had been his Personal Assistant in Italy and it was through McCreery's personal support that Stewart was given the authorship of the *Regimental History*.[19] Stewart covered two significant periods in the shaping of the Regiment's understanding of 1940.

The first one was the mechanisation of the Regiment in the chapter 'The Years Between,' a story he would have understood from his own Regiment, the 11th Hussars, as it went through the same process as the 12th Lancers. The inter-war period saw both regiments rotate with each other, in and out of Egypt, where the regiments were identically equipped. Both were issued with the Rolls-Royce 1920 Pat. armoured cars which Stewart described as being 'in their own way... beautiful machines: fast, mechanically reliable and responsive to good treatment.' When the regiments received their Morris armoured cars in 1936, Stewart wrote that they were looked on 'with much dissatisfaction' and were a complete contrast to all previous types. The Morris had an open turret and was less 'heavily armoured' than 'the vintage Rolls-Royce.' The car was 'only' equipped with a Boyes anti-tank and a Bren gun: it had 'hardly a spare part to its name' and it was known in disgust as the 'Suicide Box.' This would appear to have been Stewart's personal opinion or possibly reflected the thoughts of the 11th Hussars, as Hunn was later to recall that he had never heard it being called

17   *12L Regimental Journal* (June 1946), p.4 and p.6.
18   *12L Regimental Journal* (April 1949), pp.165-166.
19   R. Mead, *The Last Great Cavalryman: The Life of General Sir Richard McCreery, Commander Eighth Army* (2012), p.104 and p.256, *n*.3

by that name in the 12th Lancers.[20] That said, Stewart introduced the phrase into the *Regimental History* and it has endured as an authoritative Regimental opinion.

The following chapter covered the period 'The World War, France.' It is relatively short and is a chronological account of the Phoney War and the 21 days of action. The chapter is accompanied by fold out black and white maps which cover the period up to 18th May in great detail, although there was only a generic map for the actions in and around Belgium and Ypres. There are many anecdotal (and unreferenced) quotes throughout the narrative but it benefits from both Lumsden's and Browne-Clayton's war diaries which are sadly no longer available. When it came to primary sources, Stewart references Gort's *Despatches*, and Clark-Kennedy's account in the 1946 Regimental Journal, however, does not reference Falaise.[21]

Three years later Stewart, *Official History of the War in France and Flanders* (1953) was published. Like all official histories, it is general and far reaching in its nature, but the representation of the Regiment's activities is fair and balanced.[22] It would be another seven years before Dunkirk found its way back into the Regiment's collective thoughts when in 1957 the Regiment was awarded its battle honours for the Second World War. For the period of 1940 it received five individual honours: Dyle, Defence of Arras, Arras Counter-Attack, Dunkirk 1940, Northwest Europe 1940, and chose to have Dunkirk 1940 and North-West Europe 1940 as emblazoned honours on its Guidon. In the same year The Queen Mother unveiled the Dunkirk War Memorial on 29th July where Major Bob McGuire and Lieutenant Colonel Bill Mabbott laid wreaths on behalf of the Regiment. A picture of the memorial was used as the front piece to the 1958 Regimental Journal.[23]

Two years later, in January 1959, the British Forces Network in Germany broadcast the story of the 12th Lancers at Dunkirk. The narrator stated that "I am going to describe some of the fighting done by the 12th Lancers in the Dunkirk campaign. I'm only going to pick out five episodes, but I hope they will give you an idea of what happened." He concluded by saying "it would be impossible to end the story without quoting this passage from the dispatches of Lord Gort. Without the Twelfth Lancers only a small part of the Army would have reached Dunkirk." The whole transcript of this broadcast, with accompanying maps and pictures taken from Stewart's regimental history, was published in the Regimental Journal.[24]

There would be another five years before Dunkirk would be featured in the Regimental Journal when it appeared in Brigadier Harold Charrington's obituary. He was not at Dunkirk, but it attributed his training, when he was the Commanding Officer during mechanisation, as contributing to the success of the Regiment. It emphasised the fact

20 Morpeth-Hunn interview and Hunn, Frederick (Oral history)/Imperial War Museums <iwm.org.uk> (accessed 9/8/22).
21 Stewart, *The History of the XII Royal Lancers* (1950), pp.348-372.
22 Ellis, *War in France and Flanders*.
23 *12L Regimental Journal* (1958), p.51 and Charrington, *Spearmen*, p.142.
24 *12L Regimental Journal* (1959), pp.47-50.

that 'it has been said that the evacuation from Dunkirk in 1940 might never have been possible had it not been for the actions of the 12th Lancers during the retreat.'[25] This statement is very close to the attributed statement of Gort and might be the origin.

Two years later in 1966, Major Bob McGuire retired from the Regiment after 32 years' service. It stated that he gained the Military Medal while 'driving the Commanding Officer of the 12th Lancers in the Dunkirk campaign.' This is incorrect, as McGuire won his Military Medal as a Troop Sergeant in 1942, and as such this is the first error to be introduced into the Regimental story.[26]

In 1970, four years after McGuire's retirement, the Regimental Journal contained an article entitled the 'Mechanisation of the 12th Lancers.' This was a detailed three-page article, illustrated with pictures describing the process of mechanisation. It stated that 'the Regiment was re-equipped with light Morris reconnaissance armoured cars in 1939 and these were taken to France with the Regiment early in 1940. All these cars were lost during the evacuation from Dunkirk.' There was no negative reference to the Morris.[27]

In the same year, Shand recounted his memories for the first time, although it cannot be counted as part of the Regimental narrative. He was one of the guest speakers on *Exercise ACROSPIRE*, a Battlefield Tour of north west France, and Belgium, which was conducted by 5th Division. No other members of the Regiment were present and his notes were not published. Shand provided four pages of text which was his brief to the attendees and was included in the exercise pack. He started his brief stating that, like marrying a widow with 13 children, 'his contribution would be meagre.'

He counselled the group that he was only 'a small element in a Regiment that had to cover an immensely wide area.' The brief contained a great amount of minor detail which only a participant could have known, and his modest and self-effacing style would be how Shand would always tell his tale. He finished by stating:

> It seems an awful long way away from the battle which you have been studying and that we had to cover these vast distances and one seldom in fact, even as a troop leader, saw one's SHQ let alone RHQ. One was left with some curious problems to deal with. I am sure there is an answer to all of them now. There was an immense problem having to deal with French and Belgian troops, and I think we should have known perhaps more about demolitions and things like that... Somebody said that officers should have at least two languages... a degree in civil engineering and some training with the Diplomatic Corps before assuming command of a troop. I am sure we made most terrible mistakes and got into fearful messes, I know we did, I know I did personally. His final statement is the most poignant, 'I can say this, we did communicate.[28]

25   *The Delhi Spearman* (1964), p.44.
26   TNA WO 373/23/142.
27   *The Delhi Spearman* (1970), pp.94-96.
28   Shand, *5th Division Exercise ACROSPIRE; Battlefield Tour; NW France, and Belgium 1940* (1970), p.75.

The statement in itself appears innocuous enough, but the very fact the Lancer's armoured cars had wireless communications as low as inter-car level, whereas the light tanks of the Divisional reconnaissance regiments did not, is missed by most historians. This, combined with its speed and mobility, was the unique capability that the 12th Lancers brought to the BEF. In addition, RHQ had HF wireless communications direct to GHQ. This provided Gort with real-time information which he was able to use to make decisions. Questions and dialogue could take place without the use of messengers and dispatch riders. It also makes one consider what would have happened to the BEF if the Armoured Car regiments had been disbanded which was the pre-war plan?

In 1976, the *Dunkirk Veterans' Association Journal* included a touching quote from the French Life Vice-President, Andre Lesieux. He said that 'the Lonely Soldier's grave he places a wreath on, when he visits his father's grave, belongs to Trooper H.J. Westrop, a 12th Lancer who died on 21st May 1940. I would like any ex-Royal Lancers if they know any of his relations, to let them know he is NOT FORGOTTEN, although he is the only British Soldier in this cemetery.' The association between the Regiment and the DVA provided a tangible link to Dunkirk and it ensured his grave, like others, were still being visited, as the veteran population were getting older and visits to France were becoming less frequent. The fact that the grave was still being visited by Lesieux some 36 years after the event also demonstrates the enduring level of French gratitude.[29]

The following year, both Andrew Horsbrugh-Porter and Kate Savill were interviewed by the Imperial War Museum (IWM) regarding their military service. Savill was interviewed specifically on the mechanisation of the Regiment in 1928 and Horsbrugh-Porter's interview covered the period from 1927, through mechanisation to May 1940. Both of these audio interviews are available online through the IWM website. However, none of the information given by either Savill or Horsbrugh-Porter can be found quoted in any subsequent publications.[30]

It would be another six years before Dunkirk would be mentioned again. In 1982, the obituary of Major Fred Fox, the RSM in 1940, alluded to the spirit of the Regiment and 'his devotion and loyalty to his Regiment [which] stemmed from the fact that as a young soldier he had absorbed the atmosphere created by Blakiston-Houston, Lawrence, and Mabbott.' It also stated that 'he became a proficient horseman and won the Young Soldiers' Cup for skill with sword, lance, and revolver. But the rifle was his real weapon. For years he coached and shot with the rifle team.' This explains his 'dashing solo action in his armoured car near Mount St. Eloi,' where he was 'able to destroy enemy lorries by fire from his Boyes rifle and inflicted at least 30 casualties on the enemy infantry.'[31]

---

29   *The Delhi Spearman* (1976), p.68.
30   Savill, Kenneth Edward (Oral history)/Imperial War Museums <iwm.org.uk> and Horsburgh-Porter, Andrew Marshall (Oral history)/Imperial War Museums <iwm.org. uk> (accessed 9/8/22).
31   *The Delhi Spearman* (1982), p.78; TNA WO 167/452, 22 May 1940.

On 14th May 1985, the Regimental Command Team led by the Commanding Officer delivered a presentation to the Reconnaissance Brigade called 'The Salvation of the BEF, 10-31 May 1940.'[32] The theme chosen was the withdrawal in contact of the 12th Lancers and they were to select one of the 10 Principles of War to illustrate. The Regiment said that the action would demonstrate all the Principles of War with the exception of concentration, as given the role it was impossible to concentrate 38 armoured cars, but the principle they chose was 'the Selection and Maintenance of the Aim.' In their introduction they used the quote that 'without the Twelfth Lancers only a small part of the Army would have reached Dunkirk,' again stating that Gort said it in his *Despatches*. The presentation drew attention to the poor relationship between Montgomery and the Regiment, taking it further back than Dunkirk, and to the Regiment's time under his command at Alexandria. This was attributed to Montgomery banning the wearing of civilian clothes for all ranks below the rank of sergeant making him cordially 'detested' by all ranks, and that this 'mutual aversion,' which began in 1932, was to have interesting repercussions in the last week of May 1940.' When referring to the Morris armoured car, the phrase 'Suicide Box,' first introduced by Stewart 35 years previously to the Regimental vocabulary, was used and therefore perpetuated. After setting the scene, the presentation was delivered concentrating on the three distinct phases of the withdrawal. It made reference to the fact that Freddie Hunn (B Squadron's Signal Sergeant) had been interviewed by OC B Squadron two months previously. In the last and final phase, they concentrated on Second Lieutenant Mann's DSO action at Dixmuide, which was 'one of the most important of many,' and which they said came down to the troop leader's 'initiative and gallantry' and deserved 'a high place in the history of those days of disaster.' The lesson's learned were measured against 9 of the 10 Principles of War, and the commanding officer summarised:

> I hope you haven't got the feeling that the 12th Lancers saved the BEF single-handedly. This is inevitably a snapshot of significant events which by huge good-fortune and much individual courage allowed an escape from wholesale disaster. We train to achieve the same qualities of cunning, flexibility and initiative in our officers and NCOs, to master the skills of effective administration and communication, and to be ready and fit when the need arises.[33]

The commanding officer saw a direct link between the role of the Regiment in 1940 and the current requirement of a reconnaissance soldier, which included the NCOs. In 1985, this was set against the backdrop of the Cold War and the Regiment's role in the Covering Force in Germany.

---

32   Lieutenant Colonel R.V. Searby, Majors Hutchins, Crofton, Morpeth and Lort-Philips.
33   9/12L Lecture Notes, 'The Salvation of the BEF, 10-31 May 1940' (1985), pp.1-33.

The significance of the 1985 presentation by the Regimental Command team was that it captured the Regiment's perception of events that happened 45 years earlier. They used it as an example which showcased the attributes of the serving Regiment and related it to the contemporary Principles of War.[34] Gort's statement and the 'Suicide Box' were starting to become part of the Regimental narrative. However, the Regiment's exploits, notable as they were, were all framed against the background of the Commanding Officer saying that Dunkirk was 'a complete and total disaster unparalleled in our nation's history either before or since.'[35] This might help explain why May 1940 was always a time that the Regiment found difficult to celebrate. This resulted in the Regimental Day, Moy Day, not being updated to Dunkirk Day to commemorate their heroic performance, as they had done at Waterloo and Diamond Hill.[36]

In 1987, the Regimental Journal featured the obituary of Major Simon Browne who joined the 12th Lancers in 1914. He served through World War 1, retiring from the Army in 1925. His obituary stated that he rejoined the 12th Lancers and was Mentioned in Despatches for his work with the Regiment in France and Belgium. During the Dunkirk period it stated that he was a liaison officer at the age of 45 and was continually on a motorbike taking messages, etc, all over northern France.[37] The significance is that it increases the number of mentions of the Regiment and would indicate he was possibly the oldest serving member of the Regiment in 1940.

Two years later, in 1989, the Regimental Journal carried Ronald Kennard's obituary, written by Shand. Kennard had been Lumsden's Adjutant at Dunkirk. It stated that 'it should be remembered that the 12th Lancers were the only armoured car regiment with the BEF and were appallingly over-stretched for the disastrous three weeks of that campaign. Herbert Lumsden carried out tasks far beyond his role of Commanding Officer and Ronnie [Kennard], during this time, conducted affairs at RHQ – which at times must have resembled an Army Intelligence Centre – with his customary even-tempered aplomb.' It states on his return from Dunkirk he was awarded the Member of the British Empire and was Mentioned in Despatches for his services. This insightful comment regarding how the RHQ handled the information which was coming in from the Squadrons gave a good indication of not only the volume but also the calm and methodical way with which the situation was handled.[38] In September of the same year, the National Army Museum (NAM) conducted an oral interview with Second Lieutenant Sir Basil Hall, who had served with A Squadron as the Squadron Transport Officer. The interview was recorded on two cassette tapes.

34   The concept of Mission Command does not feature in the text, which was being informally introduction prior to the first issue of the *British Military Doctrine* in 1989.
35   9/12L Lecture Notes, p.1.
36   The Regiment had three previous Regimental Days, Waterloo (1815), Diamond Hill (1900) and Moy (1914).
37   *The Delhi Spearman* (1987), p.81.
38   *The Delhi Spearman* (1989), p.138.

Hall donated his 'journal of events' to the NAM, but it would be another 27 years before the Regiment had its own copy.

In the Regimental Journal 1990, Shand wrote an article entitled 'May 1940 – A Memory'. The account was six pages long and written 50 years after the start of the Second World War. The article was exactly what it said it was, an account written from memory and as a result contained small errors. In it he stated that:

> I think the quota of armoured cars was 39 [38]... I think this burnt out quite effectively later... I think all Squadron Headquarters consisted of soft vehicles only, the armoured cars having been sacrificed to make up troop losses... We had one day of rest here and I think it was then that we first heard something of the intended evacuation... This was not an easy journey and I think lasted some six or seven miles but, as we approached Malo-les-Bains I have absolutely no recollection of the journey back at all as I think I slept the whole way.[39]

The same year, Shand would publish a more accurate version of events in his autobiography *Previous Engagements* which was dedicated to 'Tom and Ben.' The Duchess of Cornwall wrote that 'we could never get him to talk about it. But when the grandchildren came along, he started talking about it and we got him to write a small book. I think it was a huge load off his mind to be able to tell people about it.[40] Shand described his own book as a:

> Monstrous comestible, a club sandwich. There are two strata of filling, and three of bread. The filling is made up of two accounts that I wrote while I was a prisoner in the latter half of the war. I managed to send these home through either the Swiss or Swedish Red Cross, but they were impounded by the Historical Section of the War Office, and I was unable to obtain possession of them until 1970.

Shand stated that the first part, France and Belgium 1940, was written three years after the event. When he was writing them, he 'was conscious that they would have to pass through both German and British censorship and that possibly imposed reticence makes them in retrospect, somewhat anaemic,' but 'they are printed as written.' The period of 1940 was written 'being entirely dependent on a treacherous memory and a few letters home.'[41]

The publisher described Shand's book as the 'narrative in the mood of class and period, light-hearted, unpretentious, and graphic in their description of active

39   *The Delhi Spearman* (1990), pp.150-155.
40   *The Duchess of Cornwall Reads Extracts from Her Father's Military Memoirs* <https://www.princeofwales.gov.uk/duchess-cornwall-reads-extracts-her-fathers-military-memoirs-ve-day> (accessed 30/8/22).
41   Shand, *Previous Engagements*, pp.7-8.

service… It is a book that should entertain at all levels and evoke memories among his friends and contemporaries.' This latter statement provides the context for the book which was written primarily for his grandchildren and a Regimental audience, financed by the Regimental Trustees and only available through Home Headquarters (HHQ). Shand states it was written while he was a prisoner and from memory and there are no footnote citations to indicate where he might have drawn upon other publications. However, it is quite apparent that his quote that 'without the Twelfth Lancers only a small part of the Army would have reached Dunkirk,' which is cited as coming from Gort's *Despatches* is incorrect, because Gort does not say this or anything closely approximating to this in either his First or Second *Despatch*. This is the phrase used in the radio broadcast in 1959, which was published in the Regimental Journal.[42]

In 1992, SQMS C.V. Hardy published his 'Memories of an Old 12th Lancer' in the Regimental Journal. Hardy had been the B Squadron SQMS at Dunkirk and he recounted being directed by Captain [sic] Browne-Clayton to take Trooper Skinner who had been seriously wounded in the leg to the pier at Dunkirk and managing to get both himself and Skinner aboard HMS *Icarus*.[43] This is the only reference to Regimental soldiers being evacuated via the East Mole and is one of the few accounts from a SNCO. The following year, three years after publishing his own autobiography, Shand edited and published Tim Bishop's posthumous 'abundant diaries,' under the title *One Young Soldier: The Memoirs of a Cavalryman*.[44] The book was published and distributed in the same way as Shand's, supported by the Regimental Association and distributed by HHQ. Bishop, like Shand, also served in A Squadron and Shand reproduces the maps from Stewart's *Regimental History* which produces a degree of duplication. However, Shand leaves large tracts of Bishop's text in their original form, including many of Bishop's personal thoughts which compliment Shand's own accounts. When reading Bishop's narrative, it is difficult to understand why his own gallantry was never formally recognised.

In 1993, 33 years after the amalgamation of the 12th Lancers with the 9th Lancers, Major General Robin Brockbank and Major Bobby Collins published a *Short History of the XII Royal Lancers* which covered the period from 1945 to 1960.[45] The title of the book theoretically put Dunkirk and May 1940 outside the scope of the book, but in Appendix C, there was a list of gallantry awards gained during the period 1939-45 which included those for Dunkirk. The list differs from that published in the War Diary as it included Kennard's MBE which was previously not listed. The citation shows that Lumsden nominated Kennard in July 1940 in recognition for his services

42   Shand, *Previous Engagements* (1990), p.62 and *The London Gazette*, 10 October 1941
      <https://archive.org/details/GortDespatches/mode/2up?q=without> (accessed 7/8/22);
      Quote from Broadcast was made over the British Forces Network in Germany in January
      1959, in *12L Regimental Journal* (1959), p.50.
43   *The Delhi Spearman* (1992), p.91.
44   Bishop, *One Young Soldier*.
45   Brockbank and Collins, *A Short History of the XII Royal Lancers*.

to the Regiment as the Adjutant. This included Dunkirk but was not Dunkirk-specific as he had already been Mentioned in Despatches.[46] The *history* also mentions that in Palestine the Regiment was directed to form a Phantom Force whose role was to provide communications between the Divisional HQ and the Parachute Brigades. This had its origins in 1940 and 12th Lancers officers, like Fane who was to command it, served with this force but no direct connection is made to 1940. The only Dunkirk reference is to the fact they returned from Palestine to England on 31st May 1947, on the seventh anniversary of Dunkirk.[47] This statement connecting the date of the anniversary was written 53 years after the event and was clearly still important to Brockbank and Collins who had both served with the Regiment during the war. In the same year there was a plea from the Royal Monmouthshire Royal Engineers Museum to exhibit any mementos of the joint action in its museum at Monmouth Castle. This, if supported, would have kept the link between the actions of Lieutenant Smith and the Regiment alive.[48]

Four years later, in 1997, the Regiment would conduct its first Battlefield Study of the campaign under the auspices of Exercise LANCERS' RETURN. The study was conducted by Major Richard Charrington on behalf of the Commanding Officer, Lieutenant Colonel Nick Everard. The background to the campaign was delivered by Mr Nigel de Lee from the War Studies Department at RMAS and Mr Mike Taylor, an amateur historian. The tour benefitted from having Lieutenant Colonel Clark-Kennedy (troop leader in B Squadron) and Major Freddie Hunn (B Squadron Signals Sergeant) in attendance. The exercise pack opened with the quote that 'without the Twelfth Lancers only a small part of the Army would have reached Dunkirk,' re-introducing the oft-repeated statement to the Regiment, 38 years previously, and which had been repeated by Shand 10 years earlier in his autobiography. The three-day tour covered 11 different stands with the first being on the River Ghette and the last ending on the beach at Bray-Dunes, Dunkirk. The tour emphasised Lumsden's 'forethought and correct assessment of Belgian intentions,' and that the 'Regiment was able to prevent much of the BEF being encircled from the north east.'[49] The link to the OODA loop (Observe, Orientate, Decide, Act) and getting inside the enemy's decision-making cycle was included in the text of the presentation, but was redlined out. It is unclear if reference was made to this during the visit.[50]

The exercise was run as a study period and the attendees were put into syndicates and role-played appointments from the Commanding Officer to troop leaders and were given 'tactical teasers.' The syndicates which role-played the Commanding Officer at Mont St Eloi had to 'plan the advance to contact as tasked to the Regiment.' At Lennick St. Quentin (after 12th Lancers became the GHQ Reserve), they had

46   TNA WO 373/75/583.
47   Brockbank and Collins, *A Short History of the XII Royal Lancers,* p.15.
48   *The Delhi Spearman* (1993), p.94.
49   *The Delhi Spearman* (1997), pp.94-97.
50   Script for Initial Brief – Exercise LANCERS RETURN, p.7.

to reorganise the 'Regiment for this role' paying 'particular attention to rest, patrol-ling and the balance to be achieved with regard to concealing GHQ presence.' As Squadron Leaders they role-played Horsbrugh-Porter and had to plan 'to cover from Tienen to Budingen,' and how they would go about this task, while giving 'considera-tion to: demolitions, orders for opening fire, Blue on Blue, and liaison with flanking units.' At Ypres they looked at the defence of Ypres and role-played Browne-Clayton: 'you have six cars left and eight tanks of the 13th/18th Hussars under command, what do you do? As troop leaders, they looked at Shand's action at Braine le Chateau, 'what is your plan for delaying the enemy in the town?' and also Mann's action at Dixmuide, 'you are the troop leader at Dixmuide with two cars. You have been told to delay and destroy the enemy. Site your position.' The overall approach was to refight the actions from a modern perspective, but there is no reference to it being specifically applied and measured against the extant doctrine.

The following year, Freddie Hunn was interviewed by the IWM. His extensive audio reels are available through the IWM website. When questioned about the Morris armoured car and its nickname of the 'Suicide Box,' he stated that he did not remember the soldiers of the Regiment ever using that name. He said that in comparison to the Lanchester, the Morris was smaller, faster, had a lower profile, more reliable and better fuel consumption than its predecessor. This is one of the few positive references to the Morris which was ideal for the Regiment's role in 1940 and for which the Lanchester would not have been suitable. Normally, the negative comments regarding the Morris are linked to the Army's fiscal constraints rather than considering it as a design feature.[51]

In the Regimental Journal of 1999, Tony Warre's obituary, written by Colonel Alex Twickel, mentioned that he had 'transferred to a rather secretive unit named GHQ Liaison Regiment. It also mentioned that he took 'with him an entire troop of 12th Lancers complete with armoured cars,' and that the organisation was later renamed more 'glamorously' Phantom. The mission of the unit 'was to patrol, at times, behind the enemy lines and report back accurate information about the enemy's strength and deployment.' The obituary stated that it was a 'highly difficult and dangerous task about which Tony seldom spoke' and his exploits 'won him a well-deserved Military Cross.' However, the obituary placed Warre's exploits within the context of the strate-gical picture, which was the campaign that 'ended in the disasters that lead up to the Dunkirk evacuation.'[52] There is no evidence to corroborate the statement regarding the move of a whole troop and its armoured cars, as Phantom Force were equipped with the Guy armoured car, although other members of the Regiment did serve with Phantom Force.[53] Although Warre did not talk publicly about his exploits, however,

51   Hunn, Frederick (Oral history)/Imperial War Museums <iwm.org.uk> (accessed 09/08/22).
52   *The Delhi Spearman* (1999), p.96.
53   Banbury of Southam, Charles William Banbury, Second Baron, as see Troopers William Chappell and Geoffrey Rudkin (Rudrin) from the Regiment in *GHQ Liaison Regiment*

he did correspond with the Regimental Secretary in 1989 regarding the death of Second Lieutenant Piers Edgcumbe who was also a member of the force.[54]

In the same year, HQ 1st Reconnaissance Brigade under Brigadier Torrens-Spence conducted their own Battlefield Tour of northern Europe, called Exercise REYNARD CHASSE aiming to 'study various armoured and reconnaissance battles from different periods.'[55] The party consisted of 20 personnel rank-ranged from the Brigade commander down to JNCO and trooper level. In the pack were two maps for 21st May and the action at Arras. It also included Shand's last page from his Exercise ACROSPIRE notes.[56] This talked about the attributes required by a troop leader, the challenges they faced and the fact that they 'did communicate.' It is unclear why this reference was chosen from an obscure publication some 30 years previously, but the ability for reconnaissance troops to be able to effectively communicate would not have been lost on the Brigade.

Two years later, in 2001, the obituary of George Delaney 'stated that in September 1939 'George was back in uniform as part of the general mobilisation prior to WW2' and that he rejoined A Squadron. It described how on his first night in France he slept in 'a 1900 horse drawn glass funeral carriage!' During the campaign it stated that 'George found himself dodging between haystacks in the Commanding Officer's staff car while under attack from Stukas' and when seven miles short of La Panne. From the obituary it would appear Delaney was mobilised as a reservist in 1939 and initially rejoined his old Squadron, but subsequently drove the Commanding Officer's staff car. It should be noted that his name is not referenced in any other sources, and that the Commanding Officer also had an armoured car crew with his normal driver being Corporal Bob McGuire.[57]

In 2001, the Regimental Museum received an account of Freddie Hunn's wartime experiences, compiled from his diaries. The transcript dealt with the period from mobilisation to the evacuation at Dunkirk in five chapters and was accompanied by photographs and 14 pages of text. Hunn's B Squadron story could now be added to Shand's hitherto sole A Squadron narrative. In terms of chronology, Hunn's transcript was the most recent element of the story to be added, albeit held in the museum and not in a published format.

In 2005, the Regimental Journal contained a book review of *Dunkirk: Fight To The Last Man*, by Hugh Sebag-Montefiore, which was to be published in 2006. It stated that the book contained 'a new angle on how the 1940 BEF came to be evacuated from Dunkirk' and 'it was not just because of the courage of the men on the beaches being rescued by the Navy and those celebrated little ships.' According to the author, 'the

RAC (Phantom) Roll Of Honour/WW2 Talk <http://ww2talk.com/index.php?threads/ghq-liaison-regiment-rac-phantom-roll-of-honour.22568/> (accessed 1/9/22).
54   *The Delhi Spearman* (1999), p.96.
55   Exercise REYNARD CHASSE, Battlefield Tour, 1-5 March 1999, Final Admin Instruction, 26 Feb 1999.
56   Exercise *ACROSPIRE*, p.75.
57   McGuire account, p.1.

evacuation would never have taken place had it not been for the bravery of the British soldiers who were left behind to hold back the Germans while the evacuation went ahead. The units who were involved included the 12th Lancer and were 'featured in the book at both the beginning and end of the campaign' although it only refers to the Regiment's and Mann's activities (Dixmuide) between 27-28 May.[58] It concludes with the statement that 'thanks to Mann's Royal Lancers and the engineer who had done the exploding, the west bank of the Yser remained a German-free zone, and the Dunkirk evacuation carried on unimpeded.'[59]

The book mentions Bishop's diary, which had been made available to him by Bishop's sister, but, does not directly reference it. He also makes no reference to Shand's *Previous Encounters*, although he does refer to Bishop and Shand sharing the bottle of Moët & Chandon but cites it within the context of two cavalry officers being 'boisterous' and 'knocking back a bottle of champagne, celebrating their 'call to arms.'[60] The reference to this incident is only contained in *Previous Encounters*. However, Sebag-Montefiore chooses a somewhat stereotypical characterisation of cavalry officers which did not reflect Shand's somewhat more serene setting of two officers sharing a lunch together.[61] He also painted his own rather embellished account of the crossing of the Regiment at Lannoy:

> 'Charge!' signal on his trumpet, as each troop of three armoured cars sped past. Thus did the horns of the proverbial bull charge into Belgium, mesmerised by a flourish of the matador's cloak.[62]

From a Regimental perspective, Sebag-Montefiore chose to draw the majority of his information from the *Regimental History* augmented by his own personal impression of the cavalry and did not reference Shand's or Bishops own autobiographies, something the reviewer failed to notice.

Sadly, on 11th June 2006, Bruce Shand passed away. His obituary stated that 'in his dispatches, Lord Gort wrote that without the 12th Lancers only a small part of the BEF would have reached the coast and Dunkirk.' Also, that in 'that phase of the fighting Lord Gort made 31 awards of which 12 went to members of the Regiment.[63] Later that year, on 15th November, HRH The Duchess of Cornwall invited a small number of former members of her late father's Regiment to a luncheon in his memory at Clarence House. Fifteen attended, including Freddie Hunn.[64]

---

58   H. Sebag-Montefiore, *Dunkirk: Flight To The Last Man* (2006), pp.332-334 and *The Delhi Spearman* (2005), pp.73-74.
59   *The Delhi Spearman* (2005), pp.73-74.
60   Sebag-Montefiore, *Flight To The Last Man*, p.59.
61   This may be how Bishop described the lunch, but there is no corroborating footnote citation.
62   Sebag-Montefiore, *Flight To The Last Man*, p.60.
63   *The Delhi Spearman* (2005), pp.73-74.
64   *The Delhi Spearman* (2006), pp.103-104.

In 2009, the Regimental Journal included the obituary of Lieutenant Colonel John Clark-Kennedy, who had been a young Troop Leader in May 1940, involved in the early fighting and the withdrawal to Dunkirk. The obituary introduced his nickname 'Haywire' which he himself had used when writing Major Tom Bailey's obituary in 1987. The obituary also mentioned the award of his Military Cross at Dunkirk and that he had had six armoured cars 'shot from underneath him' during the course of the war, including the two in 1940.[65]

The following year in 2010, a visit to Clarence House reinforced the link between Bruce Shand and The Duchess of Cornwall. Those who attended were a combination of serving soldiers and their families and members of the Old Comrades' Association. The day was concluded with The Duchess of Cornwall giving an address and a short resumé of her father's career and said 'how her father enjoyed his time with the Regiment and how he would be so pleased that she had invited the Regiment for lunch'. The Duchess of Cornwall concluded in extending her best wishes to the Regiment and their forthcoming operational tour.[66]

The visit to Clarence House also coincided with Colonel Richard Charrington's publication of *Spearmen: The History of the 9th/12th Royal Lancers* in what was the 50th anniversary year of the Regimental amalgamation. Charrington offered the new *history* not only to mark the anniversary but as a means of including new material relating to the human side of Regimental life which would add colour to the somewhat 'bare bones' of the previous histories. The book is beautifully illustrated and well referenced and Charrington was also prepared to acknowledge the Regiment's 'occasional shortcomings.'[67] The period France 1939-1940 brought together quotes from Falaise, Shand and Bishop and included a map for the whole period of operations filling the gap from 18th May to 31st May that Stewart did not cover in detail. Charrington includes Lumsden's quote with reference to his relationship with Montgomery and why he was sacked from the Eighth Army, 'you may think the Desert is a huge place but there wasn't enough room for two shits in it and, as I was junior, I had to go.'[68] The Gort quote regarding the role of the Twelfth and the fact that 'only a small part of the BEF would have escaped the continent' is repeated. Also, the phrase 'Suicide Box' was repeated and introduced to a new audience.[69] This narrative written by Charrington was the last real attempt to draw together the story of Dunkirk. Charrington is a third generation Lancer, with both his father and grandfather having served in the 12th Lancers. He clearly understood the story he was trying to tell: that without the Twelfth, the BEF would not have escaped.[70]

65   *The Delhi Spearman* (2009), pp.107-108.
66   *The Delhi Spearman* (2010), p.59.
67   Charrington, *Spearmen*, passim.
68   *The Delhi Spearman* (2006), p.119.
69   Charrington, *Spearmen*, p.132, p.142.
70   Charrington, *Spearmen*, p.143.

On the occasion of the Officers' last Regimental Dinner in 2014 at the Drapers' Hall, prior to the amalgamation with the Queen's Royal Lancers, The Duchess of Cornwall spoke to the 9th/12th Lancers Regimental Officers. In her speech she referenced her 'Papa's' service with the Regiment and made reference to the amusing incident during the Retreat to Dunkirk which involved him assisting in the delivery of a French woman's baby. She stated that she knew he would be drinking a toast to the Regiment that night 'in which he was so proud to have served.' Sadly, the same edition of the Regimental Journal carried the obituary of Freddie Hunn. With his death, the last living link with the Regiment to Dunkirk was broken.[71]

In 2016, notwithstanding the fact that Sir Basil Hall had deposited his 'journal of events' in the NAM, Home Headquarters received a copy of the transcript of Hall's 13-page War Diary for the period of 1939-1940 from Brian Davis. In the accompanying email it stated that 'the original exercise book was held by the Inns of Court and City Yeomanry Association. It is still unclear if the 'journal of events,' the 'War Diary of Sir Basil Hall' and the 'original exercise book' are the same document.[72] Although, theoretically, Hall's account was new to the Regiment, it had been publicly available since 1989 and Hunn's was the last to be written. Neither of these sources have been cited in any available works and while Hunn's account add balance to Shand's, Hall's account is written from the perspective of a Transport Officer, which adds a dimension that neither Shand nor Hunn can offer.

The final piece of the story is Exercise DUNKIRK LANCER which was the catalyst for this book. Exercise DUNKIRK LANCER was the Battlefield Study which took place in September 2022 and was aimed at approximately 50 officers and NCOs (mostly reconnaissance vehicle commanders) from the Regiment. The Regiment had just been resubordinated to the Deep Recce Strike (DRS) Brigade Combat Team and become one of three Divisional Reconnaissance Battlegroups (DRBG), or Deep Recce Strike Reconnaissance Battlegroups (DRS BG). This coincided with the delay in the delivery of the new Ajax Reconnaissance vehicle and saw the Regiment converting to Warrior (as a surrogate platform). However, the Regiment's primary vehicle at the time was Jackal, a wheeled reconnaissance vehicle with similar capabilities and limitations to the Morris armoured car. The Commanding Officer, Lieutenant Colonel Richmond, observed:

> Nature of warfare has not changed – and so many of the precepts which we believe underpin DRS are already enshrined in Regimental experience. For example, fighting at reach, delaying the enemy's advance, and covering withdrawals… Opportunities to remind ourselves of these skills and learn how they might be integrated into DRS are crucial.[73]

---

71   *The Delhi Spearman* (2014), p.27 and p.122.
72   Email Pocock-Davis, 2 March 2016.
73   Exercise DUNKIRK LANCER Study Guide (2022), p.4.

The exercise author, Major Pritchard, wrote that the 12th Lancers:

> Circumstances are all too easily compared to ours and applying contemporary
> doctrine to this campaign is more than an academic exercise; it is illuminating.
> We will look at the series of actions through the lens of ADP Land Operations
> which, as our capstone doctrine, sets the framework for all subordinate doctrine.[74]

The study retraced the withdrawal of the 12th Lancers from the River Dyle back to
the beach at Dunkirk over three and a half days, which included Shand's action at
Baine-le Chateau, and revisited Villers-Sir-Simon and the farm where B Squadron
had been billeted in October 1940 (picture 41). The study also went to Mont St. Eloi,
and looked at RSM's Fox's action and the site of RHQ and the Observation Post. The
study also went to the site of the Wormhout Massacre and then discussed the circumstances around the death of Lieutenant Edgcumbe. The study also took in Mann's and
Glarvey's action at Dixmuide, Shand's action at Renescure and a joint Anglo-Belgian
service of remembrance was held at the church yard in Lynde, at the grave of Second
Lieutenant Roddick. At each location, once the historical context had been set, the
syndicates discussed how the situation of 1940 might be similar to something they
may encounter in the DRS role and how they might either take lessons away or react
differently. As a result, a detailed list of Tactical Lessons and Considerations was
produced, the exercise author thought that:

> Exercise DUNKIRK LANCER was a successful exercise. The aims were
> achieved and the Commanding Officer's intent was met. All those involved in
> this battlefield study are now better placed to understand current and future
> operations by relating the lessons of our predecessors to the modern day.[75]

Summary

The original story of Dunkirk remained known only to the Regiment for 30 years
until the 1970's, when the War Diary and the *Bartholomew Committee* report were
made available to the general public. The only supporting narrative of the Regiment
was in the *Official History* which was balanced and fair. For the Regiment the story has
remained in its sub-conscious for over 80 years. As with all stories of the period, as the
veterans have passed away it is only the texts of their obituaries, diaries and autobiographies which are left to tell their story. The challenge for the Dunkirk veterans was
how to place their own actions inside the context of what was an unmitigated military
disaster. The subsequent campaigns in Africa and Italy were perceived to have been

---

74   Exercise DUNKIRK LANCER Study Guide, p.5.
75   Exercise DUNKIRK LANCER – Post Exercise Report (3 October 2022).

more successful and for those who continued to serve beyond 1940, and whose careers benefited from their subsequent successes in the desert and Italy.

The influence of Bruce Shand on the Regimental narrative should not be under-estimated, from his first notes written for a Battlefield Study in 1974 to the editing of Tim Bishop's diaries in 1993. His writings have been used in all significant works for the last 50 years and a copy of his book is given to young officers at Sandhurst before they join the Regiment. In January 2008, the Regiment funded a second print run of Shand's book. The diaries of Hall and Hunn and the audio interviews of Savill, Horsbrugh-Porter, Kidston-Montgomerie, and Hunn all seemed to have remained unsourced between 1977 and 2010. They only feature in *Spearmen* (2010), *Everything Worked Like Clockwork* (2016) and *Armoured Warfare in the British Army 1914-1939* (2022). It should also be noted that the latter two focus on mechanisation, not Dunkirk.[76]

The two Regimental studies conducted in 1985 and 1997 are both a snapshot of the Regiment's understanding of its own story. It is some 25 years since the period was last formally studied by the Regiment. The presentation to the Reconnaissance Brigade in 1985 linked the action to the Principles of War, but the timing pre-dated the Army's articulation of its formal command philosophy of mission command in 1989. The independent actions of both Lumsden and Mann during this period will serve as excellent examples for study periods to come through the prism of Mission Command.[77]

There is sadly no evidence to prove that Gort ever wrote in his *Despatches* that 'without the Twelfth Lancers only a small part of the Army would have reached Dunkirk.' The true origin of this statement was a radio broadcast on the British Forces Network in 1959, repeated by Shand in 1990 and since embedded in the Regimental narrative. However, this does not make the statement untrue and the battle honours of Dunkirk and North-West Europe 1940 are still carried on the Guidon of The Royal Lancers to this day.[78]

It would appear that, notwithstanding all of the Regimental autobiographies and audio recordings, the Regimental story has not made its way into popular or academic writings and as such the mainstream narrative is unlikely to change. At a Regimental level, however, we can look back with immense pride and a new understanding of the key role played by the 12th Royal Lancers in saving the BEF, potentially helping to prevent the anticipated German invasion.

76 R. Salmon, *'Everything Worked Like Clockwork': The Mechanisation of British Regular and Household Cavalry, 1918-1942*, (2016) and D. Taylor, *Armoured Warfare in the British Army 1914-1939* (2022).
77 Mission Command was being taught and lectutred prior to its official appearance officially in 1989
78 Broadcast quote was made over the British Forces Network in Germany in January 1959. See *12L Regimental Journal* (1959), p.50.

Bibliography

Archival Sources

The National Archive (TNA)

Reports
CAB 106/220, Bartholomew Committee Final Report (1940)
Gort, First Despatch (25 April 1940)
Gort, Second Despatch (25 July 1940)

War Diaries
TNA WO 167/29/28 GHQ War Diary (19–25 May 1914)
TNA WO 167/452 12L War Diary
TNA WO 167/454 15/19H War Diary
TNA WO 167/778 101st Royal Monmouth Royal Engineers War Diary
TNA WO 373/23/142 McGuire, Military Medal Citation
TNA WO 373/75/583 Kennard, Member of British Empire Citation
TNA WO 373/92/164 Willis, Military Cross Citation

Home Headquarters, The Royal Lancers Archive
9/12L Lecture notes: Corps Recce Study Day, 'Salvation of the BEF 10-31 May 1940' (1985)

B. Hall Diary
Pocock-Davis email correspondence, 2 March 2016
Exercise REYNARD CHASSE, Battlefield Tour, 1-5 March 1999, Final Admin Instruction, 26 Feb 1999

F. Hunn Diary
Hunn – Morpeth interview
J. Thurston, Account (1990)
Smith to Charrington correspondence, 12 April 1997
The Royal Lancers Museum Derby correspondence
R.C. Maguire, Account

Script for Initial Brief – Exercise LANCERS RETURN

Shand, 5th Division Exercise ACROSPIRE; Battlefield Tour; NW France and Belgium 1940 (1970)

Miscellaneous

CADOGAN No. 117413 (1917-1940)

II. Her Majesty's Stationery Office (HMSO)

War Office, *Armoured Car Training War, Vol. 2, 1931*

Armoured Car Training: Training and War, 1921 (Provisional)

—— *Cavalry Traiing (Horsed), 1937*

—— *Cavalry Training (Mechanised) Pam. No. 1 – Armoured Cars, 1937*

—— *Field Exercise, 1870*

—— *Tank and Armoured Car Training, Vol. 2, War (Provisional), 1927*

—— *Training Regulations, 1934*

Secondary Sources

Anglesey, M. *A History of the British Cavalry, 1816-1919, Vol. 4, 1899-1913* (London: Leo Cooper, 1986)

Atkin, R. *Pillar of Fire: Dunkirk 1940* (London: Sidgwick & Jackson, 1990)

Badsey, S. *Doctrine and Reform in the British Cavalry 1880–1918* (Aldershot: Ashgate, 2008)

Blaxland, G. *Destination Dunkirk: The Story of Gort's Army* (Barnsley: Pen & Sword, 1973/2019)

Brereton, J.M. *The History of the 4th/7th Royal Dragoon Guards 1685-1980* (Catterick: Published by the Regiment, 1982)

Brockbank, R & Collins, R.M. *A Short History of the XII Royal Lancers 1945-1960* (Wigston: Published by the Regiment, 1994)

Bryant, A. *The Turn of the Tide 1939-1943* (London: Collins, 1957)

Charrington, R.A. *Spearmen: The History of the 9th/12th Royal Lancers* (Wigston: 9th/12th Royal Lancers Charitable Association, 2010)

Courage, G. *The History of 15th/19th The King's Royal Hussars 1939-1945* (Aldershot: Gale & Polden, 1949)

Ellis, L.F. *The War in France and Flanders 1939-1940* (London: HMSO, 1953)

Forsyth, M. *The Etymologicon* (London: Icon Books, 2013)

Harris, J. *Dunkirk: The Storms of War* (London: David & Charles, 1980)

Jones, S. *From Boer War to World War: Tactical Reform of the British Army, 1902-1914* (Norman, Oklahoma: University of Oklahoma Press, 2013)

Miller, C.H. *History of The 13th/18th Royal Hussars (Queen Mary's Own) 1922-1947* (London: Chrisman, Bradshaw, 1949)

Procter, A.A. *Legends, and Lyrics: A Book of Verses* (London: George Bell & Sons, 1892)

Salmon, R. *"Everything Worked Like Clockwork": The Mechanisation of British Regular and Household Cavalry, 1918-1942*, (Solihull: Helion & Company, 2016)

Sebag-Montefiore, H.

Dunkirk: Flight To The Last Man (London: Penguin, 2006/2016)

Sheppard, E.W. *The Ninth Queen's Royal Lancers 1715-1936* (Aldershot: Gale & Polden, 1939)

Stewart, P.F. *History of the XII Royal Lancers* (Oxford: Geoffrey Cumberlege Oxford University Press, 1950)

Taylor, D. *Armoured Warfare in the British Army 1914-1939* (Barnsley: Pen & Sword, 2022)

------------ *Armoured Warfare in the British Army 1939-1945* (Barnsley: Pen & Sword, 2022)

Thompson, J, *Dunkirk: Retreat to Victory* (London: Pan Books, 2009)

Periodicals

Barrow, G. 'The Future of Cavalry', *The Cavalry Journal* (April 1929)

Charrington, H.V.S. 'Where the Cavalry Stands Today, *The Cavalry Journal* (January 1927)

Chenevix Trench, R. 'Wireless with Cavalry', *The Cavalry Journal* (January to October 1929)

Clark-Kennedy, A.J. 'Record of Service of the Regiment During the War, France 1940', *The Journal of The XII Lancers* (1946)

Croft, W.D. 'Notes on Armoured Cars', *The Cavalry Journal* (January 1926)

Hume, E.G. 'Mechanical Aids to Cavalry', *The Cavalry Journal* (July 1935)

Hume, E.G. 'Some Thoughts on Modern Reconnaissance', *The Cavalry Journal* (January 1928)

Mulliner, A.R. 'Cavalry Still an Essential Arm', *The Cavalry Journal* (October 1927)

Pitman, T.T. 'Back to the Chariots', *The Cavalry Journal* (April 1928)

Robson, J. 'Some Memories of Lieutenant General Herbert Lumsden', *The Delhi Spearman* (2006)

Shand, B. 'May 1940: A Memory' *The Delhi Spearman* (1990)

Journals

Aberdeen Press and Journal, Wednesday 14th March 1928
Delhi Spearman (1964, 1966, 1970, 1973, 1974, 1976, 1980, 1981, 1986, 1987, 1989, 1990, 1992, 1993, 1997, 1999, 2000, 2001, 2005, 2006, 2009 , 2010, 2014)
The Marlburian, July 1940 (vol. LXXV nos. 986 and 987)
12L Regimental Journal (1927, 1928, 1930, 1946, 1947, 1949, 1957, 1959, 1960)

Electronic Sources

An Officer and a Gentleman: The Life of John Clark Kennedy 1918-2010 <https://www.carsphairn.org/CarsphairnArchive/files/original/c9db07c01e683d6 261b500c81fd24c7f.pdf>
GHQ Liaison Regiment RAC (Phantom) Roll Of Honour <GHQ Liaison Regiment RAC (Phantom) Roll Of Honour/WW2Talk>
History of the Public Records Acts – The National Archives <https://www.nationalarchives. gov.uk/information-management/legislation/public-records-act/history-of-pra/>
Duchess of Cornwall Reads Extracts from Her Father's Military Memoirs <https://www. princeofwales.gov.uk/duchess-cornwall-reads-extracts-her-fathers-military-memoirs-ve-day>
GHQ Liaison Regiment RAC (Phantom) Roll of Honour <http://ww2talk.com/index. php?threads/ghq-liaison-regiment-rac-phantom-roll-of-honour.22568/>
Hunn, Frederick (Oral history)/Imperial War Museums <iwm.org.uk>
Kidston-Montgomerie, George Jardine (Oral history/Imperial War Museums <iwm. org.uk>
Savill, Kenneth Edward (Oral history)/Imperial War Museums <iwm.org.uk>
The Forgotten Tragedy: The Story of the Sinking of HMT Lancastria <briancrabbmari-timebooks.co.uk>

Index